The New Charismatics II

Other Books by the Author

The Young Evangelicals

The New Charismatics

The Worldly Evangelicals

I Found It! The Story of Bill Bright and Campus Crusade

By What Authority

RICHARD QUEBEDEAUX

The New

Charismatics

II

1817

HARPER & ROW, PUBLISHERS, SAN FRANCISCO
Cambridge, Hagerstown, New York, Philadelphia
London, Mexico City, São Paulo, Sydney

Grateful acknowledgment is made to the following for permission to use copyrighted material:

Alumni Association of Fuller Theological Seminary—"The Old Pentecostalism and the New Pentecostalism" by Richard Quebedeaux, printed in Vol. 20, no. 1 (March 1974) issue of *Theology, News and Notes.*

Augsburg Publishing House—*The Pentecostals* by Walter J. Hollenweger; copyright Augsburg Publishing House; used by permission.

Ave Maria Press—*The Pentecostal Movement in the Catholic Church* by Edward O'Conner; copyright © 1971 Ave Maria Press, Notre Dame, Indiana; used with permission of the publisher.

Fountain Trust—Editorial from *Renewal* magazine, December 1970–January 1971; reprinted by permission.

Humanities Press and Oslo University Press—*The Pentecostal Movement: Its Origin, Development and Distinctive Character* by Nils Bloch-Hoell, 1964; reprinted by permission of Humanities Press Inc.; Atlantic Highlands, N.J. 07716.

Logos International—*The Era of the Spirit* by J. Rodman Williams; copyright © 1971 by Logos International. *These Are Not Drunken, As Ye Suppose* by Howard M. Ervin; copyright © 1968 by Howard M. Ervin. *The Spirit Bade Me Go* by David J. du Plessis; copyright © 1970 by Logos International. *Walk in the Spirit* by Michael Harper; copyright © 1968 by Michael Harper. *None Can Guess* by Michael Harper; copyright © 1971 by Michael Harper; reprinted by permission.

National Council of Churches—The *Revised Standard Version of the Bible*, copyrighted 1946, 1952, © 1971, 1973.

Paulist Press—*Catholic Pentecostals* by Kevin and Dorothy Ranaghan; copyright © 1969 by The Missionary Society of St. Paul the Apostle in the State of New York. *As the Spirit Leads Us* by Kevin and Dorothy Ranaghan; copyright © 1971 by The Missionary Society of St. Paul the Apostle in the State of New York; reprinted by permission.

This book is a completely revised edition of *The New Charismatics*, originally published by Doubleday & Company, 1976.

FIRST HARPER & ROW EDITION, 1983

Designed by Catherine Hopkins

Library of Congress Cataloging in Publication Data
Quebedeaux, Richard.
  THE NEW CHARISMATICS II.

  Bibliography: p. 237
  Includes index.
  1. Pentecostalism—History. I. Title.
BR1644.Q43 1983   270.8'2   82–48417
ISBN 0–06–066723–0

83 84 85 86 87 10 9 8 7 6 5 4 3 2 1

The Lord hath more truth and light
yet to break forth from his holy Word.
—*John Robinson*, pastor to the Pilgrims

Contents

Preface   *ix*

Introduction: **The Nature of Charismatic Renewal**   *xiii*

Chapter One: **The Background**   *1*
Pentecostalism Old and New   *3*
Penetration of "Established" Churches   *7*
The Spiritual Gifts   *12*
The Miraculous and the
    Nonmiraculous   *16*
The Charismatics in History   *18*

Chapter Two: **Beginnings in North America**   *23*
Black and White Origins   *26*
Distinctive Religious Style   *31*
Basic Theology and Ethics   *35*
Recruitment   *38*
Mainline Ecclesiastical Disapproval and
    Rapid Spread   *39*
Diffusion of the Movement   *46*
In Great Britain: An Early Unitive
    "Experiment" That Failed   *52*

Chapter Three: **The Path to Renewal**   *59*
Beginnings   *59*
"Outburst of Tongues" at St. Mark's   *61*
An Increasingly Recognizable
    Movement   *64*
Rapid Spread to Other Parts of the
    World   *67*
All Roads Lead to Rome: Catholic
    Pentecostals   *72*
The New Pentecostalism Today   *81*

Chapter Four: **The Leadership of Charismatic Renewal**   87
The Trusted Authority Figure   90
Prominent Charismatic Leaders   92
Organizational Leaders   92
Editors and Publishers   94
Preachers and Lecturers   97
Important Early Leaders   99

Chapter Five: **Faith and Practice**   127
Prominence of the Laity   128
Young People and Women   129
Spiritual Authority   131
Human Authority   135
The Josephine Ford Controversy   137
The Rise of "Shepherding"   138
Evangelism   142
Fellowship   147
Prayer Meetings   147
Unity in Diversity   151
General Theological Orientation   153
Baptism in the Holy Spirit   155
Water Baptism and Confirmation   159
Sacramental Intercommunion   161
Neopentecostal Culture: Accommodation of Holiness to the Middle Class   162
Spirit Baptism and Social Change   166
Patterns of Worship   170

Chapter Six: **The Development of Classical Pentecostalism and Charismatic Renewal in Contrast**   175
Theology   179
Worship   181
Ecclesiastical Stance   185
Mind and Spirit   187
Christ and Culture   189
Constituency   190

Chapter Seven: **From Opposition to Acceptance**   *193*
Early Opposition Within Historic
    Denominations   *194*
Gradual Acceptance by Ecclesiastical
    Authorities   *196*
Changing Attitudes   *199*
Reactions from Classical
    Pentecostalism   *208*

Chapter Eight: **The Reasons for Success**   *211*
The Ecumenical Movement   *212*
Vatican II   *213*
Wider Acceptance of Theological
    Dissent   *215*
General Spread of Secularization   *216*
Young People   *218*
In the Middle Class   *219*
Statistics   *220*
Religious Experience and "Instantism" in
    Modern Culture   *222*
Increased Leisure Time   *224*
Antiinstitutionalism   *226*
"Rediscovery" of the Supernatural   *227*
Charismatic Renewal and Other
    Contemporary Movements   *228*

Conclusion: **The Achievement of Charismatic
Renewal**   *233*

Annotated Bibliography   *241*

Index   *257*

Preface

Unlike a more or less clearly defined "church" or "denomination," the new religious "movement" poses distinct research hazards to scholars who wish to study it. One of these is the fact that a movement's structural, ideological, and behavioral bounds are often not easily circumscribed. In the particular case of charismatic renewal as a movement within Christianity, its very contemporaneity has presented a *major* problem to the academic researcher; namely, the fact that until just a few years ago it was still in the process of development. Furthermore, its heterogeneity of self-understanding and expression has never permitted more than a "provisional" evaluation of dominant theological and organizational trends at any given time. In addition, once neopentecostalism had actually achieved its primary goal by the late 1970s—that of making the once-despised pentecostal experience acceptable within mainline Protestantism and Catholicism—there was no longer any need for its continued existence *as a movement*. Because charismatic renewal had rejected the idea of forming a new "Spirit-filled" denomination from the beginning, it very simply lost its distinctive identity and became part of the larger, concurrent "evangelical resurgence." Even though there may be more new charismatics than ever today, the differences between them and other mainline Christians have become fewer and farther between.

The scope of the present study embraces an historical, sociological, and ecclesiastical assessment of neopentecostalism, primarily in the United States, where it began, and in Great Britain, where it spread shortly thereafter. Although this investigation does deal with pertinent theological and exegetical views of the movement's most articulate leaders, it does not stress the strictly "doctrinal" aspects of charismatic renewal, except where they have had more than a little impact on the movement's development.

When the original edition of *The New Charismatics* was published in 1976, it was the first comprehensive treatment of neopentecostal leadership, faith, and practice as a whole, as well as the first study of its kind to propose causes of the movement's emergence and success in relation to trends in the wider society. The present edition, written *after* charismatic renewal's visibility had peaked, follows essentially the same progression of topics and argumentation as the first. But the text and documentation have been thoroughly updated, revised, and corrected. In addition, the highly sophisticated recent scholarship of younger pentecostal academics—Gerald T. Sheppard and James Tinney, in particular—has forced me to reconsider some of my earlier interpretations, especially those pertaining to the *essence* of classical pentecostalism as a movement and its relationship to neopentecostalism. Those who have read the first edition will find this revised version, in some respects, at least, an altogether new book.

The bibliography has also been completely updated and revised. Although by no means exhaustive, it does include almost all of what I think are the most important journalistic, apologetic, and scholarly-critical sources for the study of charismatic renewal available to date—with special (but not exclusive) reference to the United States and Great Britain. A few significant works on classical pentecostalism and other related issues are included as well. More importantly, however, I have annotated the bibliographical entries in this edition for which author, title, place, publisher, and date do not convey sufficient information about the work. Most of the important books and articles cited in the footnotes are also listed in the bibliography, with the sole exception of articles printed in classical pentecostal and neopentecostal magazines themselves. These appear only in the documentation.

All the sources used in the present and original editions of *The New Charismatics*—some, exceedingly hard to locate in even the best research collections—can be found in the Holy Spirit Research Center of the Oral Roberts University Library, Tulsa, Oklahoma. These do not circulate, however, and have not yet been placed on microfiche. Another excellent collection of pentecostal sources is held by the new Graduate Theological Union Library, Berkeley, California, and many of its books and magazines in that specialization do circulate. Finally, it should be noted that most books published by Logos International, and still in print when it collapsed in 1981, are now available from Bridge Publishing, Plainfield, New Jersey.

For their assistance in helping me with the research for the original edition of *The New Charismatics*, I am especially indebted to Christian Aid (London), Michael Harper, Walter Hollenweger, Kilian McDonnell, J. Robert Welsh, Bryan Wilson, and the World Council of Churches. And for substantial help on this revised edition, I must also thank Roy M. Carlisle, my editor at Harper & Row San Francisco, and Gerald T. Sheppard, in particular, who prepared for me an invaluable page-by-page critical commentary on the first edition.

Richard Quebedeaux
Berkeley, California
June 1982

The Nature of Charismatic Renewal

Someone has said that the problem with the present is the future. If the future is merely the continuation of the present, will there be any future at all? It is almost a truism to say that we are living in very distressing times in which even our wildest fantasies cannot provide solutions to present dilemmas—the population explosion; the "energy crisis," and the general depletion of natural resources; uncontrolled inflation, and the widening economic gap between rich and poor nations; the rapid increase in pollution, corruption in government, and competition for employment; and the demise of the family. All these enigmas vex rich and poor, educated and uneducated, white and black, male and female, alike. No one is exempt. At another level, the persistence of racism, sexism, militarism, and totalitarianism indicates that humankind is still riddled by grave uncertainty and fear—no less for the present than for the future. The once-powerful hope that science and technology would save us has turned out to be illusion. In fact, the "civilization" produced by technology and science tends to dehumanize rather than save men and women. It deprives them of an identity, and reduces them to an economic entity at best, and exploits and tortures them at worst.

The central message of the Christian gospel is "new life" now, and "new heavens and a new earth in which righteousness dwells" in the future. But somehow the institutional church has failed notably in getting this message across—in making it believable—to contemporary men and women. The church needs renewal. Many Christians, no less than others, find themselves dehumanized by our present society. They live frustrated and incomplete lives of faith, believing that they are forgiven and have been made new by God, but not sensing in themselves the *certainty* that this has really happened. Likewise, many Christians are encouraged by the New Testament promise that Christ has come into their lives to give them a fulfilling and abundant expression of himself, and that, ultimately, the Kingdom of God will prevail; but they are burdened because they have little or no *experience* of the joy that would confirm this promise. Yet others believe that God has called them to a life of responsibility toward the oppressed for whom Christ also died; but they do not feel assured that he is actively affirming their decisions and actions to bring about reconciliation, healing, and liberation.

When Christ promised his disciples that he would bestow on them his Holy Spirit after departing from them, he anticipated three practical needs the Spirit would satisfy in their lives: (1) empower them to fulfill the Great Commission, (2) bring joy in the midst of suffering as a foretaste of better things to come, and (3) assure, guide, and teach those who would choose to follow Christ. Yet to many, if not most, Christians, Christ's promise of his indwelling Spirit may be accepted intellectually, but it is not received experientially. Hence the promise is meaningless, and the question is raised again and again, "How do I *know* that the Holy Spirit dwells within me?" Charismatic renewal has offered an answer to this question—baptism in the Holy Spirit, a powerful experience that *convinces* the recipient that God is real, that God is faithful to what he has promised, and that the same "signs and wonders" described in the Book of Acts can happen today—to *me!*

Charismatic renewal has rejected the liberal, nonsupernatural god who really isn't there anyhow, but it also has rejected the rational evangelical god of the intellect—the great giver of propositional truth—in favor of the God you can feel, respond to, and love, the God who *cares* about our present and our future. It is the knowledge of this God, given through the experience of his Holy Spirit, that has bound charismatics together.

In a word, charismatic renewal has been a celebration in our generation that God has not forgotten his promises, that he is, in fact and deed, a living God, totally committed to work in *evidential* ways through the lives of those committed to him. This is the theme of the present work and the topic to which we shall now give our attention.

Chapter One

The Background

Secularization may be understood to include two related transformations in the way people think. First, there is an increasing "worldliness" in the attitude toward persons and things. What is fundamentally involved here is the abandonment of emotional commitment found in the religious response, the response to the sacred and holy. Second, there is a rationalization of thought, the repression of emotional involvement in thinking about the world. Rationalization suggests a manner of thought that is comparatively free of emotion and in which logic replaces emotional symbolism in organizing reflection and speculation. The secularization of culture indicates that a religious world view is no longer dominant as the frame of reference for thought.[1] By the mid-1960s, even theologians had come to accept, if not celebrate, the "secular" understanding of the world. But since that time, something has happened to indicate that "modern humanity" might not, in fact, be so free of religious needs and aspirations as was hitherto supposed. Already in 1948, Kingsley Davis suggested that the "tendency toward secularization probably cannot continue to the point where religion entirely disappears. Secularization will likely be terminated by religious revivals of one sort or another."[2] It is doubtful, however, that secularization can ever be *terminated*. But it is also apparent that secularization is not in all respects an irreversible process. The recent upsurge in the popularity of

---

1. Thomas F. O'Dea, *The Sociology of Religion* (Englewood Cliffs, N.J.: Prentice-Hall, 1966), p. 81.

2. Quoted in ibid., p. 17.

Eastern and other new religious movements, astrology, and the occult, the renaissance of evangelical and enthusiastic Christianity, affecting seemingly all strata of Western society, together point to the reemergence of what Andrew Greeley has called "unsecular man."[3]

Religion is nothing less than a symbolic transformation of experience. If the design religion gives to life is looked on by the skeptic as a set of rules and practices concealing chance events and cosmic indifference to human concerns, that same design is viewed by the believer as a revelation, often supernatural in nature, of the deeper meaning of experience—which is at the heart of religion.[4]

In the religious experience, men and women respond to the extraordinary, to power, to spontaneity and creativity. That experiential response, characterized by intense attraction and awe, leads to stable forms of thought, feeling, action, and relationship.[5] The religious experience is an attempt by humankind to respond to, and enter into, a relationship with what lies behind and beyond mere appearance.[6]

Yet basic to the very essence of religion is an unavoidable dilemma. Religious men and women must always live in relationship with two contrary realms of experience. They must relate both to the sacred and to the profane. And they must concern themselves both with the ultimate and the mundane, the spirit and the flesh. Out of this situation comes a multitude of problems for the church in all ages—not the least of which is the persistent effort to preserve the spirit of the New Testament and the primitive church in the changing conditions of each ensuing generation.[7] It is in this context that we shall examine closely one contemporary attempt to maintain and renew that spirit—"charismatic renewal," pentecostalism in its most recent expression.

---

3. See Andrew M. Greeley, *Unsecular Man* (New York: Dell, 1972).

4. O'Dea, p. 13.

5. Ibid., p. 24.

6. Ibid., p. 26.

7. Ibid., p. 24.

PENTECOSTALISM OLD AND NEW

The beginnings of the modern pentecostal movement can be traced back to 1906. "Classical pentecostalism" (or traditional pentecostalism), to distinguish it from the more recent charismatic renewal or "neopentecostalism," arose at the turn of the century out of various Baptist bodies and "holiness" groups that were reacting against the secularism and rationalism then seemingly dominant in the institutional churches. Pentecostal denominations that later developed from the early movement stressed an experience called "baptism in the Holy Spirit" as a second or third stage (after "conversion," or conversion and "sanctification") in the life of the believer. Evidence of this experience was most often assumed to be the *initial* speaking in tongues or glossolalia (Greek, *glossa*, "tongue"; *lalia*, "a talk") "as the Spirit gives utterance." "Spiritual gifts" outlined in 1 Cor. 12–14, for instance, including the *gift* of tongues (glossolalia as a *recurring* phenomenon), were understood as likely to follow in due course. Classical pentecostalism led to a wide variety of new denominations or "movements," despite its early condemnation of denominations as "sectarian" and "formalistic" and its critique of a divided Christian church feuding over nuances of doctrine. These new organizations also included highly independent congregations and storefront missions. The manner of church government varied. For instance, the early black Church of God in Christ had an episcopal form with bishops and elders, while the white Assemblies of God tried to find a balance between congregational and presbyterian structures to assure the absolute autonomy of local churches from the control of the larger denominational hierarchy. In the latter case, however, time led to a steady capitulation of local church autonomy to the judgment of a national general presbytery, a centralized structure aimed, in particular, at excluding certain "heretical" pentecostals like the "Jesus only" unitarians. Classical pentecostalism originated as a revivalistic movement, principally among the poor and disadvantaged. Dominant within the movement were blacks, poor whites in the South, and white immigrants from the South to the

North, East, and West. It lacked roots in a single tradition and was itself a reaction against the "historic denominations." Hence, sociologists have often designated traditional pentecostalism as "sectarian."[8]

Because of their low social status and the "crude negroisms" of their religion, the classical pentecostals were neither recognized by nor accepted in the historic denominations, so they developed their own. Although integrated at first, white and black pentecostals soon went their own separate ways as well, forming distinctively black and white church organizations. White pentecostalism, in its traditional expression, separated itself as much as it could from the wider society ("the world") and its institutions and values. The movement also gradually aligned itself with the essential doctrines of nonpentecostal fundamentalism (another movement of marginalized whites) in opposition to the liberalism gaining ascendance in the historic denominations. This alliance emerged despite the vicious attacks on pentecostalism and its "emotionalism" by fundamentalist leaders such as Reuben Archer Torrey, who termed the movement "the last vomit of Satan." Black pentecostalism, however, like the black church in general, was left out of the concurrent fundamentalist-modernist controversy because of the cultural ghettoizing of the time due to racism. Hence, black pentecostals were not all that aware of the issues so important to fundamentalists and liberals in their heated debate, and fundamentalist doctrine did not become a hallmark of identity within black pentecostal churches as it eventually did in white pentecostalism.

Although grounded in the same religious experience, neopentecostalism differed markedly in its development from its classical forerunner and counterpart. In principle, charismatic renewal began and maintained itself as a "transdenominational" movement of enthusiastic Christianity that emerged and became recognizable in the historic denominations only in 1960. It has been theologically diverse but generally orthodox, unified by a common experience

---

8. Gerald T. Sheppard, unpublished "Commentary on *The New Charismatics* (First Edition)," December 1981.

—baptism in the Holy Spirit—with accompanying *charismata* (Greek, "gifts") to be used personally and corporately in the life of the church. Evangelistic and conversionist in character, charismatic renewal, like early classical pentecostalism, has also been a reformist movement. But because of its upper-middle-class origins in the white community, neopentecostalism found much quicker acceptance in the historic denominations in its time than the traditional form did at its inception. Thus, sectarianism has never been a dominant characteristic in the development of charismatic renewal.

It should also be noted here that there has not been a comparable neopentecostal movement in the historic black denominations, because black religion was already so expressive in worship and so open to spontaneity (including that of the Holy Spirit) that such a spiritual "renewal" was simply unnecessary. Indeed, some black Baptist congregations conduct services in a manner indistinguishable from the black pentecostal churches.[9]

Charismatic renewal has been, first of all, neither a church nor a denomination. It developed, as Edward O'Connor, professor of theology at the University of Notre Dame, suggests, as a "movement" (although not without qualification):

> The term *movement* . . . implies that numbers of people have joined forces in more or less concerted effort on a common project. This supposes a goal that is aimed at and a deliberate pursuit of that goal; usually it connotes a considerable degree of organization and method . . . [neopentecostalism] did not originate by the deliberate adoption of any goal, is not an organized enterprise, and it does not consist in a method. It is indeed a movement, inasmuch as it consists of a multitude of people moving in the same general direction, and influencing one another. But their unity does not derive, at least basically and originally, from any intention or plan of their conceiving. In fact, what is most remarkable about this movement in its early days is how unexpectedly it arose and how spontaneously it spread. Most of those who were involved in it at the beginning found themselves taken quite by surprise.

9. Ibid.

It is true [however] that in the course of its development it has become more aware of its aims, more deliberate in its efforts, and more methodical and organized.[10]

Nevertheless, charismatic renewal's general direction *was* set by its early leaders in terms of "proper" (that is, middle-class) ritual for worship and the distinctively neopentecostal exercise of spiritual gifts—more regulated and less spontaneous than in traditional pentecostalism. The movement very quickly developed its own particular ways of conducting small groups, and key leaders established the pattern repeatedly wherever they went. So there was more than a measure of organized and methodical spirituality from the beginning, but this did not hamper the "unity in diversity" that would continue to mark the movement.

A sense of relative freedom was maintained over against the potential tyranny of a single leader by the large number of small "prayer groups" that catered to people of quite different needs and dispositions. Within a cluster of such groups, an observer could identify one group as more ecclesiastically oriented, another whose activity centered more on teaching the Bible, another on evangelism, and yet another whose emphases were focused more on eschatology, the doctrine of the "Last Days." Charismatics have tended, over a period of time, to move from one group to another, and from one emphasis to another, as a matter of personal choice. Yet, despite these differences, the very plurality of groups identifying themselves as "charismatic" has compensated for the potential exclusiveness of each particular one. In the common meetings of charismatic congregations and parishes, and in large ecumenical rallies, the leaders would cooperate to find some common denominator to accommodate the diversity.[11]

Michael Harper, Great Britain's foremost early neopentecostal leader, emphasized in 1972 that "there are few signs yet of [the movement's] being bureaucratised into impotence. Its main

---

10. Edward D. O'Connor, *The Pentecostal Movement in the Catholic Church* (Notre Dame, Ind.: Ave Maria Press, 1971), pp. 33–34.

11. Ibid.

strength, and for many its attractiveness, lies in its spontaneity, and in the fact that it is so far comparatively unstructured."[12] By and large, Harper's words remained true—with a few notable exceptions—throughout the ensuing decade.

PENETRATION OF "ESTABLISHED" CHURCHES

If neopentecostalism has been a proper movement, its essential nature has been transdenominational. Roman Catholics, Eastern Orthodox Christians, Anglicans, and Protestants of virtually all the historic denominations are included. Here the pentecostal experience is understood to transcend denominational walls, while it clarifies and underscores what is authentically Christian in each tradition without demanding structural or even doctrinal changes in any given church body. Hence, charismatic renewal is also ecumenical, although not in the sense that it openly seeks institutional unity as a goal. Harper stresses that the movement has been more concerned with *spiritual* unity at the "grass roots" level than with organic union engineered by ecumenical planners:

> There is a sharing together at the deep levels of worship, prayer, spiritual gifts and ministries, and testimony, as well as biblical teaching. This is not to disguise the fact that there are still many differences between Christians and many difficulties in the pathway to unity. But those involved believe that this is where Christians should *begin* in their quest for unity, not at the conference table or the debating chamber. . . . The ecumenical movement seems to put the cart before the horse; whereas this new move of the Holy Spirit is indicating what we should be doing first.[13]

Nevertheless, neopentecostalism has been generally friendly in its attitude toward the ecumenical structures such as the World Council of Churches and its regional counterparts. Furthermore, the

12. Michael Harper, "On to Maturity," *Renewal* (December 1972–January 1973), p. 34.

13. Michael Harper, *None Can Guess* (Plainfield, N.J.: Logos International, 1971), p. 154.

Protestant-Catholic encounter within charismatic renewal has been so intense and heartfelt that it is probably unparalleled in contemporary ecclesiastical experience. In view of this fact, Harper again has asserted "that this movement is the most unifying in Christendom today ... *for only in this movement are all streams uniting, and all ministries being accepted and practised.*"[14] Already in 1952, David du Plessis, then secretary of the Pentecostal World Conferences, called for a reconciliation of pentecostals and other Christians:

> After nearly half a century of misunderstanding and ostracism, for which they recognized they have not been entirely without blame on their own part, the Pentecostal Churches offer their fellowship in Christ to the whole of His Church in this grave hour of her history. They believe they have something to gain by larger fellowship with all who truly belong to Christ. They are greatly encouraged by many world-wide tokens that old prejudices are melting and a new era of mutual appreciation dawning. Brethren, let us receive one another, as Christ also received us to the glory of God.[15]

The real beginnings of that reconciliation took eight years to materialize. And when the rapprochement finally did occur, it was no mere "dialogue" between pentecostal and nonpentecostal churches; rather, it was a totally unanticipated *penetration* or diffusion of the pentecostal experience into the "established" denominations.

Another characteristic of neopentecostalism has been its theological diversity. Protestants and Catholics, conservatives and liberals, do not automatically discard their own theological and ecclesiastical differences when they come together in this movement. Nor do the movement's leaders themselves agree on a precise definition of baptism in the Holy Spirit or the exact nature of the charismata and their operation. Nevertheless, charismatic

---

14. Ibid., pp. 149, 153.

15. David J. du Plessis, "A Statement by Pentecostal Leaders," in Norman Goodall, ed., *Missions Under the Cross* (London: Edinburgh House, 1953), pp. 249–250.

renewal is indeed firmly rooted in "historic orthodoxy."[16] Furthermore, this implicit orthodoxy is enhanced by the fact that whether one is theologically liberal or conservative, it is felt that he (or she), as a neopentecostal, will invariably come to have a more vivid sense of God as a *person,* since in Spirit baptism God has *demonstrated* his reality to someone in a personal way. Likewise, it is expected that the pentecostal experience will initiate or restore a person's interest in serious Bible study and will also give him or her a new awareness of the efficacy of prayer. Neopentecostals, regardless of their theological and ecclesiastical outlook, must cultivate a fresh *openness* if they are to continue successfully within the movement.[17] Charismatic renewal manifests a kind of "unity in diversity"—grounded in Spirit baptism, the pentecostal experience. To the majority of neopentecostals, this experience is so dynamic that it produces an all-embracing religious enthusiasm and renders denominational and theological barriers insignificant as deterrents to Christian fellowship.[18]

A further aspect of neopentecostalism has been its nature as an evangelistic movement. Activity often centers on an evangelism that calls people to a personal (although variously understood) "acceptance of Jesus Christ as Savior and Lord," and that is expected to result in a new relationship with God. This must always come prior to baptism in the Holy Spirit, although it is felt that individuals are initially brought to that point in their lives through the activity of the Spirit. The Holy Spirit is understood to provide the *power* necessary to convince persons of their need for the experience, whether the latter is regarded as a "first-time decision" or a profound "renewal" of what has already happened in water baptism and confirmation. Charismatic renewal has been also evangelical in spirit. By *evangelical,* we refer to those who actively seek to bring others what they see as a "God-human encounter."

---

16. See, for instance, Jamie Buckingham, "Breakthrough in Unity," *Logos Journal* (September–October 1972), pp. 37–39.

17. O'Connor, *The Pentecostal Movement in the Catholic Church,* p. 159.

18. Harper, *None Can Guess,* pp. 154–155.

But the term describes a theological spirit as well, a kind of mediating position between the legalistic, literalist, and very exclusive tenets of religious (or politicoreligious) "fundamentalism" and the humanistic naturalism of religious "liberalism."[19] This mediating evangelical spirit has been demonstrated by the readiness of neopentecostals to participate in discussion with Christians of other persuasions, with the knowledge, of course, that such discussion itself can be a form of evangelism. The former believe that the person with an experience need never feel themselves to be at the mercy of the person with an argument.[20]

Charismatic renewal, moreover, has been thoroughly reformist in character. There is very little if any interest in separating from old ecclesiastical structures and building new ones according to the classical pentecostal pattern. Rather, present institutions are to be "renewed" by the charismatic activity of the Holy Spirit as it affects the membership of a church or other group through the continued presence *within* that structure of individuals who have been baptized in the Spirit. This stance as a norm of neopentecostalism was first articulated by Dennis Bennett, a pioneer of charismatic renewal, in his letter of resignation as rector of St. Mark's Episcopal Church, Van Nuys, California, in 1960—a resignation motivated by the strong disapproval of his pentecostal experience voiced in powerful quarters of the parish:

I am sorry for the furor, and for the pain that has been caused. I ask every person in St. Mark's whether they be for me or against me, *not to leave the Parish or cancel their pledge*. This is a spiritual issue, and will not be settled in this way. I myself am going to stay strictly out of Parish work until the matter has been clarified one way or the other. Support whatever interim pastorate the Bishop and Vestry set up. . . .

Any rumors that reach your ears that in any way imply that I am

---

19. See Richard Quebedeaux, "Evangelicals: Ecumenical Allies," *Christianity and Crisis* (December 27, 1971), pp. 286–288; and *The Young Evangelicals* (New York: Harper & Row, 1974).

20. McCandlish Phillips, "And There Appeared to Them Tongues of Fire," *Saturday Evening Post* (May 16, 1964), p. 40.

leaving the Episcopal Church are false.... What I am standing for is to be found within the Episcopal Church; no one needs to leave the Episcopal Church in order to have the fullness of the Spirit. But it is important that the Spirit be allowed to work freely in the Episcopal Church, and it is to this that I bear witness, and will continue to bear witness.[21]

Initially, there were a few neopentecostals who discouraged others new to the experience from remaining in the more theologically inclusive denominations. In England, the typical argument used by "dissenters" from the established church (appropriately modified) was even raised.[22] But such vocal opinions were few and far between. The stage had clearly been set for the continued diffusion and "settling in" of pentecostal phenomena in the historic ecclesiastical structures as "normative procedure" for the movement.[23]

Finally, we can say that charismatic renewal has been characterized by a very large representation of individuals from the middle and upper-middle socioeconomic levels of society. Among those in the movement, there have been wealthy businesspeople and other professionals, "mainline" clergy, even intellectuals—a fact manifestly apparent from the beginning. St. Mark's Episcopal Church serves an affluent community. And the Blessed Trinity Society, Van Nuys, California—one of the first fellowship and publishing organizations the movement produced—had several well-to-do patrons. An early sampling of the society found Republicans in a ratio of seven to one.[24] When neopentecostalism began to diffuse

21. Quoted in Walter J. Hollenweger, "Handbuch der Pfingstbewegung," unpublished doctoral thesis, Faculty of Theology, University of Zurich, 1965–1967, pp. 824–825 (02a.02.206).

22. See D. G. Lillie, "Renewal in Historic Churches," *Renewal* (October–November 1966), pp. 7–9.

23. See Michael Harper, "First Edify, Then Evangelize," *Trinity* (Whitsuntide 1965), p. 25.

24. See Robert L. Dean, "Strange Tongues: A Psychologist Studies Glossolalia," *Trinity* (Trinitytide 1964), pp. 37–39; and, for instance, Pat Boone, *A New Song* (Carol Stream, Ill.: Creation House, 1970); Thomas R. Nickel, *The Shakarian Story*, 2nd ed. (Los Angeles: Full Gospel Business Men's Fellowship Internation-

within the Roman Catholic Church in 1967, most of the first participants from that tradition were part of the academic community—undergraduates, graduate students, and university instructors (including theologians). With the growing involvement of Catholic bishops, priests, nuns, and laypeople, the "WASP" (White Anglo-Saxon Protestant) stereotype of the movement no longer applies. And although *some* representatives of the poor and minority groups are to be found in the ranks, no one can rightly designate charismatic renewal as a movement of the economically deprived and disadvantaged—a description that still might, to a large degree, fit (at least black) classical pentecostalism.

Having looked at the essential nature of neopentecostalism and, in broad terms, a few *dominant* attributes distinguishing it from its classical forerunner and counterpart, we shall now examine the character of the pentecostal phenomena themselves, their biblical justification, and their historical incidence.

THE SPIRITUAL GIFTS

At the heart of the pentecostal experience is baptism in the Holy Spirit. It should be clarified from the start, however, that the expression "baptism in the Holy Spirit" does not occur in the New Testament. The noun "baptism" is never used in that way. A few times the verb "baptize" is employed in this connection with the Greek preposition *en,* which the Revised Standard Version (RSV) translates "with" (Matt. 3:11, Mark 1:8; Luke 3:16; Acts 1:5, 11:16). All these refer to the same saying ascribed to John the Baptist that the coming Messiah would "baptize with the Holy Spirit." The one other appearance of the phrase is in 1 Cor. 12:13, where it is declared that "by (Greek *en*) one spirit we were all baptized into one body" (that is, the church).[25]

---

al, 1964); and George Otis, *High Adventure* (Van Nuys, Calif.: Time-Light Publishing, 1971).

25. United Presbyterian Church, U.S.A., *The Work of the Holy Spirit* (Philadelphia: United Presbyterian Church, U.S.A., 1970), p. 30.

Pentecostals believe that certain sayings and incidents recorded in Acts are a fulfillment of the prophecy that the Messiah (that is, Jesus) would baptize with the Holy Spirit. Luke reports that at Pentecost, Peter proclaimed that the gift of the Spirit was now available to all who repent and are baptized in the name of Jesus Christ (Acts 2:38)—a teaching very much in harmony with the basic implications of the New Testament as a whole. But in the case of Cornelius and his household, the Spirit "fell on" the converts immediately, before they were baptized (Acts 10:44–48). We can also point out the case of the Samaritan converts who were baptized by Philip, yet whose reception of the Spirit was delayed until Peter and John had come from Jerusalem and had laid their hands on those new believers (Acts 8:12–17). Somewhat similar to the last incident is the status of various disciples Paul met in Ephesus (Acts 19:2–6) who had been baptized with only "John's baptism." They had not received the Holy Spirit "when they had believed" (that is, had been converted—the King James Version rendering, "since ye believed," is incorrect). These individuals were then baptized by Paul "in the name of the Lord Jesus," and "when Paul had laid his hands upon them, the Holy Spirit came upon them; and they spoke with tongues and prophesied" (Acts 19:6).[26] Thus it is difficult to ascertain any one consistent pattern in Acts of the sequence of conversion, reception of the Holy Spirit, and water baptism. In this respect, it is clear that (as an interpretive principle) pentecostals give primary attention to the *historic* parts of Acts as normative over, perhaps, other *doctrinal* portions of the New Testament which some critics believe are more important.[27]

For pentecostals, the physical action of "laying on of hands" by clergy or laypeople (or both) who are already "filled" with the Holy Spirit in a manifest way, during prayer, is usually (but not

---

26. Ibid., p. 36.

27. Ibid., p. 37. See Gordon D. Fee, "Hermeneutics and Historical Precedent," in Russell P. Spittler, ed., *Perspectives on the New Pentecostalism* (Grand Rapids, Mich.: Baker Book House, 1976), pp. 118–132.

always) the manner in which individuals receive their Spirit baptism (an action that is not regarded by Catholic theologians as sacramental or even quasi-sacramental in character.[28]) Although the candidates pray, it is generally (but again, not always) anticipated that they will experience at least an initial outburst of glossolalia in the course of their prayer—when they actually receive "the blessing." Such speaking in tongues is viewed as evidence of the manifest "fullness" of the Holy Spirit and may in due course, if not immediately, be followed by reception of the *gift* of tongues (recurring glossolalia) or other spiritual gifts. Edward O'Connor describes the laying on of hands as follows:

> When a person is seeking the "baptism of the Holy Spirit," it is a common thing for others, especially those who have already been thus blessed, to lay their hands on his head and to pray for him. The same form of prayer is frequently used when other graces [or gifts] and needs are being sought for also.
>
> The adoption of this gesture has been inspired by biblical precedents, especially those in which the Holy Spirit was given to someone through the laying-on-of-hands. However, its continued use is motivated above all by the power that it seems to have. De facto, God seems to use it in a remarkable way to bestow grace . . . the effects of this prayer are quite manifest, in the gift of tongues, or in a sudden powerful experience of the grace of God, or even in a miraculous healing. These occur often enough that people in the movement are deeply convinced of this form of prayer and strongly attached to its use.[29]

Glossolalia, although generally the most observable, is certainly not the *only* spiritual gift for which an individual baptized in the Holy Spirit may aspire. "Spiritual gifts" is a comprehensive term for all the extraordinary and sometimes "miraculous" powers possessed by many Christians in the Apostolic era. These charismata had their origin in the gracious (Greek *charis*, "grace") action of

---

28. Edward O'Connor, *The Laying on of Hands* (Pecos, N.M.: Dove, 1969), pp. 5–7.

29. Ibid., pp. 3–4.

the Holy Spirit and were given in order "to equip God's people for work in his service" (Eph. 4:12, New English Bible).

The most important section of the New Testament dealing with spiritual gifts is 1 Cor. 12–14. Here Paul presents three lists of such gifts (1 Cor. 12:8–10, 28, 29–30). It is useful to compare the lists, starting with Verse 28, in which the apostle enumerates the first three gifts in a definite sequence ("first . . . second . . . third"). 1 Cor. 12:28: (1) apostles, (2) prophets, (3) teachers, (4) workers of miracles, (5) healers, (6) helpers, (7) administrators, and (8) speakers in various kinds of tongues. Somewhat analogous is the sequence found in 1 Cor. 12:8–10 and 29–30 (numerals in parentheses refer to the list in 1 Cor. 12:28, and to the same or similar gifts). 1 Cor. 12:8–10: (1) utterance of wisdom, (3) utterance of knowledge, faith, (5) gifts of healing, (4) working of miracles, (2) prophecy, ability to distinguish between spirits, (8) various kinds of tongues and the interpretation of tongues. Then, 1 Cor. 12:29–30: (1) apostles, (2) prophets, (3) teachers, (4) miracles, (5) gifts of healing, (8) speaking with tongues and interpreting (tongues).[30]

In 1 Cor. 12:29–30, "a word of wisdom" and "a word of knowledge" seem to refer to discourses or briefer utterances that either express Christian truths and their relations to one another or that put forward ethical instruction and practical exhortation. "Faith" here can hardly mean mere "saving faith" but must indicate some exceptional degree of potent faith that can work miracles (compare with 1 Cor. 13:2). "Prophecy" in the primitive church was not so much the predicting of future events; rather, it was primarily the gift of understanding and expressing by teaching or preaching the nature of the will of God for a particular situation, resulting in "upbuilding and encouragement and consolation" (1 Cor. 14:3). The "ability to distinguish between spirits" refers to an intuitive power enabling its possessor to discriminate between true and false prophets—to judge whether their teaching comes from God or is an illusion (compare with 1 John 4:1).

---

30. United Presbyterian Church, U.S.A., p. 37.

THE MIRACULOUS AND THE NONMIRACULOUS

What is clear is the fact that, in general, the gifts may be divided into the miraculous and nonmiraculous. Included among the former are workers of miracles and healers; among the latter are gifts of character and mental and spiritual endowments—exhortation, contributing, giving aid, and administering, for instance.[31] By way of summary, charismata can be defined as endowments and capacities needed for the edification and service of the church—given by the Holy Spirit—through which its members are enabled to use their natural faculties to serve the church or are endowed with new abilities and powers for that purpose.[32]

Pentecostals firmly believe that they have a biblical warrant for their exercise of the spiritual gifts. A special significance is attached to the prophecies of Joel, to which Peter referred on the Day of Pentecost.[33] Feeling compelled to account for the strange manifestations that puzzled onlookers, Peter declared that

> this is what was spoken by the prophet Joel: And in the last days it shall be, God declares, that I will pour out my Spirit upon all flesh, and your sons and your daughters shall prophesy, and your young men shall see visions, and your old men shall dream dreams; yea, and on my menservants and my maidservants in those days I will pour out my Spirit; and they shall prophesy [Acts 2:16–18; Peter is citing Joel 2:28–32].

It is because of their zealous use of the charismata that pentecostals are often characterized as prone to ecstasy and enthusiastic demonstrations. If glossolalia appears to be "ecstatic utterance," however, it is probably only so in the sense that the speaker "may feel emotionally lifted, inspired by God's Spirit, not that one behaves in an irrational and trance-like manner."[34] Pentecostalism

---

31. Ibid., p. 38.

32. Ibid., p. 39.

33. John T. Nichol, *Pentecostalism* (New York: Harper & Row, 1966), p. 9.

34. United Presbyterian Church, U.S.A., p. 5. This is, of course, subject to disagreement, and perhaps also to cultural conditions.

is indeed an enthusiastic form of Christianity; but the caricature of the "holy roller" (one who literally "rolls" in the aisles during services of worship) is applicable only to classical pentecostalism in its very extreme manifestations. Kilian McDonnell, a Benedictine monk and scholar, points out—without pejorative intent—that the typical activities associated with pentecostal worship, including hand-clapping, shouting, marching around the assembly, and "dancing in the Spirit," are merely examples of classical pentecostal "cultural baggage" and are not to be confused with what is essential to the nature and operation of the spiritual gifts.[35]

In charismatic renewal, the pentecostal experience has been subdued. Not only has much of the cultural baggage been suppressed, but the protracted sequence of events in the spiritual life characteristic of classical pentecostalism has been shortened as well. Gone are the days when an individual might have to "seek" or "tarry" perhaps months or even years in order to become experientially "sanctified," freed from sin, and then receive baptism in the Holy Spirit—often "praying through" the night and waiting patiently for evidence of the blessing to appear. For the neopentecostal, reception of the Spirit in a manifest way is generally accomplished after only a brief session of prayer with the laying on of hands. Likewise, other classical pentecostal practices such as fasting and exorcism, though not discarded in charismatic renewal, have been modified or put under restraint. In the matter of exorcism, some neopentecostals believe that Christians can be obsessed or possessed by demons and, therefore, encourage and provide a ministry of "deliverance." Others totally disagree. But in all aspects of the charismatic operation, strict emphasis is placed on Paul's dictum that "all things should be done decently and in order" (1 Cor. 14:40).[36]

---

35. See Kilian McDonnell, "Catholic Pentecostalism: Problems in Evaluation," *Dialog* (Winter 1970), pp. 35–54.

36. Sociologically, there is a point to be made here. "New" religious movements and new styles of religiosity, particularly if they involve emotional display, almost always appear to be avenues of spiritual mobility—faster ways to reach desired but hitherto hard to attain goals. Classical pentecostalism itself was that

THE CHARISMATICS IN HISTORY

If it seems that pentecostal phenomena disappeared altogether during the period between the Apostolic era and the twentieth century, this is not really the case at all. But references to the phenomena are often unclear, and it is probable that manifestations of the more spectacular charismata in (and outside) Christian history were fewer and farther between than some pentecostals have maintained.[37] Although reports of healings and other miracles are not uncommon in the corpus of surviving Christian literature, evidence for the appearance of glossolalia, at least from the late second century to the eighteenth or nineteenth century, is scarce and frequently obscure. Quite often, for example, speaking in tongues is not clearly differentiated from the gift of prophecy. After the first century until the modern period, there are only a few references to glossolalia in Christian discourse. Hence, some authorities believe that the gift of tongues was insignificant in the development of the early church. Others feel that because glossolalia was easily misunderstood by nonspeakers, the divulgence of such a gift would arouse public hostility. It does seem certain, however, that the Montanists of the second century, a schismatic group of Christians in Phrygia—ardently apocalyptic—practiced speaking in tongues and other charismata as well, although we have only a few cryptic "sayings" of Montanus and his disciples to examine as primary sources (the writings of such movements in the church considered less than orthodox were often destroyed). In fact, most of our information about the Montanists comes from

---

—getting further and with more certainty than was possible in the formalized churches. There is often a "spiritual inflation" with a consequent debasement of the existing spiritual coinage and a demand for its faster circulation and availability. Status inflation is an interesting social phenomenon; and it is possible to see pentecostalism as two waves of a demand for a wider redistribution of spiritual statuses than the formal organization of the churches otherwise would admit.

37. See, for instance, R. Leonard Carroll, "Glossolalia: Apostles to the Reformation," in Wade H. Horton, ed., *The Glossolalia Phenomenon* (Cleveland, Tenn.: Pathway Press, 1966), pp. 67–94; and Vessie D. Hargrave, "Glossolalia: Reformation to the Twentieth Century," *The Glossolalia Phenomenon*, pp. 95–139.

the comments of orthodox writers and historians (such as Eusebius) who were clearly antagonistic toward the movement and must be read with much caution.

There is some question concerning the espousal of glossolalia by Tertullian, a major formulator of Christian doctrine during the early third century. Some authorities feel that he was quite specific as to its existence and real values. Others find the references less specific or even ambiguous—also pointing out the passing influence of Montanism on his writings. Origen, in the third century, and Chrysostom, in the fourth, both disparaged the accounts of speaking in tongues, and rejected its continued validity. Augustine, early in the fifth century, asserted that glossolalia was a sign adapted only to biblical times—although some scholars believe that he did, in fact, uphold the legitimacy of speaking in tongues, and that it was still practiced in his lifetime.

Biographies of such great missionary saints as Vincent Ferrer (1350–1419) and Francis Xavier (1506–1552) have long perpetuated the notion that these people possessed the gift of tongues —in the sense that they could speak existing foreign languages previously unknown to them (some people define glossolalia in this way). But careful study of the facts indicates that the biographies in question were subject to the power of myth.

Data exist suggesting that speaking in tongues was practiced infrequently in sixteenth-century Germany by the Anabaptists, and in seventeenth-century France by the Jansenists. In 1685, Louis XIV of France called on the Protestant Huguenots to return to the Roman Catholic Church, and reinforced his urgings with severe persecution. During this time, some of the Huguenots (the Camisards) reported phenomena among them such as "strange sounds in the air; the sound of a trumpet and a harmony of voices." Those affected were known as "prophets of the Cévennes mountains," and the episodes continued until 1711.

The French prophets also toured England and probably influenced Mother Ann Lee and the Wardleys, originators of the Shakers (evidence points to the possibility of glossolalia among the Shakers in mid-eighteenth-century America). According to clergy who examined her, Ann Lee, although only semiliterate, spoke in several known languages. Various splinter groups of the early Quakers espoused speaking in tongues as a significant religious experience—among these, the so-called Ranters in England.

In the course of the nineteenth century, the Irvingites (founders of the Catholic Apostolic Church, which still exists in Germany and the United States) practiced glossolalia—as did others in Sweden, Norway, and America. Especially interesting here are the obvious similarities between the Irvingites and classical pentecostals. First, it is thought that the Irvingites believed that the occurrence of speaking in tongues among them was of the same nature as that which took place on the Day of Pentecost—an evidence of Spirit baptism. Second, they appear to have regarded such an experience as a prerequisite for obtaining one or more of the spiritual gifts mentioned in the New Testament. Third, the Irvingites insisted that the charismata manifested at Pentecost and in the primitive church were a permanent possession of the church—withheld only because of the unfaithfulness of Christian believers. And fourth, Edward Irving and his charismatic followers were expelled from the Presbyterian Church and were forced to establish a new denomination.[38]

Belief in the gifts of the Spirit ("the gift of tongues, prophecy, revelation, visions, healing, interpretation of tongues, etc.") is indicated in the "Articles of Faith" of the Mormon Church, founded in 1830 by Joseph Smith. Finally, scattered references are found suggesting that glossolalia occurred in Orthodox Russia in the nineteenth century (for example, among Presbyterians in the Armenian village Kara Kala in 1880 and thereafter).[39] And, even today,

---

38. Nichol, p. 24.

39. See Cyril G. Williams, *Tongues of the Spirit* (Cardiff: University of Wales Press, 1981); John P. Kildahl, *The Psychology of Speaking in Tongues* (New York: Harper & Row, 1972), pp. 14–18; Morton T. Kelsey, *Tongue Speaking* (New York: Doubleday, 1964), pp. 32–68; George H. Williams and Edith Waldvogel, "A History of Speaking in Tongues and Related Gifts," in Michael P. Hamilton, ed., *The Charismatic Movement* (Grand Rapids, Mich.: Eerdmans, 1974), pp. 61–113 (these scholars find more glossolalia in Christian history than most others do); Émile Lombard, *De la Glossolalia chez les Premiers Chrétiens et*

speaking in tongues is a common phenomenon among the indigenous religious traditions of Africa and Latin America.

Other possible occurrences of speaking in tongues in Christian history (and in non-Christian cultures as well) could be cited. But in so many cases—those mentioned, and others—we cannot be certain at all that the verbal behavior alluded to was anything like modern glossolalia.[40] Whatever importance may be attached to the historical incidence of speaking in tongues and pentecostal phenomena in general since the end of the Apostolic era, it is only since this century began that the church as a whole has been confronted by a widespread manifestation of the pentecostal experience within its ranks. Once more, that confrontation (especially since the advent of charismatic renewal in 1960) has increasingly attracted the interest of psychologists, historians, sociologists, anthropologists, and theologians, who have produced notable scholarship on pentecostalism both from within the movement and from the outside. It is also worthy of comment, moreover, that most of the best and most influential works have appeared just since 1964. What is striking about the more recent investigations by nonpentecostal scholars is the relatively large amount of favor shown toward the pentecostal movement as a whole (even toward glossolalia), which was not evident in most earlier studies.

---

des Phénomeñes Similaires: Étude d'Exégèse et de Psychologie (Lausanne: Imprimeries Réunies, 1910); and Eddison Mosimann, Das Zungenreden geschichtlich und psychologisch untersucht (Tübingen: Mohr, 1911).

40. William J. Samarin, Tongues of Men and Angels: The Religious Language of Pentecostalism (New York: Macmillan, 1972), p. 13.

Chapter Two

Beginnings in

North America

Nils Bloch-Hoell, a Norwegian scholar, puts forth a number of cultural and religious facilitating circumstances that he considers underlie the rise of the pentecostal movement in general, and its emergence in the United States at the turn of the century in particular.

The first underlying circumstance was the pervasive diversity characteristic of American church life. At the beginning of this century, the United States represented an immigrant conglomerate, and each national or ethnic group had its own heritage. There was no one dominant religious style; yet, unconventional appearance and antiritualism were common features of American Christianity as a whole. In this context, pentecostalism was from the start opposed both to regularity and orderliness.

Second, religious tolerance and denominations—again, distinguishing features of American life—greatly facilitated the rise and prosperity of the pentecostal movement, which itself then contributed to the ever-increasing number of American religious denominations.

A third underlying circumstance in the emergence of pentecostalism was the principle of voluntary association distinctive of American life. Voluntary church membership has promoted intense religious activity in the United States—activity that, especially on the frontier, produced fervent evangelism in the form of revival campaigns. Traditional churches and clergy did not exist on the frontier, where preaching was undertaken largely by uneducated laypeople or "circuit riders" who appealed more to the emotions than to the intellect. From 1800 onward, revivalism was closely connected with "camp meetings," which attracted thousands of people for days at a time. Mass conversions, both at rural camp meetings and, later, in urban revival campaigns, were the consequence. Pentecostalism reemphasized the old camp meetings, and its advance was associated with the persistence of revivalism in general—predominantly in the southern and western states, where the pentecostal movement reaped its richest harvest.

Fourth, the general climate of American individualism—a product of the frontier—indirectly contributed to the rise of pentecostalism. Fundamentalism, of course, has often led to individualism. But the increasingly popular theological liberalism of the nineteenth century, with its principle of critical evaluation, was often also decidedly individualistic. Denying both biblical and creedal authority, it ended up as a form of religious subjectivism. The empiricism of natural science demanded that something had to be proved by observation, verified by the senses, or demonstrated by logical argument. Like individualism, subjectivism favored the emergence of the pentecostal movement whose empiricism became emotional. Religious truth was confirmed by experience.

A fifth underlying circumstance was the pervasive optimism of the nineteenth century. This optimism—motivated by great discoveries and inventions, social awakenings, and long periods of peace —profoundly influenced religious and ethical thinking. No less than the Social Gospel,[1] the holiness movement (as the precursor of pentecostalism) was an outcome of the optimistic belief that

---

1. "An international movement that reinterpreted moral norms, found primarily in the teaching of Jesus, and the Old Testament prophets, and applied them to the issues that emerged with industrialization and the working classes. Although the movement was strongest from 1890 to 1920, it continues to exert an influence." (In Keith Crim, ed., *Abingdon Dictionary of Living Religions* [Nashville: Abingdon, 1981], p. 697.) Walter Rauschenbusch (1861–1918), an American Baptist clergyman, was considered the father and chief theologian for the movement. (Webster's Biographical Dictionary, p. 1239.)

moral perfection—entire sanctification—was indeed a very real possibility.

Sixth, the rootlessness connected with the Industrial Revolution and the mass immigration to the United States in the late nineteenth and early twentieth centuries contributed to the emergence of the pentecostal movement. The sudden change in milieu—from Europe to America, from country to city life—led almost inevitably to political and social rootlessness. Many immigrants may have had unsatisfied religious needs met more readily by an enthusiastic form of Christianity than by that represented by a static church.

A seventh underlying circumstance in the rise of pentecostalism was the thoroughly democratic character of American society, which affected religion deeply. This democratic attitude resulted in the predominance of low-church principles and practices, as well as an esteem for personal religious experience and "nonliturgical," informal worship. When university-trained clergy replaced the circuit riders and brought with them formality and "culture" to many churches, several groups of believers no longer felt at home —socially and at worship—and reacted by forming their own associations, some of which became pentecostal (*emphasizing* enthusiasm and informality).

Eighth, the new structure of industrial society itself may have facilitated the emergence of the pentecostal movement. With an apparent increase in class prejudice, the poor naturally became more open to "radical" and oppositionist movements. Pentecostalism was, in a sense, a class movement of the poor and uneducated.

A ninth underlying circumstance in the rise of pentecostalism (as well as the holiness movement before it) was the stiffening institutionalism, secularism, and "modernism" of the greater American churches. As the masses of people became seemingly indifferent, there arose a strong desire on the part of numerous Christians to *demonstrate* by some palpable evidence the truth of Christianity to an unbelieving society. The pentecostal movement found that phenomena such as glossolalia and divine healing (the latter of which was also stressed in the holiness movement) strengthened revival work by offering "proofs" of God's presence and activity to antagonists, removing intellectual doubts about Christianity, and providing additional means to conversions.

Tenth and finally, the pentecostal movement was facilitated by the interdenominationalism of American revivalism, which allowed it to cross ecclesiastical boundaries and to spread among Christians of various denominations—especially Methodists and Baptists, who were the prime supporters of the revivals. In so doing, pentecostalism was generally influenced by Baptist congregationalism, antisacramentalism, and biblicism, while it adopted Methodist sanctification and empiricism.

Thus, whatever other circumstances may have helped usher in the pentecostal movement, it is clear (if we accept Bloch-Hoell's assertions) that pentecostalism has been characteristic of certain elements of American Christianity and culture as a whole, and it has absorbed and intensified many features of American religion particularly apparent at the turn of the century.[2]

BLACK AND WHITE ORIGINS

With the dawn of the new century, there were signs of a revival of religion, especially in Wales, other parts of the British Isles, India, and elsewhere. The Welsh revival attracted the most attention, and several prominent evangelists from the United States traveled to observe it firsthand in the hope they could bring the vision back home. In America, a somewhat mysterious and mystical man named Charles Fox Parham was on a spiritual pilgrimage of his own.

Parham was born on June 4, 1873, and was licensed to preach

---

2. Nils Bloch-Hoell, *The Pentecostal Movement* (Oslo: Universitetsforlaget, 1964), pp. 5–17. In making these assertions, Bloch-Hoell relies heavily on the works of a number of prominent American religious historians such as Willard L. Sperry, *Religion in America* (New York: Macmillan, 1946); Kenneth Scott Latourette, *A History of the Expansion of Christianity*, vol. 4 (New York: Harper & Row, 1941); William W. Sweet, *The American Churches* (London: Epworth Press, 1947), and *The History of Religion in the United States* (New York: Macmillan, 1924). For specific citation of sources, see the relevant notes in Bloch-Hoell (chap. 1).

in the Methodist Church, North, in 1892. His ministry was a real disappointment, and he left the denomination in 1894, after rejecting orthodox doctrines such as water baptism and hell as a place of eternal punishment. Parham then became an itinerant holiness minister, emphasizing divine healing. However, a strong dissatisfaction with his own spirituality led him on a search for the "true" baptism in the Holy Spirit. After fairly extensive travels, he settled in Topeka, Kansas, and opened "The College of Bethel" with about thirty-six individuals, including "students" and their children. Parham was the only teacher, and the Bible, the only textbook.

Events surrounding the "outpouring of the Spirit" at the school are obscure. According to Parham, he left Topeka for a three-day campaign in Kansas City in late December 1900, and instructed his students to study, in solitude, baptism in the Spirit, especially as it was recorded in the second chapter of Acts. When he returned, much to his surprise, they all had the same story: and although each account of the pentecostal blessing was different, "the indisputable proof on each occasion was that they spoke with other tongues." The students and their teacher immediately began to pray and fast, seeking the experience; and on January 1, one of the students, Agnes Ozman, began to speak in tongues after Parham prayed and laid hands on her. Two nights later, the whole company, including Quakers, Methodists, and holiness people, began to speak in tongues and praise the Lord in a variety of languages.

It is hard to find any scholarly refutation of this basic account. But some objections *have* been raised. Robert Mapes Anderson charges that around 1900, Parham himself had already reached the conclusion that speaking in tongues was the evidence of Spirit baptism, and deliberately led his students in such a way to make them believe that the doctrine was not his own, but came, rather, by revelation. He set the stage for their "discovery" by directing them to focus their studies on Acts 2, where speaking in tongues is most closely associated with the descent of the Holy Spirit.

Less than a week after this pentecostal outpouring, one of Parham's students, S. J. Riggins, left the company and told the newspapers that the school was a "fake," an account that attracted widespread press coverage. Although newspaper reports were not favorable (the "new religion" was referred to as "queer and strange"), Parham took advantage of his visibility to launch out with his message. But he was singularly unsuccessful and returned to Topeka only to have the school sold out from under his feet. A new school in Kansas City, moreover, also ended in failure as the faithful began to leave one by one. Finally, Parham was deserted by all except his wife and sister, and things did not improve for him until 1903, when he changed the emphasis of his ministry back to healing. The reports of many healings at this time attracted large audiences, and this set the stage for a more favorable reception of Parham's message about Spirit baptism and speaking in tongues. Thus, the movement slowly gained adherents in scattered parts of the Midwest, and in 1905, the evangelist journeyed to Houston, the largest city in Texas. Here he organized yet another school for the training of Christian workers along the same lines as the earlier one in Topeka.[3]

Charles Fox Parham was white, but the pioneer leader of pentecostalism—as a full-fledged movement—was a black man, a one-eyed former slave named William Joseph Seymour, who was one of Parham's students in Houston. Seymour stayed in the school a relatively short time before accepting a call as assistant pastor of a storefront mission that had broken away from a black Baptist church over the question of sanctification ("cleansing from sin") as a second work of grace after conversion. Although Parham wanted Seymour to stay, the latter finally prevailed. Oddly enough, however, the former slave himself had not yet spoken in tongues, and neither man knew that Seymour would soon eclipse his teacher in the advent of the pentecostal movement.

3. Robert Mapes Anderson, *Vision of the Disinherited: The Making of American Pentecostalism* (New York: Oxford University Press, 1979), pp. 47–60; and John Thomas Looney, unpublished master of divinity thesis, "Nondenominational Charismatic Churches: Visions of a New Testament Community," Union Theological Seminary, New York, December 1981, pp. 3–6.

In his first sermon after reaching Los Angeles early in 1906, Seymour boldly proclaimed that no one could be baptized in the Spirit without speaking in tongues (which the evangelist had yet to do). Accounts differ on the group's reception of the message, but Seymour was banned from any further meetings, because some, including the pastor, Sister Hutchinson, "believed the baptism and sanctification were one and the same experience and that they had already obtained it." But the black preacher continued to proclaim his message in private homes. Parham was contacted for assistance in March, and soon Lucy Farrow and J. A. Warren arrived from Houston, with the result that several people, including Seymour himself, received their pentecostal experience.

The home meetings then began to grow, so Seymour rented a hall in early April at 312 Azusa Street (the rundown site of a former African Methodist Episcopal Church). But the work went slowly for almost six months, with an average attendance of about a dozen people at the meetings, until the newspapers picked up the story in September, giving the fledgling movement valuable free, though negative, publicity (the Los Angeles Times called it a "weird babble of tongues"). With the arrival of the concerned, the curious, and numerous hecklers and mockers, Seymour and his small band finally realized the revival they were praying for.

The mission stayed open around the clock. Meetings started at ten in the morning and ran continuously until midnight, and were often extended until two or three the following morning. Africanisms in worship—including "shout songs," the holy dance, and speaking in tongues itself—long suppressed by slavers and hidden from white view by captive black people, suddenly came out in the open. Spontaneity was the notable characteristic of the services that featured healings, testimonies, prophecies, visions, casting out of demons, and songs composed spontaneously "in the Spirit." Sermons were not announced ahead of time; rather, messages were given when someone felt anointed. In the midst of it all was Seymour, who, curiously, hardly ever preached, and kept his head covered with an empty shoebox behind the pulpit much of the time.

It is difficult to fully understand its attraction, but the humble mission on Azusa Street became a subject of international press coverage. As the news spread, hundreds and then thousands from all over the continent (and foreign countries, too) flooded to the ramshackle building. But as time passed, more and more became critical of the emotion and enthusiasm that characterized this early pentecostalism and its adherents who came from among the poorest, least-educated classes—"the 'scum' of society...habitual drunkards, veteran gamblers and even immoral women and infidels" were touched. Such physical manifestations as the "jerks" and "treeing the devil" became commonplace, while spiritualists and mediums soon joined in the services, contributing their seances and trances.

In time, Seymour apparently became disturbed by the runaway eclecticism of the meetings and invited Parham to help him sort things out. But after Parham arrived and denounced the "extremes and fanaticism beyond the bounds of common sense and reason" and condemned the "hypnotists and spiritualists" in the meetings, he was ordered to leave and never come back. This conflict precipitated a breach between Seymour and Parham that was never healed.

If Parham and other whites were appalled by what was happening at Azusa Street, many (especially those from holiness backgrounds) went away convinced that a genuinely Christian revival was taking place. Visitors and recent migrants carried the message of the pentecostal movement back to their hometowns with evangelical fervor. Aside from these volunteers and "free-lancers," the Azusa Street Mission, now organized as the "Apostolic Faith Gospel Mission" under a governing committee of twelve elders, dispatched a number of workers to various parts of North America (some also journeyed overseas, believing the Spirit would empower them to speak foreign languages they had never studied). In addition, a monthly paper, *The Apostolic Faith,* was soon being sent free to over 80,000 individuals, especially those of holiness persuasion. And in a relatively short period of time, several other pentecostal publications, also mailed free of charge, inundated holiness people in North America and abroad. The secular press aided local efforts by its sensationalist coverage, which continued to attract large numbers of the curious, only a few of whom actually remained to seek baptism in the Holy Spirit. And short-term Bible schools sprang up to train additional workers.

One of the most important characteristics of early pentecostalism was the lack of segregation along racial lines. However, as early as 1907, blacks and whites in the movement gradually began to separate. By 1912–1914, the mission and congregation had become entirely black; William Seymour died in 1923; and the work ended in 1928, when the building was demolished. But numerous evangelists whose ministries were "revolutionized" at Azusa Street in those early years carried the pentecostal message from there to the world—and that is why it is remembered even today.[4]

DISTINCTIVE RELIGIOUS STYLE

From the beginning the pentecostal movement was marked by a distinctive religious style that still characterizes large segments of contemporary pentecostalism. Services of worship were not untypical of the black worship experience as a whole. There began to take shape a rather precise oral liturgical process in which some activities were allowed and others ruled out. For example, people could not arbitrarily interrupt the sermon with the holy dance or speaking in tongues without being recognized. The order of certain

---

4. Anderson, pp. 60–76; Vinson Synan, *The Holiness-Pentecostal Movement in the United States* (Grand Rapids, Mich.: Eerdmans, 1972), pp. 108, 110–112; Looney, pp. 6–8; James S. Tinney, "The Blackness of Pentecostalism," *Spirit* 3, no. 2 (1980), 28, 29, 31, 32; and his groundbreaking "Black Origins of the Pentecostal Movement," *Christianity Today* (October 8, 1971), pp. 4–6. For a contemporary account of the Azusa Street revival by a participant, see Frank Bartelman, *Another Wave Rolls In!* (formerly *What Really Happened at Azusa Street?*), ed. John Walker and John G. Myers (Monroeville, Pa.: Whitaker Books, 1970).

activities meant explicit things to the participants, and the spontaneity—even in very early pentecostalism—was *limited* within that order. For a person to violate that order would be to betray unfamiliarity with the group worship or to be making a prophetic judgment about something currently in progress.

Pentecostalism has vigorously promoted evangelism. And although the stress has clearly been on "soul winning," sanctification, and, of course, Spirit baptism, pentecostals have also emphasized the "reclaiming" of "backsliders" fallen from grace. Pentecostal theology has always been Arminian,[5] and thus the fall from grace has not been an uncommon occurrence. Every pentecostal believer was expected to be an evangelist—evangelism itself being an integral part of every service of worship.

Pentecostalism took on other theological and cultural features of revivalism as well. Revivalistic preaching, the use of "gospel songs" (such as "I'll Fly Away" and "The Meeting in the Air") in place of traditional hymnody, and a thoroughgoing biblical emphasis prevailed. By and large, the culture of the wider society—particularly its amusements, mores, and education—was rejected. "Separation from the world" was the watchphrase.

The pentecostal movement emerged with an inherent subjectivism. Individuals did, however, conform to the dominating role of the group. This conformity was not so much ideological in character (as in fundamentalism) as it was ritualized in the form of worship, style of prayer, and conduct in the world. Thus, the group dictated the actions of its own membership. Despite the emphasis on biblical authority, it was really personal experience that validated religious belief and commitment. Experience and testimony preceded doctrine. Individual piety took the form of moral negativism (for example, taboos against drinking, smoking, and

---

5. Jacob Arminius was a sixteenth-century Dutch theologian who opposed the absolute predestination of strict Calvinism. Rejecting the notion that Christ died only for "the elect," he maintained that salvation is open to all by an act of "free will," which must be continually reaffirmed by a godly life. Arminians do not accept the Calvinist doctrine of "eternal security" applied to believers who fall back into sin.

social dancing), while adherence to the Protestant ethic ("hard work, little play") remained firm.

In one sense, pentecostalism was a product of nineteenth-century optimism. It upheld the possibility of ethical perfection, but in a privatized way that did not reflect the "social holiness" of John Wesley nearly so much as it did the culture-rejecting, even gnostic elements of later revivalism. Yet pentecostals were very active in missions to alcoholics and prisoners, in founding and running orphanages. Seymour himself identified the Azusa Street revival with an antiracist eschatological event. In time, however, the pentecostal movement was affected by the dispensational[6] pessimism about social reform that permeated fundamentalism in general, at least after the appearance of the Scofield Reference Bible in 1909, if not before then.

Pentecostalism was a basically democratic movement from the beginning. Rooted in antisacramentalism, there was never much distinction made between clergy and laity in the pentecostal concept of ministry. "Brother" or "Sister" seemed a more appropriate ministerial title than "the Reverend" or even "Pastor." Nevertheless, in one sense, at least, the sacramental issue *was* a prominent one. Most often, only ordained ministers (usually men) could serve the elements of communion—unless no ordained men were present. Lack of formal education was no bar to ordination (although pentecostalism established its own Bible schools), and a sense of "calling" was often enough to warrant local or congregational ordination. And because of the informality and spontaneity of worship, the laity could easily assume an important role in services—almost as great as the minister himself. Women, like ordinary workingmen, also became pastors, missionaries, and evangelists (half of the staff of the Azusa Street Mission in 1906 were women), but in a number of large pentecostal denominations

---

6. Dispensationalism originated in Great Britain in the early nineteenth century with the writings and ministry of J. N. Darby, founder of the Plymouth Brethren. This school of theology divides history into several "dispensations," each of which signifies a *different* way in which God relates to humanity, and in which humanity utterly *fails* to please God.

(including the Church of God in Christ and the Church of God [Cleveland, Tennessee]), women were not ordained, only "licensed," a limited form of "ordination."[7] To the average pentecostal layman or laywoman, a full-time ministerial vocation offered a measure of social status denied that person in the workaday world. Pentecostalism was clearly a working-class movement in which even oppressed minorities, no less than physically, economically, or socially disadvantaged and deprived whites, could find recognition.

If the religious style of the pentecostal movement was indeed grounded in elements of the American cultural and religious experience dominant at the turn of the century, that style was also reflected in its organizational character. Like revivalism in general, pentecostalism emerged largely among Baptists, Methodists, and holiness people as an interdenominational movement; but, given the ease of legitimation for leadership through spiritual gifts, it soon became structured into a large number of denominations distinct and separate from each other. And although pentecostalism was integrated at first, it was but a short time before racially segregated churches and denominations were established. Within denominational structures, low-church principles predominated. Some denominations, such as the Assemblies of God, took on the congregationalism of their Baptist parents; while others, like the Church of God (Cleveland, Tennessee), retained a strong, centralized ecclesiastical polity characteristic of their Methodist forebears. Like fundamentalism, but even more so because of holiness influence, the pentecostal movement created its own "society" and "culture" as a substitute for that offered by "the world"—a "haven of the masses."[8]

---

7. See Bloch-Hoell, p. 48. But also see Charles H. Barfoot and Gerald T. Sheppard, "Prophetic vs. Priestly Religion: The Changing Role of Women Clergy in Classical Pentecostal Churches," *Review of Religious Research* (September 1980), pp. 2–17.

8. See Kilian McDonnell, "The Ideology of Pentecostal Conversion," *Journal of Ecumenical Studies* (Winter 1968), pp. 105–126.

BASIC THEOLOGY AND ETHICS

A close kinship exists between pentecostalism and the holiness movement from which it emerged. Holiness as a movement was an outgrowth of "perfectionist" teaching and revivalism both before and after the Civil War. Its development was greatly facilitated by certain Methodists (and others) who revived a faded interest in John Wesley's doctrine of sanctification (Christian perfection) neglected in Methodism by that time; and although the movement grew largely under Methodist leadership, it actually operated on an interdenominational basis—to stimulate religious piety as an antidote for the "worldliness" thought to prevail in an "apostate" institutional church.[9] In this connection, Prudencio Damboriena, a Roman Catholic scholar, puts forward five basic reasons for the evolution of the holiness-pentecostal movement in the late nineteenth and early twentieth centuries. These include (1) an apparent departure from "the true faith" in the historic churches (signaled by their increasing acceptance of Darwin's evolutionism, Kant's rationalism, Schleiermacher's religion of experience, Bushnell's theories on Christian nurture, and Rauschenbusch's Social Gospel); (2) the dead formalism of the established denominations; (3) the pervasive worldliness in the churches, especially in Methodism, where separation from the world was by then a dead issue, and in which traditional prohibitions—from card playing to drinking—had been rescinded; (4) the substitution of personal religion by mere knowledge and external profession; and (5) the resistance of endorsement of urgently needed reforms by denominational hierarchies.[10]

William Boardman, an American Presbyterian, and Robert Pearsall Smith conducted holiness meetings in England that resulted in the famous Keswick interdenominational conferences for the deep-

---

9. Nichol, p. 5; and Donald W. Dayton, "The Evolution of Pentecostalism," *Covenant Quarterly* (August 1974), pp. 29–32.

10. Prudencio Damboriena, *Tongues as of Fire: Pentecostalism in Contemporary Christianity* (Washington, D.C.: Corpus Books, 1969), pp. 29–30.

ening of spiritual life. In America, the holiness movement was greatly aided by the use of media fast disappearing in the established churches—revival campaigns, camp meetings, and inexpensive printed literature. Its theological thrust was the belief that when the Holy Spirit makes his abode in the heart, it will be evidenced by a definite emotional experience—a "second blessing" Spirit baptism.[11]

It eventually became expedient for these holiness bands to withdraw from the already established churches and form their own denominations—such as the Church of the Nazarene, Church of God (Anderson, Indiana), and the Christian and Missionary Alliance. The reasons for this shift were mainline ecclesiastical opposition, recurrent outbursts of seeming fanaticism among holiness fellow travelers, increasing attacks on the holiness doctrine of sanctification, and the growing activity of urban holiness preachers in city missions and social work.[12]

In terms of theology and ethics, the debt owed by pentecostalism to the holiness movement is sizable. In fact, a number of holiness churches in the South finally came to believe that speaking in tongues is indeed the outward sign of Spirit baptism and thus joined the emerging pentecostal movement. Among these were the Pentecostal Holiness Church, and the Church of God (Cleveland, Tennessee). But more generally, the doctrinal influence of holiness on pentecostalism can be summarized by the following points suggested by John Nichol: (1) There is a second blessing to be sought and received *after* conversion; (2) a believer must seek the Spirit's leading in all of life; (3) revivals and camp meetings are crucial not only for evangelism but also for the rejuvenation of the spiritual lives of believers; (4) believers ought always to expect the imminent return of Christ (a doctrine repopularized in the late nineteenth century); and (5) Christians should shun "the world" and all manifestations of worldliness (including any "appearance of

---

11. Nichol, pp. 5–6.

12. Damboriena, p. 24.

evil"—1 Thess. 5:22, King James Version) such as luxuries, cosmetics, jewelry, amusements, alcohol, and tobacco.[13]

Over the course of the twentieth century, white pentecostal theology and ethics have gradually reflected the basic tenets of American fundamentalism. Important here is the acceptance of what became known as "the five fundamentals of the faith"—biblical infallibility, the virgin birth of Christ, and his substitutionary atonement, physical resurrection, and imminent, visible, and personal second coming. In addition, a strict biblical literalism—reinforced by dispensationalism—and a moral negativism have been equally important. Pentecostal distinctiveness, however, lay in the emphasis on sanctification and the present-day operation of charismata (particularly glossolalia and divine healing) in the life of the church as the result of Spirit baptism. In due course, to be sure, a number of white pentecostal denominations "officially" rejected the cultural and theological *excesses* of fundamentalism by aligning themselves with the emerging neoevangelical movement and joining the National Association of Evangelicals (NAE) at its inception in 1943. (It is interesting to note here that the Assemblies of God affirmed in their creedal statements the fundamentalist doctrines of the virgin birth, substitutionary atonement, and bodily resurrection of Jesus Christ only in 1962, the year after the denomination's titular head was elected president of the NAE. Prior to that time, there were no such declarations in the Assemblies' "Statement of Fundamental Truths." Even the earlier official statements on the "infallibility of Scripture" reflected the wording of the Westminster Confession of Faith, where infallibility pertained only to "matters of faith and practice," not like those of the fundamentalists who wanted the "inerrancy" of Scripture to speak to *all* matters, including history and the cosmos.)[14]

---

13. Nichol, p. 7. See also Damboriena, pp. 20–36.

14. See Gerald T. Sheppard, "Word and Spirit: Scripture in the Pentecostal Tradition—Part One," *Agora* (Spring 1978), pp. 4, 5, 17–22; and "Part Two" (Summer 1978), pp. 14–19.

RECRUITMENT

The initial (and continued) success of pentecostalism can be tied directly to its ideology and method of recruitment—aggressive evangelism. In the early years, the pentecostal message was directed at the nominal Christian, the apathetic believer, rather than the unconverted. It was felt strongly that baptism in the Holy Spirit would provide the means of more effective Christian service for those who were already followers of Christ. The initial non-denominational character of the pentecostal movement allowed it to infiltrate various segments of the church. And pentecostal belief in the imminent second coming of Christ brought a sense of urgency to evangelism; all pentecostal believers were expected to be evangelists in that they were obligated to "witness" boldly to their faith and experience.

Feeling uncomfortable in the increasingly middle-class Baptist and Methodist congregations, many people from lower-income groups severed their affiliation with these churches. It was primarily from the masses of such alienated working-class men and women that pentecostalism recruited its membership in ways that attracted *their* interest particularly. Like the Methodist circuit riders of a bygone era, pentecostals did not wait for individuals to come to them; they went out eagerly to meet the people where they were—singly or collectively.

Early in the movement's development, pentecostal leaders discerned the potential good effect mass meetings of various sorts could have on their followers. Tent meetings and camp meetings, it was thought, would not only offer an opportunity to evangelize nonpentecostals, but would also function as a means for pentecostal believers themselves to experience a sense of belonging to a community—a fellowship often denied them in the wider society. Thus American pentecostals employed evangelistic and healing revivals as a primary method of recruitment.

In addition to mass meetings, inexpensive tabloid newspapers became an effective means of pentecostal evangelism. These early religious newspapers dealt chiefly with the nature of the pentecostal experience, and presented moving testimonies by people who had been baptized in the Spirit or who had experienced a dramatic healing. Distributed throughout the world, the newspapers also conveyed information and announcements concerning pentecostal activities and institutions—from newly founded missions to revival campaigns.

In early pentecostalism, there was little discrimination on the basis of sex, race, national origin, or social status—a fact that certainly aided recruitment. Pentecostals had in their worship a rich experience of the divine presence that made pentecostalism attractive to people who underestimated the power of religious experience more generally.

More than anything else, perhaps, it was the certainty of their convictions, the vivid sense of reality emanating from them, that attracted people to the pentecostals. They were convincing, because they themselves were convinced. And in other lands, pentecostals often found a special welcome both for their missionaries and their message largely because of the pentecostal movement's manner of establishing indigenous churches, allowing local people to conduct their work, ministry, and worship in a manner that conformed best to the latter's own interpretation of the Christian faith.[15]

MAINLINE ECCLESIASTICAL DISAPPROVAL AND RAPID SPREAD

Luther Gerlach and Virginia Hine, anthropologists at the University of Minnesota, have suggested that a key factor in the success of a modern religious movement is the perception of opposition among its adherents.[16] Without a doubt, the

---

15. Nichol, pp. 54–69.

16. See Luther P. Gerlach and Virginia H. Hine, "Five Factors Crucial to the Growth and Spread of a Modern Religious Movement," *Journal for the Scientific Study of Religion* (Spring 1968), pp. 23–40; and *People, Power, Change: Movements of Social Transformation* (Indianapolis, Ind.: Bobbs-Merrill, 1970), pp. 183–197.

pentecostal movement was aided by the tactics of its opponents.

From its early days, pentecostalism became the object of abusive attacks from the pulpits of established churches and from the religious and secular press. Ministers and missionaries, both participants and sympathizers, were summarily removed from their pastorates and dismissed by their mission boards. Some pentecostal leaders were even subjected to violence. These occurrences took place not only in the United States, but also in Canada, Sweden, Great Britain, Chile, and in other countries.

Many denominational leaders were disturbed by the apparent "transient" character of pentecostalism. They were unhappy about their own members' withdrawing to join a tent meeting or a storefront mission only to see the tent soon folded up, the mission abandoned, and the itinerant pentecostal evangelist move on his way. This caused mainline pastors to refer to pentecostalism as a "fly-by-night" religion. But they also condemned the movement as inherently antiintellectual and spiritually elitist. The early pentecostals did emphasize the fact that they themselves were the special recipients of both baptism in the Holy Spirit and the charismata. Yet it has to be underscored here that this feeling was motivated by the attitude of other Christians toward *them*. Mainline clergy most often viewed pentecostals as "the scum of society" and their religious posture as something suitable only for poor whites and minorities (especially blacks).

Of course, there were other reasons why the established churches quickly became hostile to pentecostalism. These included its African style of emotive worship, asceticism, divine healing, its opposition to ornamentation—from neckties to jewelry—and its aggressive (and seemingly questionable) methods of evangelism.[17]

We have said that mainline ecclesiastical disapproval helped rather than hindered pentecostal expansion, which advanced at a fast pace. Technically, pentecostalism became the last great wave of "sectarian orthodoxy" and the first religious movement to have the *full* advantage of telegraph, telephone, and inexpensive mass

---

17. Nichol, pp. 70–80.

media. We have noted already, for instance, the publicity given the movement by the secular and religious press that, although uncomplimentary, served to draw attention to its progress and aroused the interest of a curious public. Likewise, we have seen that pentecostalism made effective use of tabloid newspapers (for example, the denominational *Pentecostal Evangel* and *Church of God Evangel* and later, the independent *Voice of Healing*) to carry its message to the far reaches of the globe, while it employed mass meetings centered on charismatic activity as a successful means of evangelism (in the United States, at least). Revival campaigns and camp meetings could be set up easily, and itinerant evangelists often were content to live "by faith"—to subsist on a marginal income derived only from the "love offerings" of the people.

It can also be said that the pentecostal movement spread rapidly because of its highly dramatic style. Although outbursts of enthusiasm did on occasion occur in services of the holiness movement, its characteristic manner was far quieter than that of pentecostalism. The holiness experience of sanctification appeared as little compared to pentecostal Spirit baptism evidenced by speaking in tongues and the consequent reception and exercise of charismata in services of worship. Supernatural signs and wonders happening among the poor and otherwise disadvantaged not only functioned to validate religious truth in their minds, they also demonstrated to these people that God has indeed "put down the mighty from their thrones, and exalted those of low degree" (Luke 1:52).

If the pentecostal movement was from the beginning opposed by the established denominations, it suffered from *internal* dissension and controversy as well. Baptism in the Holy Spirit was not enough of a unifying experience to prevent fragmentation from occurring almost immediately. Pentecostalism had received no one organizational form. Its spirit was in itself antiorganizational. Thus there was no one beginning, no basis for agreement, but rather diverse, simultaneous, local, varied, uncoordinated, and perhaps finally irreconcilable positions taken by different churches and congregations.

Pentecostal believers in America (and in Europe) very early came to associate their initiation into the movement with the particular ministry of an outstanding personage in their own general locality (for example, Charles Parham in Kansas and Texas, and William Seymour in Los Angeles; and, as we shall see, Alexander Boddy in England). These leaders soon captured the allegiance of their followers to the point that adherents even copied the mannerisms of each respective leader. Partisanship arose already at Azusa Street, and not one single leader could ever speak for the pentecostal movement as a whole. Furthermore, some pentecostals insisted on following the Spirit's "direct" leading apart from *any* human authority; but waiting for a voice from within, or charismatic announcements alone, only added to the confusion. These people tended to ignore human direction completely. Finally, much dissension was rooted merely in the fact that the early pentecostal leaders themselves had come from a variety of ecclesiastical backgrounds (for example, Methodist, Baptist, Lutheran, Anglican, and holiness) and saw no reason to renounce (entirely, at least) their inherited views and preferences regarding baptism, liturgy, and church polity.

One important controversy had to do with church organization itself. Some leaders favored the continuance of a decentralized movement structure, while others discerned serious problems in independence—doctrinal instability, conflicting ethical standards, vulnerability of local congregations to unscrupulous pastors, and financial inefficiency. Thus, to this day, there exists side-by-side in pentecostalism a multitude of denominations, some weak and others stronger, as well as numerous completely independent local assemblies.

Another divisive issue early in the movement's development was the doctrine of sanctification. Pentecostals who had emerged from the holiness movement stressed sanctification as a distinct, experiential "second work of grace" subsequent to conversion—whereby one's inner nature was thought to become "dead to sin," totally free from sinful inclinations. But pentecostals from a Baptist background, for instance, felt that a second work of grace was really superfluous; for them, conversion (salvation) changed people's hearts as well as their natures. Basically, the problem centered on chronology. Holiness people were used to thinking that Spirit baptism is imparted only after a period of cleansing (sanctification). Pentecostals of Baptist background, on the other hand, were quick to point out large numbers of nonholiness people who had been baptized in the Spirit—*without* the experience of sanctification after conversion. They understood sanctification not as distinct from, but as somehow related to the conversion experience itself—or as an ongoing process in Christian life. The present-day Church of God (Cleveland, Tennessee) and the Pentecostal Holiness Church reflect the former view; the Assemblies of God, the latter.

In Great Britain and Germany, there also occurred early dissension over the prominence of certain spiritual gifts—particularly glossolalia, the interpretation of tongues, and prophecy—in the life of the church. There was a tendency here for a minority of pentecostals to say that the gift of prophecy was actually coequal with the authority of scriptural revelation—even as the basis for church government. But this tendency never became popular in the United States.

Another important controversy was designated in mainstream pentecostalism: the "Jesus only" heresy. Spokespersons for the "Jesus only" school of thought (best represented today by the United Pentecostal Church) denied the doctrine of the Trinity, and baptized with water in the name of Jesus alone. They felt that although God is indeed a threefold *being*—Father, Son, and Holy Spirit—there is only one *person,* Jesus. The emphasis of these people on the name of Jesus, with the promise of additional power to all who would embrace their doctrine, greatly facilitated the popularity of "Jesus only" groups in the course of pentecostal development.

Yet another early area of dissension had to do with cultural attitudes—the degree of strictness concerning characteristic prohibitions. Pentecostal believers from a holiness background most often held very strict views—regarding dress, entertainment, eating habits, medicine, and the like—that other pentecostals did not always accept. To the list of such views might be added the use of wine (rather than unfermented grape juice) in communion, footwashing as an ordinance (adopted by the Church of God [Cleveland, Tennessee]), baptism by immersion (optional in the Pentecostal Holiness Church), divorce and remarriage (the latter generally forbidden until the death of one spouse), the use of tobacco (a special problem in the tobacco-growing South), eating of pork, drinking of coffee and "soda pop," and participation in the military and labor unions (prohibited by some denominations in their early development).

Even the doctrine of the necessity of glossolalia as an accompaniment to Spirit baptism was not held *universally* among pentecostal groups. The Elim Pentecostal Alliance (in England), for instance, endorsed the view that there *may* be signs of baptism in the Holy Spirit other than tongues alone.

It should be manifestly clear by now that the widespread diversity of opinion within early pentecostalism and its fragmentation into groups favoring different degrees of spontaneity and ritual, ecclesiastical independence and hierarchical control, legalism and tolerance, would seemingly preclude the development of a unitative pentecostal movement. The establishment of separate pentecostal denominations—distinct not only from those already existing in Protestantism, but also from each other—was inevitable.[18] Nevertheless, by 1920, the aforementioned decisive debates and consequent splitting had essentially ended, so that thereafter we see quite familiar groups living out their early decisions about their own identity.

We can say, therefore, that the pentecostal movement arose as separate denominational organizations for the following reasons: (1) the virulent and belittling opposition raised especially by the increasingly middle-class established denominations toward pentecostal phenomena and adherents; (2) the internal diversity of the movement itself; and (3) the feeling among pentecostals that their

---

18. Ibid., pp. 81–93.

testimony would be hindered without the establishment of some kind of ecclesiastical regulation of polity and doctrinal-ethical norms.

The oldest and most prominent holiness-pentecostal bodies in the United States include (1) the Church of God (Cleveland, Tennessee),[19] (2) the Church of God in Christ, and (3) the Pentecostal Holiness Church. All three have strong central hierarchies after the Methodist pattern. The Assemblies of God,[20] structured by a curious combination of (congregational) Baptist and Presbyterian elements, constitute the most important pentecostal body holding to a "progressive" rather than instantaneous doctrine of sanctification. Another very significant American pentecostal denomination is the International Church of the Foursquare Gospel, founded by an ex-Assemblies of God minister, Aimee Semple McPherson.[21] Although this denomination reflects characteristic Assemblies of God theology, it has a strong central bureaucracy, now led by Sister Aimee's son, Rolf McPherson. Finally, we should mention the most important "Jesus only" (unitarian) denomination in America, the United Pentecostal Church, which also has developed a powerful central administration.

In Great Britain, the oldest and most prominent denominational organizations include the strictly hierarchical Apostolic Church,[22] which relies largely on prophetic utterances in matters pertaining to church government; the Elim Pentecostal Alliance (or Elim Church),[23] founded as the result of George Jeffreys' revivals and later molded into the most centralized pentecostal denomination in

---

19. See Walter Hollenweger, *The Pentecostals* (Minneapolis, Minn.: Augsburg Publishing, 1972), pp. 29–46.

20. See ibid., pp. 47–62.

21. See Aimee Semple McPherson, *The Story of My Life,* ed. Raymond L. Cox (Waco, Texas: Word, 1973).

22. See Hollenweger, *The Pentecostals,* pp. 191–193, 196.

23. See ibid., pp. 197–205; and Bryan R. Wilson, *Sects and Society* (London: Heinemann, 1961).

Great Britain; and the Assemblies of God.[24] The British Assemblies of God, interestingly enough, have not incorporated in their services of worship the American revivalistic altar call. At the same time, unlike their American counterparts, they *emphasize* the ordinance of communion, which is celebrated every Sunday morning with very little (if any) preaching. As a whole, British pentecostal congregations are smaller than those in the United States, less enthusiastic in worship, and constitute a far smaller percentage of the total ecclesiastical constituency than do American classical pentecostal churches. There are, no doubt, cultural as well as purely theological reasons accounting for these differences.[25]

DIFFUSION OF THE MOVEMENT

The pentecostal movement, as we have said, spread rapidly from Azusa Street (and later from New York City as well) to other parts of America, and soon crossed the Atlantic. Great Britain was fertile ground for the new pentecostal thrust—having had its own holiness movement, best represented by the Keswick conventions of the late nineteenth century, and the Great Welsh Revival of 1904, led by Evan Roberts. To these British conclaves came many continental clergy, who returned to their own pastorates challenged by the message of holiness. Reuben Archer Torrey, the Yale- and Leipzig-educated American fundamentalist evangelist and pastor, took the holiness doctrine to Germany—stressing baptism in the Holy Spirit (sanctification) as necessary for an effective Christian witness. News of the pentecostal movement's beginnings in Los Angeles thus created a great deal of interest both in Germany and Great Britain.

Thomas Barratt, a native Englishman who had been resident since childhood in Norway, where he was a Methodist minister,

---

24. See Hollenweger, *The Pentecostals*, pp. 206–217.

25. See Nichol, pp. 94–122, 180–186; and Frank S. Mead, *Handbook of Denominations in the United States*, 7th ed. (New York: Abingdon, 1980).

visited the United States in 1905–1906 to solicit funds for his work. Just before returning to Norway, Barratt received the pentecostal Spirit baptism in New York City (he may have also visited Azusa Street), and returned to Kristiania (now Oslo), where he introduced pentecostalism to Norway and founded the Filadelfia Church in 1916. In January 1907, a young Baptist pastor in Sweden, Lewi Prethus, became intrigued by a newspaper account of Barratt's revival in Kristiania. Prethus later traveled to the Norwegian capital and experienced baptism in the Holy Spirit, which led him to spread the pentecostal message within his own country—assisted already in 1907–1908 by Barratt himself, who held several revivals in Sweden during those years.

Partly because the happenings in Kristiania had often been featured in the secular press, Barratt's fame spread widely. Another visitor to Kristiania to observe the happenings there was an English Anglican vicar from Sunderland, Alexander Boddy, who had been influenced by the Welsh Revival. Boddy returned to his home parish in Sunderland to advance the pentecostal experience in England. Subsequently he invited Barratt to preach at All Saints Church, Monkwearmouth, where people from all branches of Christendom flocked in 1907, as they had done a year earlier at Azusa Street. Word of the Sunderland revival was quickly broadcast throughout the British Isles in the newspapers and by word of mouth.

Yet another person drawn to the Norwegian capital was Pastor Jonathan Paul of Berlin, who took the pentecostal message back to Germany and began to preach it throughout that country—supported by the efforts of Barratt and two Norwegian evangelists, Dagmar Gregersen and Agnes Thelle, who traversed Germany and Switzerland in 1907–1908.[26] Pentecostalism was popularized in Finland no later than 1912 through the evangelistic work of Pastor Gerhard Smidt from St. Paul, Minnesota, and William Pylkkanen, a Lutheran missionary who had recently returned from China. Although it does appear that a small amount of pentecostal

---

26. See Hollenweger, *The Pentecostals*, pp. 218–243.

activity developed in France and a larger incidence of pentecostal phenomena occurred in the Netherlands in that time, no major pentecostal revival took place in other European countries until 1923 in Austria, and 1925 in Poland and the Baltic States.[27]

The Far East, Africa, and Latin America, together, are another matter completely. By 1909, pentecostalism had spread to India (and even beyond, as far as Korea) by the initial efforts of a well-educated Christian woman, Pandita Ramabai of Mukti, and through the labors of pentecostal missionaries from Great Britain and the United States. The pentecostal movement took root in China—Hong Kong, Canton, and Shanghai—in 1908–1910, furthered initially by American "graduates" of Azusa Street and later by pentecostal missionaries from Scandinavia, the Netherlands, and Canada.

Sometime before 1910, the pentecostal message took hold in Johannesburg, South Africa, through the efforts of two American evangelists, John Lake and Thomas Hezmalhalch, and soon spread across that country both among whites and nonwhites.[28] Central Africa was evangelized by pentecostals no later than 1914–1915—by two Englishmen, William Burton and James Salter. In the western part of the African continent, Nigeria has been the most receptive to pentecostalism. The majority of pentecostals there affiliated either with the Apostolic Church (Great Britain) or the Assemblies of God of Nigeria (established initially in 1940 with the help of American missionaries).

In Latin America, Chile and Brazil were permeated with the pentecostal ideology very early. Pentecostal phenomena first appeared in a Methodist church in Valparaiso, Chile, in 1907. Its pastor, an American named Willis Hoover, was finally ordered back to the United States by his distraught Methodist superiors in 1910; but he remained in Chile instead to help found the Methodist Pentecostal Church there. Later, the ranks of Chilean pentecostalism

---

27. On pentecostalism in the Soviet Union, see ibid., pp. 267–287.

28. See ibid., pp. 120–122, 124–125.

began to swell dramatically.[29] In Brazil, the pentecostal revival has continued unabated since 1910. The work in that country was begun by Louis Francescon, who left for São Paulo from the United States in 1910, and by two Swedish-American missionaries, Daniel Berg and Gunnar Vingren, who arrived in Pará from Chicago in the same year. The latter two were joined in a short time by Nels Nelson and Samuel Nystrom, pentecostal missionaries from Scandinavia.[30]

With respect to North America, once more, Canada was evangelized for pentecostalism in the early years of the movement's history. The Pentecostal Assemblies of Canada received a Dominion charter in 1919—and two years later affiliated with the Assemblies of God (U.S.A.). Unlike the Americans, Canadian pentecostals did not emphasize their differences and thus did not proliferate nearly so much. The movement also spread through Mexico during the early years of its growth, attracting, for the most part, men and women of the masses—peons on haciendas, common people on ranchos, in pueblos, and the ciudades.

Returning to South America, we note that the pentecostal message was first introduced to Argentina by a group of Italians from Chicago who brought the experience in 1909 mainly to their own people who had settled there. But the larger work in Argentina was undertaken only in 1921 with the arrival of Swedish and Canadian missionaries in Buenos Aires.

Pentecostalism was slow to develop in Australia. Although there had been isolated cases of pentecostal phenomena in Victoria during the first decade of this century, no widespread pentecostal revival occurred in Australia until American and British evangelists such as Smith Wigglesworth (1921), Aimee Semple McPherson

---

29. Nichol, pp. 40–53. For an excellent recent study of pentecostalism in Chile, see Christian Lalive d'Epinay, *Haven of the Masses: A Study of the Pentecostal Movement in Chile* (London: Lutterworth Press, 1969). On the movement in Colombia, see the important work by Cornelia B. Flora, *Pentecostalism in Colombia: Baptism by Fire and Spirit* (Rutherford, N.J.: Farleigh Dickinson University Press, 1976).

30. Nichol, pp. 40–53. On Brazil, see Hollenweger, *The Pentecostals,* pp. 75–100.

(1922), and A. C. Valdez (1925) arrived to conduct large campaigns in Melbourne, Sydney, and Brisbane. The pentecostal movement was introduced in Indonesia by two American missionaries in 1921, and its growth over the decades since then has been especially significant.

During World War II, pentecostalism entered a "settling down" period during which its rapid expansion subsided. After that time, the pentecostal movement experienced a late growth in Latin (Roman Catholic) Europe—although it had been introduced in France already in 1909, and in Italy in 1908.[31] Until recently, its development in these lands (including Spain and Latin America) had been, more or less, hampered by the Catholic Church;[32] but with the diffusion of pentecostalism within Roman Catholicism itself since 1967, opening channels of communication between Catholics and pentecostals, Catholic opposition to pentecostal Christians has abated.[33]

John Nichol stresses that the post–World War II period has not only been marked by substantial pentecostal gains throughout the world, but also by what he feels are significant trends within classical pentecostalism suggesting a gradual modification of its once characteristically sectarian traits. Among these, he includes (1) the decision of the Assemblies of God (U.S.A.) and the Church of God (Cleveland, Tennessee) to join the National Association of Evangelicals in 1943; (2) the organization of regular Pentecostal World Conferences since 1949; (3) the formation of the Pentecostal Fellowship of North America (PFNA) in 1948–1949 and other national and international cooperative ventures; (4) the admission in 1961 of two Chilean pentecostal denominations to the World Council of Churches (followed later by a Brazilian pentecostal body); (5) the increasing pervasiveness of highly structured liturgical order in pentecostal worship; (6) a growing interest among

---

31. On Italy, see Hollenweger, *The Pentecostals*, pp. 251–266.

32. See Nichol, pp. 158–207.

33. On Latin American pentecostalism in general, see C. Peter Wagner, *Look Out! The Pentecostals Are Coming* (Carol Stream, Ill.: Creation House, 1973).

pentecostals in higher education; (7) the emphatic reemergence of social concern in pentecostalism—seen most dramatically in the efforts of Assemblies of God Pastor David Wilkerson to rehabilitate teenagers of the drug and delinquent subculture (by organizing in the ghettos of New York City his now international Teen Challenge organization); and (8) the new willingness of pentecostals to engage in a measure of self-criticism.[34] Furthermore, the development of strong bureaucratic pentecostal denominations in the noncommunist countries of the world, and the advent of neopentecostalism in 1960, together have made it impossible to neatly categorize pentecostalism as a "sectarian" religious movement by whatever definition.

The purpose here has been just to sketch briefly the diffusion of classical pentecostalism since its beginning in 1901. In so doing, I have merely touched on the introduction of the pentecostal message to various (but not nearly all) nations in North and South America, Europe, Africa, and Asia.[35]

Reliable statistics on world pentecostal growth and present constituencies are most often lacking. Nevertheless, thanks to Prudencio Damboriena and Walter Hollenweger's work, we can offer a very approximate estimate of total pentecostal adherents in the late 1960s, in nations where the movement has had a measurable impact, as follows (for example): United States, 1,400,000; Great Britain, 70,000; Scandinavia, 200,000; Italy, 200,000; India, 190,000; Nigeria, 130,000; Zaire (the former Belgian Congo), 200,000; South Africa, 470,000; Indonesia, 1,000,000; Mexico, 120,000; Chile, 460,000–1,000,000, where 80 percent of the Protestant population is pentecostal; and Brazil, 4,000,000.[36] These

---

34. Nichol, pp. 208–239.

35. For details concerning the establishment of classical pentecostalism and its later denominational development in specific countries of the world, the reader is referred especially to Hollenweger's "Handbuch der Pfingstbewegung"; and also Damboriena's *Tongues as of Fire: Pentecostalism in Contemporary Christianity*; Nichol's *Pentecostalism*; and Bloch-Hoell's *The Pentecostal Movement*.

36. See Damboriena, Hollenweger, and, most importantly, David B. Barrett, ed., *World Christian Encyclopedia: A Comparative Survey of Churches in the Mod-*

statistics are for classical pentecostalism alone, and they should be adjusted upward, in some cases dramatically.

What is particularly noteworthy is the phenomenal growth of pentecostalism in Indonesia, Chile, and Brazil. Within Latin America as a whole, classical pentecostalism is clearly the fastest-growing religious movement of any kind, and it continues to make important advances elsewhere as well (especially in the Third World). There is no doubt that pentecostalism in its denominational expression is indeed a significant Third Force (in addition to Catholicism and Protestantism) in contemporary Christendom.

IN GREAT BRITAIN: AN EARLY UNITIVE "EXPERIMENT" THAT FAILED

We have talked about the rapid change in pentecostalism from a nondenominational movement to a distinct form of (now increasingly moderated) denominational sectarianism in the United States. But this same process took much longer to occur in Great Britain.

Alexander Boddy, an Anglican priest and one-time lawyer and author of travel books, became vicar of All Saints Church, Monkwearmouth, Sunderland, in 1886. In later years, he became a staunch supporter of both the Keswick movement and the Great Welsh Revival. During March 1907, Boddy visited Thomas Barratt in Norway and was deeply impressed by the pentecostal happenings in Kristiania—with the result that when the Anglican vicar attended the convention at Keswick later in 1907, he distributed thousands of tracts he had written entitled *Pentecost for England*. This undertaking, however, met with a very cool reception there.

In August 1907, the vicar of Monkwearmouth welcomed Thomas Barratt, whom he had invited to conduct a preaching mission (or revival) at All Saints Church. Barratt preached the same evening that he arrived in Sunderland (August 31), and the first three members of All Saints were baptized in the Spirit that night (the

---

ern World, A.D. *1900–2000* (New York: Oxford University Press, 1982) for exact statistics relevant to specific countries of denominations in those countries.

service lasted until 4 A.M. the next day), "speaking in other tongues as the Spirit gave them utterance." Without delay, the national press carried the sensational news.

Barratt's mission in Sunderland lasted seven weeks. Meetings, all comparatively quiet and orderly, were held in the church's large vestry. During this time, both Alexander Boddy and his wife were actually baptized in the Holy Spirit, and Mrs. Boddy introduced the experience to a plumber from Bradford who was destined to become one of England's great pentecostal evangelists—Smith Wigglesworth. Before long, All Saints Church had become a mecca for those seeking the pentecostal experience, no less than Azusa Street had become the previous year.

Although Alexander Boddy encountered much opposition, he also did not lack support. Mail *poured* into his Sunderland vicarage, forcing him to hire two full-time secretaries. In 1908, Boddy decided to hold a Whitsun (Pentecost) convention at Sunderland— the first of many such gatherings. The vicar himself sent out invitations, and admission was by ticket only, restricted to people in full sympathy with the pentecostal message. Strict rules regarding order at the meetings were drawn up and kept. At about the same time, the Anglican vicar first published *Confidence,* a magazine on the pentecostal movement that, although originally intended just for England, was rapidly circulated throughout the world.

Associated with Alexander Boddy's leadership was another Anglican, Cecil Polhill, who inherited Howbury Hall (an eighteenth-century country house near Bedford with extensive grounds) in 1903. Educated at Eton and Cambridge, Polhill had experienced an evangelical conversion in 1884, and became a missionary to China the following year. On a visit to Los Angeles after pentecostalism emerged there, the squire of Howbury Hall was baptized in the Spirit, returned to England, and immediately joined forces with Boddy. In 1909, he commenced the well-known nondenominational pentecostal meetings at Zion College, London. This "college," on the Thames Embankment near Blackfriars, had been founded in the seventeenth century by a vicar of St. Dunstan's Church in Fleet Street as a place where clergy could "maintain love by conversing together." Smith Wigglesworth was one of the first speakers at Zion College in 1909, and the regular meetings there (like the Sunderland conventions) became recognized as a place where one might expect to hear pentecostal speakers from all over the world. According to Donald Gee, the British Assemblies of God leader, writing shortly before his death in 1966, a hall of the college was still available for religious gatherings. He declares, "Pentecostal people have appreciated the gracious hospitality of this Church of England establishment for many years."[37] But nondenominational pentecostalism in Great Britain did not last after World War I.

The Sunderland pentecostal conventions ended in 1914 and moved to Kingsway Hall (Methodist), London, where Cecil Polhill took the chairmanship from Alexander Boddy. By 1918, Boddy's leadership in pentecostal circles declined measurably. And although he remained vicar of Monkwearmouth until 1922, Boddy played no further active role in the pentecostal movement. By the end of World War I, pentecostalism in Great Britain followed its American counterpart into separate denominations. The Church of England and the Free Churches had barely been touched. Like Cecil Polhill, Alexander Boddy never left the Church of England; but as an Anglican pentecostal, in the words of Michael Harper, he was a "prophet few listened to, and most forgot."[38]

Why did the pentecostal movement in Great Britain take so much longer to become denominationally sectarian than its counterpart in the United States? We can argue that the pervasive respectability of a national ecclesiastical establishment in Great

---

37. Donald Gee, *Wind and Flame* (formerly *The Pentecostal Movement*) (Nottingham, England: Assemblies of God Publishing, 1967), p. 50.

38. See Larry Christenson, "Pentecostalism's Forgotten Forerunner," in Vinson Synan, ed., *Aspects of Pentecostal-Charismatic Origins* (Plainfield, N.J.: Logos International, 1976), pp. 15–37; Michael Harper, *As at the Beginning* (Plainfield, N.J.: Logos International, 1905), pp. 34–39; and Gee, *Wind and Flame,* pp. 20–50. For an interesting exegetical and theological treatise on the charismata by an English Anglican (vicar of Ham, Surrey, and sometime chaplain of Clare College, Cambridge) sympathetic to the basic pentecostal stance, see J. R. Pridie, *The Spiritual Gifts* (London: Robert Scott, 1921).

Britain (the Church of England) often has tended to discourage the formation and subsequent growth of new denominations side by side. In America, on the other hand, initial resistance to a nonsectarian pentecostalism was no doubt facilitated by the absence of such a national church and by the general ease in starting new religious organizations—especially in the West, Midwest, and South. There is no evil connotation to the concept of religious sectarianism. With respect to the case of Alexander Boddy in particular, we have to remember that it was he, as a Church of England clergyman in good standing, who primarily influenced the early development of the pentecostal movement in Great Britain; and Boddy never left the Anglican Church.

Modern Anglicanism has had a reputation for inclusiveness. For instance, the Church of England has been able to keep under one roof at least two very contrary ecclesiastical parties—Evangelicals and Anglo-Catholics—without a great deal of conflict. Furthermore, it was also the case that after the nineteenth century, Anglican bishops as a whole tended to display more tolerance of seemingly aberrant priests who themselves found it inherently difficult to leave the national church—because in so doing, the latter would not only lose their stipend and position, but their *respectability* as well. This fact, of course, may have constituted one reason why Alexander Boddy always remained faithful to the Church of England.

Donald Gee puts forward a few suggestions why the sectarian process in British pentecostalism developed rather slowly. He emphasizes again that the dominant leaders in the earliest years of the pentecostal movement in Britain never encouraged the formation of separate pentecostal assemblies or denominations as such. The counsel usually was given, rather, to "receive the baptism in the Holy Spirit, but remain in your church, whatever the denomination may be."[39] Gee points out that Alexander Boddy was particularly fortunate in having an exceptionally lenient bishop in the person of Handley Moule, bishop of Durham, who allowed the

---

39. Gee, *Wind and Flame*, p. 88.

pentecostal meetings at All Saints Church to continue unabated. And Cecil Polhill, though not an ordained priest, found his denomination connection as an Anglican layman no hindrance to his roving pentecostal activities. With such early pentecostal leadership in Great Britain, denominationalism was simply not encouraged.

Yet other factors did lead ultimately to the organization of British pentecostal denominations. Gee goes on to declare that in Britain "the Pentecostal Movement probably received the most determined, capable, and prejudiced opposition that it encountered anywhere in the whole world."[40] As in the United States, therefore, vehement opposition fostered the establishment of separate, exclusive pentecostal denominations in Great Britain. Furthermore, Gee suggests that the pentecostal message there had actually been hindered in the early years for lack of proper ecclesiastical control. He states that a "crude, and ungifted ministry" emerged in many areas of the British Isles:

> Consecration was deemed enough, not only for personal discipleship, but for leadership also. The baptism in the Spirit was construed as making its recipients not only "witnesses," but competent preachers in the assemblies. . . . A handful of kindred spirits [following a devoted but incompetent minister] could make a happy little company to enjoy fellowship among themselves; but it scarcely seemed to be realized that there was a complete lack of any ministry sufficiently powerful to attract and move the masses outside.[41]

Some kind of bureaucratic authority over the increasing number of independent pentecostal assemblies, therefore, became necessary to regulate pockets of "fanaticism," set qualifications for the ministry, and foster overseas missionary work.[42]

Thus, nonsectarian pentecostalism in Great Britain came to an

---

40. Ibid.

41. Ibid., p. 89.

42. Ibid., pp. 87–91. Gee feels that the lack of pentecostal denominations in the early period actually hindered the movement's growth in Great Britain and the influence of British pentecostalism throughout the world.

end by the conclusion of World War I. It had been an "experiment" that failed. For the rebirth of nondenominational pentecostalism, the world had to wait until 1960, when—in an Anglican parish in California—another Alexander Boddy emerged to lead a new pentecostalism, with very different consequences for the church.

Chapter Three

The Path

to Renewal

Although charismatic renewal, as a recognizable movement within Christendom, became recognizable only in 1960, the beginnings of neopentecostalism can really be traced to isolated incidents of pentecostal phenomena among clergy and laity of the historic denominations by the mid-1950s[1]—but very little documentation for these incidents exists.

BEGINNINGS

The groundwork for the new diffusion of pentecostalism within mainline Christendom had been laid during the 1950s through the activities of (1) the Full Gospel Business Men's Fellowship International and (2) David du Plessis. The FGBMFI was born in Los Angeles in 1951 as a nondenominational fellowship of "full gospel" (pentecostal) businesspeople and professionals. Supported ini-

---

1. Kilian McDonnell, "The Ecumenical Significance of the Pentecostal Movement," *Worship* (December 1966), p. 628. See also, for instance, Dennis Bennett, *Nine O'Clock in the Morning* (Plainfield, N.J.: Logos International, 1970), pp. 33–35, 78; James Brown, "Every Christian Must Become a Pentecostal," *Full Gospel Business Men's Voice* (September 1959), pp. 7–8; David du Plessis, "Pentecostal Revival Inside the Historic Churches," *Pentecost*, no. 50 (1959), pp. 1–2; "The World-Wide Pentecostal Movement," *Pentecost*, no. 53 (September–November 1960), back cover; Harper, *As at the Beginning*, pp. 56–66; Kelsey, pp. 102–104; O'Connor, *The Pentecostal Movement in the Catholic Church*, pp. 24–25; and Phillips, pp. 32–33.

tially by Demos Shakarian (a wealthy California dairyman) and Oral Roberts (the faith-healing evangelist), local chapters of the FGBMFI emerged throughout America in the 1950s. In 1953, the organization began issuing its monthly "testimony" magazine, now called *Full Gospel Business Men's Voice* (or just *Voice*). Meetings of the fellowship's local chapter and interchapter conventions eventually attracted mainline clergy and laity who had received the pentecostal experience or who were merely interested in it. These meetings provided an opportunity for fellowship with "respectable" pentecostals (that is, businesspeople and professionals) without the explicit or even implicit demand of affiliation with any particular pentecostal denomination or church. Later, *Full Gospel Business Men's Voice* magazine was distributed among mainline laity and clergy—featuring personal testimonies of Christians from the historic denominations who had been baptized in the Spirit.

David du Plessis, a leader in the pentecostal movement throughout the world, and then an Assemblies of God (U.S.A.) minister, spent much of the 1950s participating as a pentecostal "observer" in the emerging ecumenical movement and, at the same time, sharing the pentecostal experience with nonpentecostal clergy and laity alike—some of whom were high-ranking ecumenical leaders. His own irenic stance as a pentecostal spokesman—in the context of his relationship with nonpentecostal ecclesiastical officials—did much to "dignify" the pentecostal experience and message in the minds of an heretofore skeptical and belittling ecclesiastical establishment. By the 1950s, some mainline church leaders had even come to regard pentecostalism as a "Third Force" in world Christianity—with Protestantism and Catholicism[2]—and du Plessis himself can be credited with the growth and spread of that attitude during the decade.

By 1960, the historic denominations had had some preparation

---

2. See Lesslie Newbigin, *The Household of God* (New York: Friendship Press, 1954); and Henry P. Van Dusen, "Force's Lessons for Others," *Life* (June 9, 1958), pp. 122, 124.

for the new diffusion of pentecostalism, which was soon to be felt within their own ranks as charismatic renewal.

"OUTBURST OF TONGUES" AT ST. MARK'S

Dennis Bennett, who was born in London, came to the United States with his family at the age of ten. His father, a Congregational minister, settled the family in central California. Following his schooling, Dennis Bennett became briefly associated with an electronics firm as a salesman, but soon decided on a ministerial career and attended the University of Chicago Divinity School, where he received the bachelor of divinity degree in 1949. In 1951, Bennett converted to the Episcopal Church—the Anglo-Catholic wing— and, in 1953, accepted a call to become rector of St. Mark's Episcopal Church in Van Nuys, California. At that time, the church was just recovering from serious financial difficulties and consisted of about five hundred members. Dennis Bennett proved to be a successful pastor. By 1960, St. Mark's membership roll stood at 2,500, services were extremely well attended, and the rector had three curates on his staff.

During 1959, John and Joan Baker, who were members of another Episcopal church, received baptism in the Holy Spirit through the witness of pentecostal friends. They were tempted, at that point, to forsake the Episcopal Church—in which they had, in any case, been only nominal members—and join a pentecostal assembly where they would be understood. They resisted this temptation, however, and remained in their Episcopal parish. Soon afterward they told their vicar, Frank Maguire, about their pentecostal experience. He took the news calmly, assuming that other "more balanced" members of the church would eventually dissuade them from further involvement in this departure from traditional Anglican orthodoxy.

The "problem" with John and Joan Baker, however, was that they seemed to have become *better* Episcopalians after their pentecostal experience than before. They thrust themselves completely into the work of the church, attended even weekday services, and began to tithe. Moreover, instead of other members of the parish influencing the Bakers, the reverse was true until, with the passage of just a few months, about a dozen members had been baptized in the Spirit and were (quietly) speaking in tongues. Before long, therefore, Frank Maguire found it necessary to seek pastoral advice on the matter.

Because Dennis Bennett was a colleague and personal friend, Maguire consulted him first. Yet, if anything, Bennett was more ignorant about the issue than Maguire—but interested. Soon, Bennett met the Bakers personally and, as a result of this encounter, received baptism in the Holy Spirit himself in November 1959, followed three days later by Frank Maguire. A pentecostal prayer group was already functioning in Maguire's parish, and Bennett began sending interested members of his own congregation to the fellowship, which was headed by John and Joan Baker. Within the next four months, eight ministers and nearly a hundred laypeople in the diocese (including a number of key members of St. Mark's) were baptized in the Spirit. By April 3, 1960, some seventy members of St. Mark's Episcopal Church had received the pentecostal experience.

Although these new Anglican pentecostals tried hard to keep quiet about their experience, news leaked out quickly within Bennett's parish and the city of Van Nuys as a whole. Rumors, dissension, and misunderstanding—centering on alleged excessive charismatic behavior (that is, rolling in the aisles)—became commonplace. Certainly, participants in the pentecostal experience *were* intensely enthusiastic. Prayer and fellowship meetings often lasted until 1:30 A.M. (even as late as 4:00 A.M.), but *order* was insisted on from the beginning, and charismatic activity was not permitted within formal services of worship.

On Passion Sunday 1960, Dennis Bennett explained everything to his parishioners openly. During the sermon, one of the curates took off his vestments and resigned publicly while walking out down the center aisle. Another curate declared that such things simply could not be tolerated in respectable churches, and the church treasurer demanded Bennett's resignation. To keep the peace, the rector of St. Mark's did resign two days later, as we have seen, and sent a long, explanatory, and irenic letter to all members of the parish explaining that he was *not* leaving the priesthood,[3] and was not encouraging parishioners either to leave St. Mark's or cancel their pledges. That, of course, was the crucial decision. Shortly thereafter, Bishop Francis Bloy of the Los Angeles Episcopal Diocese banned any more speaking in tongues under church auspices; and later, the remarkable news of the outburst of tongues at St. Mark's was carried in both *Time* and *Newsweek*.[4]

Dennis Bennett thus found himself without a job and branded throughout the Episcopal Church as a religious fanatic and crank. However, the then bishop of Olympia, Washington, invited him to become vicar of a small mission church in Seattle that was redundant and, in fifty years, had made no noticeable impact on its community. Bennett accepted the call, and arrived on July 1, 1960, at the bankrupt St. Luke's Episcopal Church to lead two hundred confused and disillusioned communicants. Twelve months later, eighty-five of the members of St. Luke's had received baptism in the Holy Spirit—practically the whole inner core of the church. Attendance had multiplied, and the building could no longer hold all the people. The budget had increased dramatically, and all outstanding debts had been paid. By the mid-1970s, over two thousand people were attending a thriving St. Luke's Episcopal Church weekly.[5] Dennis Bennett's "defeat" had turned out to be a victory for the movement he symbolized.

---

3. See Hollenweger, "Handbuch der Pfingstbewegung," pp. 823–828. (02a.02.206); and Harper, *As at the Beginning,* pp. 60–65.

4. See "Rector and a Rumpus," *Newsweek* (July 4, 1960), p. 77; and "Speaking in Tongues," *Time* (August 15, 1960), pp. 53, 55.

5. Harper, *As at the Beginning,* pp. 56–66. See also Bennett, *Nine O'Clock in the Morning;* and Frank Farrell, "Outburst of Tongues: The New Penetration," *Christianity Today* (September 13, 1963), pp. 3–7.

AN INCREASINGLY RECOGNIZABLE MOVEMENT

Dennis Bennett took the pentecostal experience with him from Van Nuys to Seattle, and the number of neopentecostals continued to increase in both areas. With the dramatic growth of St. Luke's Episcopal Church, Seattle, after Bennett's arrival in 1960, the fame of its rector spread accordingly—both locally and nationally. Bennett soon became a very popular speaker in the Episcopal Church itself and in other denominations and interdenominational groups where the pentecostal message was beginning to attract attention. As a neopentecostal facilitator, this Episcopal priest became a modern-day Alexander Boddy and was himself responsible for much of the early growth of charismatic renewal—especially among Episcopalians, Lutherans, and Presbyterians.[6]

But the focal point of the development of neopentecostalism remained, oddly enough, in Van Nuys, California, until 1966. Among those who had received baptism in the Holy Spirit at St. Mark's before Bennett's resignation was Jean Stone, a lifelong Episcopalian whose husband was a prominent corporate officer of Lockheed Aircraft. Stone organized in Van Nuys the first charismatic renewal fellowship, which existed from 1961 to 1966—the Blessed Trinity Society ("Trinity" to emphasize the "newly rediscovered" work of the third person, the Holy Spirit). David du Plessis was an original member of the board of directors of this organization. In addition to fellowship activities for neopentecostals, the Blessed Trinity Society offered a sophisticated and (at the time) expensive quarterly ($1.50 per issue), *Trinity,* to inform its readership of current news of the movement and to introduce charismatic renewal to nonpentecostals in the historic (especially Anglican and Lutheran) denominations. Eventually, *Trinity* magazine was sent to interested clergy and laypeople in countries throughout the world (although its cost prevented widespread distribution in some areas—Great Britain, for instance). Then, motivated in part by Ralph Wilkerson (now pastor of Melodyland Christian Center, Anaheim, California), the Blessed Trinity Society

---

6. See Bennett, *Nine O'Clock in the Morning,* pp. 66–122.

launched in 1962 the first interdenominational teaching seminars dealing with charismatic renewal—"Christian Advance." These gatherings and conferences were directed at the historic churches and attracted laity and clergy from all parts of the United States. As the movement continued to spread, Jean Stone, editor of *Trinity,* was invited to speak to interested groups throughout the country, including the National Council of Churches' staff in 1964.[7]

By 1963, it was estimated that about two hundred Episcopalians in the Los Angeles diocese were speaking in tongues,[8] and 6 out of 225 congregations of the American Lutheran Church in California had been affected by the glossolalia phenomenon.[9] Soon afterward, the pentecostal experience became known in two of the most prominent Presbyterian churches in Los Angeles—Bel Air, and Hollywood First (then the nation's largest—with 600 speakers in tongues in 1964).[10] Both are still very affluent congregations.

During the first few years of the movement's growth, a number of important leaders emerged who spread the message of charismatic renewal throughout America and abroad as well. We have already mentioned Dennis Bennett, Jean Stone, and Ralph Wilkerson. Also included in this group of neopentecostal leaders were Harald Bredesen, then pastor of the First Reformed Church, Mt. Vernon, New York;[11] Howard Ervin, an American Baptist clergyman, who now teaches in the Department of Religion at Oral Roberts University;[12] Larry Christenson, pastor of Trinity

---

7. See, for instance, *Trinity* (Trinitytide 1961); and *Trinity* (Eastertide 1963), pp. 30–33.

8. *Trinity* (Eastertide 1963), p. 32.

9. Ibid., p. 33.

10. Kelsey, pp. 110–112.

11. See Harald Bredesen, "Leaves from a Campus Diary," *Trinity* (Transfiguration 1963), pp. 6–9; and his spiritual autobiography, *Yes, Lord* (Plainfield, N.J.: Logos International, 1972).

12. See *Trinity* (Whitsuntide 1964), pp. 50–51; and, especially, Howard M. Ervin, *These Are Not Drunken, As Ye Suppose* (Plainfield, N.J.: Logos International, 1968).

Lutheran Church, San Pedro, California;[13] Robert Frost, then professor of biology at Westmont College, Santa Barbara, California;[14] Graham Pulkingham, former rector of the Church of the Redeemer (Episcopal), Houston, Texas, who is still doing renewal work in Texas;[15] and Todd Ewald, the now retired rector of Holy Innocents Parish (Episcopal), Corte Madera, California.[16] When the Blessed Trinity Society collapsed in 1966, and Jean Stone passed from neopentecostal leadership, the focal point of charismatic activity in California moved to the nondenominational Melodyland Christian Center in Anaheim and its pastor, Ralph Wilkerson.

In the early 1960s, charismatic renewal became a widespread topic for the secular and religious press, radio, and television, because glossolalia was for the first time in America being practiced by sophisticated, middle-class church members. Neopentecostal leaders and their churches were the subject of numerous interviews and discussions in the media.[17] In October 1962, as a result of two campus visits by Harald Bredesen, the glossolalia phenomenon broke out in the academic community—at Yale University, among members of the evangelical Inter-Varsity Christian Fellowship there. Included in this neopentecostal revival were Episcopalians, Lutherans, Presbyterians, Methodists, and even one Roman Catholic. Five were members of Phi Beta Kappa, and some were

---

13. See Christenson, "Speaking in Tongues," *Trinity* (Transfiguration 1963), pp. 13–16; and, especially, *Speaking in Tongues and Its Significance for the Church* (Minneapolis, Minn.: Bethany Fellowship, 1968).

14. See *Trinity* (Eastertide 1963), pp. 4–16; and, especially, Robert C. Frost, *Aglow with the Spirit,* rev. ed. (Plainfield, N.J.: Logos International, 1971).

15. See "Church of the Redeemer: Miracle in the Inner City," *Acts* 1, no. 5 (1968), 21–30; and, especially, W. Graham Pulkingham, *Gathered for Power: Charisma, Communalism, Christian Witness* (New York: Morehouse-Barlow, 1972).

16. See *Trinity* (Transfiguration 1963), pp. 32–33; and Donovan Bess, " 'Speaking in Tongues': The High Church Heresy," *Nation* (September 28, 1963), pp. 173–177.

17. See, for instance, *Trinity* (Eastertide 1963), pp. 48–49; *Trinity* (Transfiguration 1963), pp. 28–39; and *Trinity* (Christmastide 1965–1966), pp. 28–33.

religious leaders on campus (soon called "GlossoYalies").[18] Thereafter, the movement spread to Dartmouth College, Stanford University, and Princeton Theological Seminary (where it was particularly significant). By May 1964, charismatic renewal prayer groups had sprung up in colleges and seminaries in at least fifteen states in the northeastern and north-central states, and on the West Coast. Four years after its inception, neopentecostalism was a clearly recognizable religious movement—affecting both clergy and laity, students and professionals, men and women, in the Episcopal Church and almost all the historic Protestant denominations in the United States.[19]

RAPID SPREAD TO OTHER PARTS OF THE WORLD

Charismatic renewal in Europe and the British Commonwealth was profoundly affected by the emerging neopentecostal movement in the United States during the early 1960s. In many countries, of course, the stage for further development had been set by the ecumenical visits and activities of David du Plessis in the course of the preceding decade.

In Great Britain, the second wind of pentecostalism occurred about 1962—again, primarily (but not exclusively[20]) among clergy and laypeople of the Church of England. In the first years of its publication, *Trinity* was circulated in a number of areas of the British Isles. Its coverage of recent charismatic happenings among Episcopalians in the United States (together with their own accounts and testimonies of those events) certainly helped to attract the initial interest of British Anglicans. As a result of

---

18. See *Trinity* (Christmastide 1962–1963), pp. 2–17; and "Blue Tongues," *Time* (March 29, 1963), p. 52.

19. Phillips, pp. 31–40. For testimonies of early neopentecostals, see, for instance, Jerry Jensen, ed., *Baptists* (1963), *Episcopalians* (1964), *Lutherans* (1966), *Methodists* (1963), and *Presbyterians and the Baptism of the Holy Spirit* (Los Angeles: Full Gospel Business Men's Fellowship International, 1963).

20. See, for instance, Lillie, *Tongues Under Fire* (London: Fountain Trust, 1966).

Trinity's circulation at that time, a small number of people received baptism in the Holy Spirit in 1962. Also, during the same year, Phillip Hughes, editor of the *Churchman* (an Evangelical Anglican periodical), visited America and, at her invitation, met with Jean Stone in California. On his return to London, Hughes wrote an important editorial in the September issue of that publication that was very favorable to the new movement—an especially influential essay[21] (60,000 copies were sold in 1962–1963) because the author was widely respected as a balanced mainline (albeit evangelical) religious thinker and churchman.

In May 1963, Frank Maguire visited Britain and addressed a privately convened ministers' meeting in London where *some* interest was shown. Later, he spoke at the Church Army Training College, where one student was baptized in the Holy Spirit. Yet another gathering was arranged in an Oxfordshire village after which a few more people received the pentecostal experience. Finally, the Episcopal priest from Monterey Park, California, was invited to preach in a West End (London) Anglican church. But altogether, Maguire's visit represented a mere beginning for the movement in Great Britain.

In August 1963, on his way home to San Pedro, California, from a Lutheran World Federation conference in Helsinki, Larry Christenson spoke at meetings both in Germany and in London. Again, a private gathering for ministers was convened in London, followed the same day by one for interested laypeople. Before returning to California, Christenson had been instrumental in leading two curates of an Anglican church in London to the pentecostal experience. (Later, an Anglo-Catholic vicar who had attended the meeting also received the Spirit baptism—followed before many months by several clergy of his diocese.) One of those two curates influenced by the Lutheran pastor was Michael Harper, then on the staff of the prestigious All Souls Church, Langham Place, London. (Harper eventually became the most prominent neopentecos-

---

21. Reprinted in *Trinity* (Christmastide 1962–1963), pp. 20–22.

tal leader in Great Britain—as founder of the Fountain Trust in 1964 and editor of its bimonthly magazine, *Renewal,* in 1966. The Fountain Trust coordinated charismatic renewal conferences and fellowship gatherings in Britain, and published *Renewal* and books dealing with neopentecostalism, distributing them throughout the world. In this way, it quickly became the Blessed Trinity Society of the British Isles.) It is perhaps especially significant that Christenson, sometime before his visit to London, had written a booklet, *Speaking in Tongues: A Gift for the Body of Christ,* which was translated into German and was widely circulated in Germany. In the autumn of 1963, with Michael Harper's help, it was first published in Great Britain.

Later in 1963, David du Plessis visited London en route from Holland to his home in the United States. Once again, a meeting was arranged—this time in a West End hotel. Several hundred invitations were sent out, the room was filled, and the audience gave du Plessis a very enthusiastic response. After that gathering, a few more individuals received baptism in the Holy Spirit.

Slowly but surely, the neopentecostal upsurge continued unabated in Great Britain. In the spring of 1964, Jean Stone accompanied her husband on a European business trip, which included London. By the time she arrived, a rather extensive itinerary had already been worked out—consisting of a press conference, two public meetings in London, a trip to Scotland, and trips to several other places in England. In Scotland alone, nearly fifty people (including several ministers) received the Spirit baptism. The London gatherings, incidentally, were the first ones open to the public and arranged by "nonpentecostals" since the days of Alexander Boddy and Cecil Polhill. Over fifty people received the pentecostal experience as a result of these meetings. Then, in the summer of 1964, David du Plessis returned to the British Isles, where he spoke at many gatherings in England, and attended the General Assembly of the Church of Scotland in Edinburgh. Interest in charismatic renewal increased in various denominations throughout Britain, particularly in the Church of England, among Anglo-Catholics no less than Evangelicals. By 1965, over a hundred ministers of the historic churches had been baptized in the Holy Spirit.[22]

During 1965 itself, two further events greatly advanced the cause of neopentecostalism in the British Isles. The first was Dennis Bennett's visit in October of that year. Bennett freely discussed his own pentecostal experience, the dramatic growth of a once-dying St. Luke's Episcopal Church in Seattle, and the nature of charismatic renewal itself as a contemporary movement within Christendom. He spoke at a number of Anglican (and one Jesuit) theological colleges in London, Oxford, and Cambridge. Bennett spent a fair amount of his time in Cambridge, where his first address was given at Great Saint Mary's, the University Church. He was welcomed there (enthusiastically) by Hugh Montefiore, then its vicar, and spoke to a congregation that included the late Bishop James Pike of California, an old friend of Bennett's. As a guest of the dean of Magdalene College, the rector of St. Luke's also preached at Holy Trinity Church, and addressed a luncheon meeting of college chaplains, a number of whom were impressed. Besides Cambridge, the charismatic Episcopal priest fulfilled numerous other speaking engagements, including one at Southwark Cathedral in London. Most of these gatherings were extremely well attended. The curate of Great Saint Mary's wrote in the *Cambridge Daily News* of October 30, 1965:

> What kind of man is Bennett? A Bible puncher? A fire eater? No, he is quiet, sincere, with a great sense of humour and a very balanced view of life. And he is a High Churchman. But his faith makes me echo that comment: "that man has got something, and I want it."[23]

Thus, Dennis Bennett's sojourn added considerably to the respectability of neopentecostalism in Great Britain thereafter.

---

22. Harper, *As at the Beginning*, pp. 80–85. See also Harper's spiritual autobiography, *None Can Guess;* "The 'New' Pentecost in England," *Pentecost* (March–May 1964), pp. 4–5; "News from Michael Harper: Visit of David du Plessis," *Pentecost* (December 1964–February 1965), back cover, p. 3; *Trinity* (Whitsuntide 1964), pp. 26–31; and *Trinity* (Trinitytide 1964), pp. 54–55.

23. *Renewal* (January 1966), pp. 16–19. See also Bennett, *Nine O'Clock in the Morning*, pp. 129–145.

The second major happening for charismatic renewal in the British Isles during 1965 was the "airlift" of hundreds of Full Gospel Business Men (and their friends among the clergy) from the United States to London in November of that year. The FGBMFI Americans wanted to share in a London convention with their British brethren (using the London Hilton Hotel as headquarters), but they also saw the visit as an opportunity for evangelism. During the first week, meetings were held in and around the capital city. Then, in the course of the second week, evangelistic teams went to many other cities throughout Great Britain—including both Oxford and Cambridge. The final gathering was at Royal Albert Hall in London, which was filled with people to hear Oral Roberts conclude the convention (among other participants during the two-week visit were Demos Shakarian, Harald Bredesen, Howard Ervin, and Ralph Wilkerson). By the end of 1965, neopentecostalism in the British Isles (including Northern Ireland[24]) had established itself as an important force with which the church would sooner or later have to make its peace.[25]

Although the United States and Great Britain constitute the focus of this study, we should also note that the movement spread rapidly in the mid- and late 1960s to New Zealand (facilitated by visits of Dennis Bennett and Michael Harper), where early developments were recorded in the periodical *Logos*[26] and the work centers on the ten-year-old Christian Advance Ministries;[27] and to

24. See "Stirrings in Northern Ireland," *Renewal* (December 1968–January 1969), pp. 20–21; John L. Wynne, *This New Pentecostalism* (Belfast, Northern Ireland: John L. Wynne, 1967); *Logos Journal* (September–October 1972), pp. 6–15; and Thomas Flynn, *The Charismatic Renewal and the Irish Experience* (London: Hodder & Stoughton, 1974).

25. "A New Breath of Life," *Renewal* (January 1966), pp. 4–10; and Full Gospel Business Men's Fellowship International, *Airlift to London* (Los Angeles: FGBMFI, n.d.).

26. See *Renewal* (December 1967–January 1968), pp. 16, 18; Bennett, *Nine O'Clock in the Morning*, pp. 156–163; and Harper, *None Can Guess*, pp. 108–118.

27. See "New Phase in New Zealand," *Renewal* (December 1981–January 1982), pp. 29–31; and J. E. Worsfold, ed., *A History of Charismatic Movements in New Zealand* (London: Puritan Press, 1974).

Australia[28] and South Africa (aided by visits of Michael Harper and, of course, David du Plessis), where the early situation was depicted in *Gift* magazine[29] and the ministry centers on the Christian Interdenominational Fellowship, founded in 1971.[30] (The Anglican archbishop of Cape Town, Bill Burnett, is a neopentecostal.[31]) In Germany, charismatic renewal has remained almost totally independent of classical pentecostalism (theologically and culturally). Early leadership there was centered largely in the Evangelical Sisterhood of Mary in Darmstadt, and in the person of Arnold Bittlinger (a pastor of the United Church of the Palatinate) and his Ecumenical Academy at Schloss Craheim, near the village of Wetzhausen (not far from the East German border).[32] More recently, neopentecostalism has also advanced significantly in Scandinavia[33] and in other countries, including France, Italy, Ireland, Canada, and Brazil.[34]

ALL ROADS LEAD TO ROME: CATHOLIC PENTECOSTALS

Long before the initial development of pentecostalism as a movement within Roman Catholicism, there were individual Cath-

28. See *Renewal* (December 1967–January 1968), pp. 18–19; and *Renewal* (April–May 1970), p. 35.

29. See "South Africa's Move of the Spirit," *Renewal* (October–November 1968), pp. 5–6; and Harper, *None Can Guess*, pp. 108–118.

30. See "Tenth Anniversary in South Africa," *Renewal* (December 1981–January 1982), pp. 9, 10.

31. "Bill Burnett—A Break with Tradition," *Johannesburg Star* (May 4, 1974), pp. 10–11.

32. James D. G. Dunn, "Spirit Baptism and Pentecostalism," *Scottish Journal of Theology* (November 1970), pp. 397–407. See also *Renewal* (August–September 1970), pp. 9, 11–12; Arnold Bittlinger, *Gifts and Graces* (1967) and *Gifts and Ministries* (Grand Rapids, Mich.: Eerdmans, 1973); and Hollenweger, *The Pentecostals*, pp. 244–250.

33. See *Renewal* (August–September 1970), pp. 8–9; and "Church Renewal in Norway," *Renewal* (August–September 1972), pp. 6–7.

34. See Meredith B. McGuire, *Pentecostal Catholics: Power, Charisma, and Order in a Religious Movement* (Philadelphia: Temple University Press, 1982), pp. 228–229, no. 20.

olics who had received the pentecostal experience[35] often through the influence of pentecostal friends. But Catholic pentecostalism as a "movement" emerged only in 1967, in the United States—this time, however, within the academic community itself. From the start, Catholic pentecostals (a number of whom had already been influenced by the evangelical Cursillo movement in the Roman Catholic Church) were determined both to remain *Catholic* and to reject all the "cultural baggage" associated with classical pentecostalism (especially its distinctive ethical taboos and fundamentalist tendencies). At the same time, they did not allow this determination to detract from the possibility of fellowship both with classical pentecostals themselves and with other neopentecostals.

In the autumn of 1966, several Catholic laymen, all faculty members of Duquesne University in Pittsburgh, were drawn together in a period of prayer and discussion about the vitality of their Christian lives. All were active churchmen. They prayed "that the Holy Spirit of Christ would renew in them all the graces of their baptism and confirmation."[36] In August, these men had been introduced by friends to David Wilkerson's book *The Cross and the Switchblade* (1964)—an account of the beginnings of his service among young gang members and dope addicts in the Bedford-Stuyvesant section of New York City (which led, ultimately, to the founding of Teen Challenge International). The latter part of the book deals with the pentecostal experience, and this interested the men. Kevin and Dorothy Ranaghan recall, "In their struggles with the apathy and unbelief among college students they realized they needed the kind of power that Wilkerson seemed to possess in the face of the agony and ugliness of the dropouts, delinquents, and addicts of Brooklyn."[37] For the

---

35. Kilian McDonnell, "Catholic Pentecostalism: Problems in Evaluation," *Dialog* (Winter 1970), p. 35.

36. Kevin and Dorothy Ranaghan, *Catholic Pentecostals* (New York: Paulist Press, 1969), p. 8.

37. Ibid., p. 10.

next two months, they shared—talked and prayed about—issues raised in *The Cross and the Switchblade*.[38]

One of the men, Ralph Keifer, then an instructor in Duquesne's Department of Theology, also had been led to read John Sherrill's *They Speak with Other Tongues* (1965)—a journalist's account of the emergence of charismatic renewal in the United States—and gave it to the others. Eventually, the group decided to become personally acquainted with local Christians who had the pentecostal experience, and they asked a nearby Episcopal priest for his advice. He introduced them to an active laywoman in his parish who was participating in a pentecostal prayer group. During their brief encounter, the men were surprised and pleased that this woman did not fit the classical pentecostal stereotype.

On January 13, 1967, the academics from Duquesne met with the prayer group—organized by another woman, a Presbyterian. Impressed by the warmth and sincerity of the meeting and its biblical tenor, two of the men attended the next gathering as well. There, Ralph Keifer and his friend asked to be prayed with for baptism in the Holy Spirit. Keifer prayed in tongues almost immediately. In the following week, he, in turn, laid hands on the other two men, who also received the pentecostal experience. This event was followed by what they feel was a dramatic interior transformation in their lives and by the reception of numerous charismata as well.

By February 1967, four Catholics in Pittsburgh had been baptized in the Holy Spirit. And as Roman Catholics, they could discern no doctrinal problem with what happened to them. Indeed, the men were convinced that the pentecostal experience could only make them *better* Catholics. The same month, a small group of students arranged a retreat with the faculty members in question. About thirty people attended this "Duquesne weekend" (as it has come to be called) and received baptism in the Holy Spirit while

---

38. It is somewhat ironic that, as late as 1974, Wilkerson still maintained very antiecumenical attitudes, and held a rigorous stance on personal ethics. See David Wilkerson, *The Vision* (New York: Pyramid Books, 1974).

there. Later, they became the nucleus of the first Catholic pentecostal "community."[39]

Within a month, what had been born at Duquesne spread both to the University of Notre Dame and to the Catholic student parish at Michigan State University.[40] In January 1967, Kevin Ranaghan (then teaching at St. Mary's College, Notre Dame) and his wife, Dorothy, heard that their good friends at Duquesne had sought the pentecostal experience, a fact that *shocked* them. In mid-February, Ralph Keifer came to South Bend, Indiana, on business and spent the weekend with the Ranaghans. For two days the discussion was entirely concerned with pentecostalism, during which time Kevin and Dorothy Ranaghan raised every intellectual, esthetic, and psychological objection to Keifer, who by this time had actually received the Spirit baptism. Then on March 5, nine people from the Notre Dame academic community met together to seek the pentecostal experience. That night, there were no manifest charismata among the group; but the "blessing" apparently had been received. The Ranaghans describe what happened to themselves and the others as follows:

In general, we all experienced and witnessed in each other the breakthrough of the love of Christ in our lives.... Many were drawn to long periods of prayer, marked by the predominance of the praise of God. Some found themselves opening the Bible anew with a real hunger for the word of God. Just about everyone found a new boldness in faith, a desire to witness about Jesus to friends and to strangers. Divisions, even hatreds, between brothers were healed.... It was like this all throughout that first week.[41]

On March 13, the new Catholic pentecostals met in prayer with

39. Kevin and Dorothy Ranaghan, *Catholic Pentecostals*, pp. 6–23.

40. O'Connor, *The Pentecostal Movement in the Catholic Church*, pp. 15–16.

41. Kevin and Dorothy Ranaghan, *Catholic Pentecostals*, pp. 40–41. For the full story of the Ranaghans' experience, see the entire book; Kevin Ranaghan, "The Essential Element in the Church," *Charismata Digest*, no. 2 (1969), pp. 14–18, 22–24; "A Roman Catholic Discovers New Life in His Church," *Christian Life* (May 1968), pp. 30–31, 57–60; and "The Power That Fell at Pentecost," *Testimony* (Second Quarter 1969), pp. 1–3.

members of the South Bend chapter of the Full Gospel Business Men's Fellowship International, where Catholic intellectuals and evangelical Protestant laypeople discovered quickly that their unity in an experience transcended deep theological and cultural differences. Many of the Catholics who attended the gathering received the gift of tongues that evening.

Through a number of house and campus prayer meetings in the weeks to come, more students and instructors (including Edward O'Connor[42] and Josephine Massyngberde Ford[43] of the Notre Dame Department of Theology), priests and nuns, laymen and laywomen from South Bend came to have the pentecostal experience. By Easter vacation 1967, about thirty Catholics in the Notre Dame area had received baptism in the Holy Spirit.

Shortly after spring break, the Notre Dame group decided to join with others from the Catholic student parish at Michigan State University, East Lansing (some of whom had recently been Spirit baptized), for a time of prayer, fellowship, and further inquiry—now known as the "Michigan State weekend." The facilities of Old College, Notre Dame, were reserved for this purpose. About forty people from Michigan State and an equal number from Notre Dame and St. Mary's participated. By the end of that weekend, in which numerous Christians received the pentecostal experience, the Catholic pentecostal movement was flourishing at Duquesne, Notre Dame, and Michigan State—and spreading elsewhere. Hundreds of Catholics across the country had been baptized in the Spirit by the end of the spring semester.

During the summer session of 1967, about three thousand students came (as usual) to Notre Dame—mostly nuns, priests, and teaching brothers. A number of the Catholic pentecostals remained on campus that summer and arranged a panel discussion on the topic that interested them most. The previous events at Duquesne, Notre Dame, and Michigan State had been reported in the Catho-

---

42. See Edward O'Connor, "The Pentecostal Movement Has Brought Joy to My Ministry," *Testimony* (Third Quarter 1969), pp. 14–16.

43. See J. Massyngberde Ford, *The Pentecostal Experience* (New York: Paulist Press, 1970), one of her earlier works on the topic.

lic press; hence, three hundred attended that discussion. Afterward, interest was such that regular prayer meetings were scheduled once or twice a week for three weeks in which hundreds of people took part; and when the participants left Notre Dame, of course, they took the pentecostal message and experience with them.[44] Catholic pentecostalism had become a clearly visible movement.

From Notre Dame and Michigan State, pentecostalism in the Roman Catholic Church spread quickly to the University of Michigan (where the Word of God community, led by Ralph Martin and Steve Clark, became particularly vigorous),[45] to Cleveland, to the University of Iowa, and to the University of Portland (Oregon). Meanwhile, similar developments were taking place in other parts of the country—outside the academic community as well—in Boston, Orlando, Seattle, Los Angeles, St. Louis, and central New York. By October 1970, there were pentecostal prayer groups among Catholics throughout the country, and possibly ten thousand Catholics were actively involved in the movement in the United States. In addition, Catholic pentecostal prayer groups were flourishing in Canada, England, New Zealand, Australia, and in several Latin American countries—with beginnings observed also in continental Europe and in Africa.[46]

Most of the early leadership of the Catholic charismatic renewal

---

44. Kevin and Dorothy Ranaghan, *Catholic Pentecostals*, pp. 38–57.

45. See Bertil W. Ghezzi, "Three Charismatic Communities," in Kevin and Dorothy Ranaghan, eds., *As the Spirit Leads Us* (New York: Paulist Press, 1971), pp. 164–186; and *New Covenant* (February 1975).

46. O'Connor, *The Pentecostal Movement in the Caholic Church,* pp. 15–19. See also Jim Cavnar, "Catholics: Pentecostal Movement," *Acts* 1, no. 5 (1968), pp 14–19; James Connelly, "The Charismatic Movement," in Kevin and Dorothy Ranaghan, eds., *As the Spirit Leads Us,* pp. 211–232; Edward B. Fiske, "Pentecostals Gain Among Catholics," *New York Times* (November 3, 1970), pp. 37, 56; James W. L. Hills, "The New Charismatics, 1973," *Eternity* (March 1973), pp. 24–25, 33; O'Connor, *The Pentecostal Movement in the Catholic Church,* pp. 13–107; R. Douglas Wead, *Catholic Charismatics: Are They for Real?* (formerly *Father McCarthy Smokes a Pipe and Speaks in Tongues*) (Carol Stream, Ill.: Creation House, 1973); and *Full Gospel Business Men's Voice* (September 1971), pp. 3–17.

emerged from the ecumenical Word of God community in Ann Arbor. Although the initial appeal was to students, by the early 1970s movement participants could be characterized mainly as middle-aged. In subsequent years, the movement seems to have had decreasing appeal to students and an increasing attraction to older people.

Catholic pentecostalism reached the attention of the national news media in May 1967, and was described sympathetically in a Catholic magazine the following month. In 1971, Ralph Martin and Steve Clark started a "pastoral letter," New Covenant, in Martin's garage, which soon became a full-fledged monthly magazine, and had a circulation of 65,000 by 1977. New Covenant's rising influence was enhanced by the organization of Charismatic Renewal Services, an extensive umbrella operation in South Bend, Indiana, supplying music, distributing books and cassette tapes (Servant Publications), and organizing conferences for the larger charismatic renewal.

The best-known external work of the Notre Dame and Ann Arbor communities was the organization of national and international Catholic pentecostal conferences, which grew out of the Michigan State weekend in 1967. In 1968, attendance was between 100 and 150. The 1969 weekend brought together about 450, including perhaps twenty-five or thirty priests (David du Plessis was a participant at this conference). In 1970, the increase was more spectacular. Almost 1,400 people attended the conference from a much wider area of North America than before (including Canada).[47] In 1971, the number of participants rose from 5,000 to 11,000 in 1972. Then, in 1973, the charismatic renewal conference at Notre Dame (June 1–3) brought together 20,000 attendees, who occupied every available room in a 50-mile radius of South Bend. In addition to the multitude of American participants, Catholics from Australia, Germany, Holland, France, Israel, Mexico, Haiti, Colombia, Korea, and India were present to

---

47. O'Connor, The Pentecostal Movement in the Catholic Church, pp. 99–101; and Rick Casey, "Charismatics II," National Catholic Reporter (August 29, 1975), pp. 1, 4, 10.

hear Léon Joseph Cardinal Suenens, archbishop of Malines-Brussels, a well-known reformer and Catholic pentecostal himself, both endorse and encourage charismatic renewal—which at this time embraced possibly 300,000 American Catholics or more.[48] The 1974 Notre Dame conference was attended by 25,000 people.[49] And the 1975 international conference, held in Rome, attracted 10,000 pilgrims from fifty countries to hear Pope Paul VI express his warm appreciation for the movement.[50] The years 1967–1977 were a period of continuing growth and visibility for the Catholic charismatic renewal. Thousands of people were attracted, many with no prior church background. Some amazingly large conferences were held. Millions of books and cassette tapes on the pentecostal experiences were sold, and thousands of charismatic prayer groups sprang up in homes and churches.

The watershed of this period of growth and expansion was the 1977 Conference on Charismatic Renewal in the Christian Churches, held in Kansas City, Missouri. The idea was to bring all the diverse Catholic and Protestant elements of the movement together by having the various denominational groups meet separately in the morning (including Jewish Christians, classical pentecostals, and black and Hispanic delegations), but together for joint rallies in the evening in the baseball stadium.

In many ways the conference was a huge success. The 1976 conference had attracted 30,000 participants, but this one drew 45,000 (only half of whom were Catholic). The doctrinal and cultural diversity of the movement, whose visibility peaked in 1977, was demonstrated in the content of plenary speeches by celebrities as diverse as Léon Joseph Cardinal Suenens of Belgium, black pentecostal Professor James Forbes of Union Theological Seminary in New York City, and Ruth Carter Stapleton, the Southern Baptist

---

48. John C. Haughey, "Holy Spirit: A Ghost No Longer," *America* (June 16, 1973), p. 551. See Léon Joseph Cardinal Suenens, *A New Pentecost?* (New York: Seabury Press, 1974); and Elizabeth Hamilton, *Suenens: A Portrait* (New York: Doubleday, 1975).

49. Mary Ann Jahr, "A Turning Point," *New Covenant* (August 1974), p. 4.

50. See *New Covenant* (July 1975).

charismatic healing evangelist who enjoyed a brief period of leadership in the movement—and a July 17, 1978, *Newsweek* cover story—while her brother, Jimmy, was President.

After the 1977 conference, however, attendance at similar gatherings decreased dramatically—to 20,000 participants in Dublin in 1978, and only 10,000 in 1980, reflecting, in part, the movement's deemphasis of international and national conferences in favor of regional gatherings. A 1979 Gallup Poll reported that 18 percent of all Roman Catholics in the United States were charismatic; and the 1981 *Directory of Catholic Charismatic Prayer Groups* listed 4,300 of those groups active in the United States that year.[51]

The dramatic emergence and growth of Catholic pentecostalism since 1967 has produced a good deal of highly sophisticated theological literature on pentecostal phenomena (specifically in the Catholic Church) by those who have been active participants, and has also resulted in the diffusion of charismatic renewal into predominantly Catholic countries both in Europe and the Third World—Latin America especially, where it is bringing together former enemies, Roman Catholicism and classical pentecostals, in a totally unexpected way.[52] Neopentecostalism is growing faster perhaps within Roman Catholicism than in any other denomination—a fact that makes Michael Harper's words early in 1970 particularly relevant at this point: "Catholic renewal could in the end out-space renewal in all other churches."[53]

---

51. McGuire, pp. 4–6; Looney, pp. 28–31; and Kenneth S. Kantzer, "The Charismatics Among Us," *Christianity Today* (February 22, 1980), p. 13.

52. See Wagner, pp. 167–169.

53. Michael Harper, "Catholic Pentecostals," *Renewal* (February–March 1970), p. 4. For early Catholic pentecostal testimonies, see Full Gospel Business Men's Fellowship International, *Catholics and the Baptism in the Holy Spirit* (n.d.) and *The Acts of the Holy Spirit Among the Catholics Today* (Los Angeles: FGBMFI, 1974); Joseph E. Orsini, *Hear My Confession* (Plainfield, N.J.: Logos International, 1971); Kevin and Dorothy Ranaghan, *Catholic Pentecostals* (New York: Paulist Press, 1969); Maria von Trapp, *Maria* (Carol Stream, Ill.: Creation House, 1972); and R. Russell Bixler (ed.), *The Spirit Is A-Movin'* (Carol Stream, Ill.: Creation House, 1974). Important recent scholarship by and about Catholic charismatics includes the following books: Patrick L. Bourgeois, *Can Catholics Be Charismatic?* (Hicksville, N.Y.: Exposition Press, 1976); James F. Brecken-

THE NEW PENTECOSTALISM TODAY

The original nonsectarian purpose and goals of charismatic renewal, broadly formulated as early as 1960, did not change in the course of its growth. The conviction persisted that the pentecostal experience was a force powerful enough to renew and revitalize the church in its full range of contemporary institutional expressions—and potent enough to unify Christians spiritually in an experience, without requiring institutional oneness.

To further its aims as a movement, neopentecostalism developed a distinct pattern of leadership. Underlying the movement, we could discern a weblike network of individual leaders and organizations—unified in the common experience of Spirit baptism. This network, then, facilitated personal ties between lay "members" and group leaders and between the groups themselves, and so justified charismatic renewal's identity as a movement. Magazines published by these organizations further strengthened the movement's identity by setting an acceptable ideological tone.

In Great Britain, important organizations associated with charis-

ridge, *The Theological Self-Understanding of the Catholic Charismatic Movement* (Washington, D.C.: University Press of America, 1980); Stephen B. Clark, *Man and Woman in Christ* (Ann Arbor, Mich.: Servant Publications, 1980); Sheila M. Gahey, *Charismatic Social Action* (New York: Paulist Press, 1977); J. Massyngberde Ford, *Which Way for Catholic Pentecostals?* (New York: Harper & Row, 1976); Donald L. Gelpi, *Charism and Sacrament* (New York: Paulist Press, 1976); and Donald L. Gelpi, *Experiencing God: A Theology of Human Experience* (New York: Paulist Press, 1978); John C. Haughey, ed., *Theological Reflections on the Charismatic Renewal* (Ann Arbor, Mich.: Servant Publications, 1978); Réne Laurentin, *Catholic Pentecostalism* (New York: Doubleday, 1978); Kilian McDonnell, *Charismatic Renewal and the Churches* (New York: Seabury Press, 1976); Kilian McDonnell, *The Charismatic Renewal and Ecumenism* (New York: Paulist Press, 1978); Kilian McDonell, ed., *The Holy Spirit and Power* (New York: Doubleday, 1975); and Kilian McDonnell, ed., *Presence, Power, Praise,* 3 vols. (Collegeville, Minn.: Liturgical Press, 1980); McGuire, *Pentecostal Catholics* (Philadelphia: Temple University Press, 1982); Heribert Mühlen, *A Charismatic Theology* (New York: Paulist Press, 1979); Edward O'Connor, ed., *Perspectives on Charismatic Renewal* (South Bend, Ind.: University of Notre Dame Press, 1975); Léon Joseph Cardinal Suenens and Dom Helder Camara, *Charismatic Renewal and Social Action* (Ann Arbor, Mich.: Servant Publications, 1979); Emmanuel Sullivan, *Baptized into Hope* (London: SPCK, 1980); and Simon Tugwell, ed., *New Heaven? New Earth?: An Encounter with Pentecostalism* (London: Darton, Longman and Todd, 1976).

matic renewal include Anglican Renewal Ministries, Baptists for Life and Growth, Dunamis Fellowship (Methodist), Group for Evangelism and Renewal (United Reformed Church), National Service Committee of the Catholic Charismatic Renewal, and the more inclusive SOMA (Sharing of Ministries Abroad). And two magazines, *Renewal* and *Theological Renewal,* center on the movement's concerns.

The most important fellowship organization linked to neopentecostalism in the United States (and internationally) is still the Full Gospel Business Men's Fellowship International, Costa Mesa, California. By means of its local chapters, its regional, national, and international conferences and "airlifts," and its publication of *Voice* magazine, this organization continues to be a worldwide recruiting arm for charismatic renewal as well. A much smaller, but comparable, organization for women is called Women's Aglow Fellowship, Lynwood, Washington, which publishes *Aglow* magazine. The intellectual centers of both classical pentecostalism and neopentecostalism today are Oral Roberts University, Tulsa, Oklahoma, founded by the eminent faith-healing evangelist, and the Society for Pentecostal Studies, a professional association of scholars in the field.

The aforementioned are ecumenical in their orientation, but there do exist a number of specifically denominational fellowships to promote charismatic renewal in the United States. Included here are Episcopal Renewal Ministries, Fellowship of Charismatic Christians in the United Church of Christ, Logos Ministry for Orthodox Renewal, Lutheran Renewal International, Presbyterian Charismatic Communion, and the nondenominational Christian Growth Ministries. News of the movement can be found in publications of these and similar organizations, and in *Charisma* and *Christian Life* magazines more generally.

By the late 1970s, charismatic renewal had become strong enough—among key lay leaders and clergy, ecclesiastical bureaucrats and theologians—to warrant the gradual acceptance of pentecostal phenomena in most of the historic denominations. Already in 1972, Walter Hollenweger could say,

> It will become harder and harder to make a clear-cut distinction between American Pentecostals and American nonpentecostals in the future, now that the experience and message of the baptism of the Spirit have found a way into all the American denominations.[54]

Neopentecostalism did penetrate virtually all the historic (and some of the "newer") denominations in the course of its development, but none so dramatically as the Roman Catholic Church, where the work is still centered on Charismatic Renewal Services and its publications, including *New Covenant* and the *National Service Committee Newsletter*. Early in 1981, Pope John Paul II, like his predecessor, expressed explicit appreciation for the Catholic charismatic renewal and its work within the church.

There is no hard evidence that the total number of self-professed neopentecostals has declined in the 1980s. Since 1977, however, neopentecostalism—as a movement—*has* lost its media visibility. Furthermore, it has lost much of its original distinctiveness by accommodation to classical pentecostalism, nonpentecostal evangelicalism, and to the "mainline Christianity" of the historic denominations.

A major step in the movement's accommodation to nonpentecostal evangelicalism came in the form of a joint statement by charismatic and noncharismatic Evangelicals in the Church of England (including Michael Harper and the eminent evangelical leaders James Packer and John R. W. Scott) in 1977, indicating a basic conciliation on the matter of Spirit baptism.[55] This statement was later enhanced by the increasing regularity with which neopentecostals and nonpentecostal evangelicals have been featured together in revival campaigns (like the "Jesus" festivals of the late 1970s), conferences (especially those relating to evangelism, church growth, and the family), and on religious radio and television programs (where the essential message of charismatic television evangelists Pat Robertson, Oral Roberts, and Jim Bakker

---

54. Hollenweger, *The Pentecostals,* p. 15.

55. See *Theological Renewal* (April–May 1977).

differs little in content from that of noncharismatics Jerry Falwell and Robert H. Schuller).

The best symbol of neopentecostal and classical pentecostal accommodation was the reinstatement of David du Plessis to the ordained ministry of the Assemblies of God in 1980. Du Plessis lost his ministerial status within the denomination in 1962 because of his ecumenical activities with Roman Catholics and mainline Protestants at a time when such was regarded as "heresy." But by the late 1970s, the Catholic charismatic renewal was totally accepted by the leadership of the Assemblies of God, as it was by that of most of the rest of classical pentecostalism, and du Plessis was vindicated.

If neopentecostalism accommodated to nonpentecostal evangelicalism and classical pentecostalism, and they to it, the movement also had to make peace with the mainline Protestant and Catholic Christianity of the historic denominations. On the heels of numerous positive denominational statements, the Church of England published a favorable book on charismatic renewal in 1981, entitled *The Charismatic Movement in the Church of England*, while the same year the World Council of Churches also published a positive book-length study, *The Church Is Charismatic*, edited by Arnold Bittlinger. In 1979, the Gallup organization could report that 18 percent of American Catholic adults were charismatic, 22 percent of all Protestants, and 19 percent of the general public identified themselves as charismatic or pentecostal.[56] Although it is still possible in the 1980s to speak of charismatic renewal as a distinctive movement, it is no longer *necessary* to do so. The pentecostal experience, no less than the born-again experience, has become just another acceptable variant in the religious life of modern Americans (and Westerners more generally), without the need of one formal movement to maintain its identity and act as a focus for the mutual support of neopentecostals.

We shall now examine the nature of charismatic renewal with respect to the development of its leadership, its characteristic faith

---

56. Kantzer, p. 13.

and practice (including structure and organization), its kinship both to classical pentecostalism and to the church as a whole, reasons for its emergence and success, and its relationship to trends in the wider culture.

Chapter Four

The Leadership of
Charismatic Renewal

The principles of charismatic renewal leadership must be discerned in the context of pentecostal organization itself. Luther Gerlach and Virginia Hine have studied the structural character of pentecostalism as a movement in *People, Power, Change: Movements of Social Transformation*. Beginning with Gerlach and Hine's structural analysis of the pentecostal movement as a whole, we can proceed to apply their findings to neopentecostalism in particular.

The pentecostal movement is, first of all, according to Gerlach and Hine, fully *decentralized*. There are widely recognized leaders within pentecostalism. And, to outsiders, these men and women often appear to be the key individuals without whom the movement would grind to a halt. Yet not one of them could rightly be called *the* leader of the movement in which they work. Pentecostal leaders disagree on matters of theological emphasis. None of them are even aware of all the groups that consider themselves participants in the movement. None of the leaders can make decisions binding on all participants; they cannot speak for the movement as a whole, nor do they have regulatory power over it. (There are, of course, no "real" members of the pentecostal *movement* as such— only "participants"—although there are members of specific classical pentecostal denominations). Pentecostal Christians recognize each other on the basis of criteria born of a common experience, not because a leader announces that a given person is a legitimate participant in the movement.[1] What gave the movement vitality was an emphasis on the autonomy of the local church, where key individuals *were* very real and demanding leaders of their own microcosm of the larger movement and *could* expel others (as Seymour put Parham out of the Azusa Street Mission). In the early days, leaders did exercise almost total control of given churches, but this phase quickly led to denominationlike groups emphasizing local church autonomy.

Leadership in a decentralized movement is, by and large, based on personal charisma rather than the fulfillment of bureaucratic training requirements and progression up through ranked positions.[2] In charismatic renewal, however, individuals who were already bureaucratic leaders in their own denominations (or academic institutions, for instance) could become recognized neopentecostal leaders far more easily than the rest—once they received and publicly shared the pentecostal experience. Furthermore, we can distinguish within charismatic renewal the development of a largely "organizational" (goal-oriented) leadership rather distinct from (but perhaps derivative of) the leadership based on personal charisma.

"Charisma," a term first used in sociology by Max Weber, was employed by him to signify supernatural or spiritual endowment as acknowledged by others. It was, thus, a social recognition of a claim to supernatural power (as in the case of Jesus Christ himself). In the pentecostal movement, however, charisma, with reference to leadership, indicates that a given individual (1) is recognized by others as possessing one or more of the spiritual gifts in special degree; (2) has a forceful personality, in that he or she, through preaching, prayer, and spiritual discernment, can evoke group experiences of pentecostal power (including speaking in tongues, healings, and prophecy); and (3) is able, through personal qualities, to exercise leadership. This is what we mean when

---

1. Gerlach and Hine, *People, Power, Change*, pp. 33–37.
2. Ibid., p. 38.

we refer to "charismatic leadership" within charismatic renewal.[3]

Second, according to Gerlach and Hine, the pentecostal movement is made up of different *segments*. It consists of a great variety of localized groups or cells that are essentially independent but that can combine to form larger configurations or divide to form smaller units. Quite often each segment will tend to recruit from different parts of the total societal population. Each will tend to develop a "religious style" of its own—and its own specific goals and means as well. These groups proliferate rather quickly because of (1) the pentecostal ideology of personal access to power (any pentecostal has direct access to the source of spiritual power, wisdom, and authority—"the priesthood of all believers" carried to an extreme), and because of (2) preexisting personal and social cleavages. Thus, a given class-, culture-, or ecclesiastical-consciousness will probably cause pentecostals having that particular consciousness to stick together in their own primary groups.[4]

Charismatic leaders in the pentecostal movement are supported financially (and otherwise) by fellow pentecostals who believe the recipients have been called by God to do a special work. The givers believe in the work fully as much as the recipients of financial support feel *obligated* to do the work well.[5]

Third, according to Gerlach and Hine, the pentecostal movement is a *weblike network*. Its structure is weblike; the cells and groups are all tied together, not at a central point, but by intersecting sets of personal relationships and other intergroup linkages. There are personal ties among participants. For instance, a pentecostal *may* attend Sunday services at one church and Wednesday night prayer meeting at another; or he (or she) may hold an interdenominational weekly "house meeting" at his home. Then there are personal ties among the leaders of various groups themselves—even invitational conferences for pentecostal leaders alone. Fur-

---

3. Gerlach and Hine apply Weber's definition of charismatic leadership to penetecostalism.

4. Gerlach and Hine, *People, Power, Change*, pp. 41–45.

5. Ibid., p. 52.

thermore, traveling evangelists link the segments together, as do ritual activities (conferences and the like), where participants gather for expressive rather than formal, goal-oriented purposes. Such gatherings promote religious fervor, intensify commitment, and express the movement's basic unity (even in much diversity). Finally, regional, national, and international associations function to link the various pentecostal groups together.[6]

The decentralized, segmentary, and weblike character of the pentecostal movement assures a constant supply of leaders and replacements should any be lost. It limits the ability of established opposition to penetrate, gather intelligence about, and counteract the movement. And this structure allows the unifying pentecostal experience to spread the movement across class, cultural, and ecclesiastical boundaries. Thus, in a sense, there is a pentecostal church or group for "everyone."[7]

THE TRUSTED AUTHORITY FIGURE

As a result of his ten-year study of glossolalia among Protestant and Anglican neopentecostals (*The Psychology of Speaking in Tongues*), John Kildahl concludes that speakers in tongues develop deeply trusting and submissive relationships to the authority figures who introduced them to the experience. He discerned that glossolalists have a strong need for external guidance from some trusted authority—someone "more powerful" than themselves who gives them security and direction, even peace and relaxation, in their lives. Kildahl also found that speakers in tongues tend to "overinvest" their feelings in their leaders to the point of "idealizing them as nearly perfect parents."[8] Thus, while national and international neopentecostal leaders (recognized to be endowed with one or more particularly evident *charismata*) command the general respect and admiration of participants, it is the *local* group

---

6. Ibid., pp. 55–60.

7. Ibid., pp. 65–70.

8. Kildahl, pp. 50–51.

leaders with a largely personal ministry who come closer to exercising "real" authority over their followers (in the context of specific requirements of the various ecclesiastical traditions to which neopentecostals adhere).

In the very beginning, a recognizable and influential neopentecostal leadership emerged almost spontaneously. Among the "first" mainline clergy and laypeople who received the pentecostal experience, certain highly committed individuals soon attracted a following of Anglicans and Protestants to whom baptism in the Holy Spirit seemed novel and exciting. The former became trusted authorities on the experience—denominational interpreters. These charismatic leaders were, of course, aided both by the positive and the negative comments of the secular and religious press, and by exposure to the media in general. Neopentecostal leaders quickly began seeking each other out for fellowship and mutual support—among them, Dennis Bennett, Harald Bredesen, Howard Ervin, and Larry Christenson, all mainline clergymen. Open classical pentecostals who already enjoyed standing in the movement—Demos Shakarian, Ralph Wilkerson, and David du Plessis (in particular), among others—soon identified themselves with the charismatic renewal participants. Jean Stone, an Episcopal laywoman, emerged as a neopentecostal leader largely through the widespread circulation of *Trinity,* which she edited and which was the first distinctly neopentecostal periodical. In Great Britain, Michael Harper, an Anglican clergyman, became a charismatic renewal leader partly through his camaraderie with early American neopentecostal personalities, but mostly by the circulation of *Renewal* and, later, his successful books.

The Full Gospel Business Men's Fellowship International provided early organizational support for the movement; so did the Blessed Trinity Society (while it lasted) and Melodyland Christian Center. In Great Britain, as noted, the Fountain Trust functioned in a similar manner to the Blessed Trinity in America. By becoming a United Methodist minister, Oral Roberts, the classical pentecostal faith-healing evangelist, identified "officially" with charismatic renewal, and his new university added a measure of academic prestige to the movement. The career of "miracle worker" Kathryn Kuhlman, a Baptist minister, was clearly enhanced by her association with neopentecostalism—as much as the movement itself was aided by her participation. The same can be said about the vocal support of celebrities such as Pat Boone and Maria von Trapp. Furthermore, Logos International, the once highly successful publisher of charismatic renewal literature, was also a significant asset to the movement's media efforts.

Thus, despite the inherent diffusion of charisma and the presence of local authority figures, charismatic renewal has had widely recognized national and international, charismatic and organizational, leaders who preach, teach, inspire, and provided (through visits, lectures, and publications) an identity for the movement and a measure of cohesiveness to a decentralized, segmentary, and weblike structure.

PROMINENT CHARISMATIC LEADERS

In a decentralized movement, as we have seen, charismatic leadership predominates. Charismatic leaders have the power of persuasive influence over others. They inspire faith and loyalty (and also aid in the recruitment process). Charismatic renewal has produced many purely charismatic leaders within its various segments, and some whose "charisma" transcends those cells and groups. The latter included celebrities such as Kathryn Kuhlman, Oral Roberts, and Pat Boone, who aided the movement no less than lesser-known neopentecostal charismatic leaders who work locally at the person-to-person level.

ORGANIZATIONAL LEADERS

With the gradual development of structure and organization since 1960, charismatic renewal produced a number of people, who, because of their close ties to specific important organizations associated with the movement, could rightly be termed "organizational" leaders. On the one hand, these individuals did not really function as classically "bureaucratic" leaders who had fulfilled *formal* bureaucratic training requirements (which do not exist in neopentecostalism), and progressed up through ranked positions (which, again, do not exist). But neither were they leaders by virtue of personal charisma alone—although most of them, perhaps, *are* endowed with charisma, which itself aided their advancement to organizational leadership. These men and women quite often are known and respected *because* of their identification with a particular organization, publication, or church (or, as in the case of David du Plessis, are simply regarded as natural "organizers" in the larger sense) rather than merely by virtue of personal charisma. Demos Shakarian is a leader because he founded and directs the Full Gospel Business Men's Fellowship International. Ralph Wilkerson, as a leader, is identified with the church he founded and pastors, Melodyland Christian Center. Michael Harper is highly regarded as a neopentecostal leader in Great Britain and elsewhere by virtue of his association with *Renewal* (and his widely circulated books). Ralph Martin is a leader because he was editor of *New Covenant;* and Eusebius Stephanou, since he edits *Logos.* Jean Stone, of course, was also an editor.

Even before his formal identification with charismatic renewal, David du Plessis (who still considers himself a classical pentecostal) had already "progressed through the ranks" of denominational pentecostalism to the point that he was the primary organizer (and secretary) of the early Pentecostal World Conferences. Thus, neopentecostals from the beginning regarded him as "Mr. Pentecost" and solicited his help as an organizing facilitator (for example, he was among the first directors of the Blessed Trinity Society). Respected participant clergy-become-lecturers (and world travelers) easily fell into organizational leadership within the movement as it manifested itself in those leaders' own denominations—aided by whatever bureaucratic standing such ministers enjoyed prior to their participation in charismatic renewal. Hence, Dennis Bennett is a leader in the Episcopal Church and among

Anglicans in general; Larry Christenson, in the American Lutheran Church and among Lutherans as a whole; J. Rodman Williams, in the Presbyterian Church in the United States and among the larger body of Presbyterians; Edward O'Connor and Cardinal Suenens, in the Roman Catholic Church; and Eusebius Stephanou, among Eastern Orthodox Christians. All of them, of course, had the requisite ecclesiastical standing before they identified with neopentecostalism.

EDITORS AND PUBLISHERS

In a decentralized movement—especially in its beginning, before a pattern of ideological consensus and a definite structure of leadership arise—the periodical editor (aided, perhaps, by a measure of personal charisma) can rather easily become an organizational leader in that movement, influencing its emerging identity. He (or she), of course, has the power to select authors and new items (and screen manuscripts) for exposure to participants and the public at large. This editor defines the parameters of ideological acceptability. If the periodical in question is indeed acceptable to participants in the movement, its circulation will increase with the growth of the movement itself. Thus, the editor achieves notoriety, which is further enhanced by widespread circulation of the periodical. Almost automatically, then, the editor becomes a spokesperson for the movement in his editorial comments. A typical modern religious movement is greatly helped (if not "carried" almost entirely) by the mass media. Yet, as a movement's ideological consensus develops (to whatever degree it does) and becomes recognizable, and as a definite pattern of leadership emerges, it becomes less likely that the editor of a *new* periodical will rise to organizational leadership simply by virtue of who he is (and his "breakthrough" journal)—unless he has already achieved leadership status by other means. For if that editor's publication merely reflects commonly publicized and accepted ideology and the views of already widely recognized leaders, it functions merely as a support and reinforcement for such ideology and leadership previously established. The editor can no longer actually help formulate and set ideology (in an "authoritative" sense). If he contradicts the underlying consensus, the editor and his journal may well get nowhere.

(One paradox in neopentecostalism is that here is a movement very largely organized around the experience of "speaking"—a very primitive form of communication. Yet one has to be impressed with the importance of the printed word in the movement, which reflects a dependence on literacy, and which itself indicates a reliance on subsidiary channels of communication. "Speaking" and "communicating" are basic means of establishing "community." For modern man, however, community depends on other techniques too. Early classical pentecostalism probably had much less dependence on journals than neopentecostalism did.)

In charismatic renewal, Demos Shakarian's leadership and the strength of his Full Gospel Business Men's Fellowship International have been aided enormously by the success of *Full Gospel Business Men's Voice* magazine (founded in 1953). Shakarian himself is not the journal's editor; nevertheless, he directs the organization for which *Voice* is the official mouthpiece. The magazine itself strengthens the organization and, with it, Shakarian's personal prestige as well; it aids the recruitment process by introducing the pentecostal experience to people (especially to FGBMFI activities for further information and fellowship). Jean Stone, of course, emerged as an organizational leader in the movement almost entirely because of the participant acceptance (and recruiting success) of *Trinity*, the first exclusively neopentecostal periodical to be published (1961–1966). Widespread circulation of the magazine that she edited made her an authoritative spokeswoman for the movement. In Great Britain, likewise, Michael Harper became an organizational leader (even theoretician) largely because of his editorship of that nation's first neopentecostal journal, *Renewal*, which was received by participants with enthusiasm. In the same way, Ralph Martin, founding editor of *New Covenant*, and Eusebius Stephanou, editor of *The Logos*, also became organizational leaders.

From the movement's beginning in 1960, charismatic renewal

employed the mass media very effectively. Especially important has been its distribution of published literature—not only periodicals, as we have seen, but also pamphlets and books. At first, books and pamphlets by neopentecostal authors and their sympathizers were most often printed privately or by small, relatively unknown "publishers." These works were then distributed to the various charismatic renewal communities, churches, and conferences by the authors themselves (often charismatic leaders) or by traveling evangelists, teachers, and lecturer-preachers. Meetings of one kind or another (for expressive purposes) have always been a characteristic mark of neopentecostalism, and they provide a natural outlet for the relevant literature. Invariably, there is a "bookstall" connected with each charismatic renewal community. And in recent years, many of the larger, growing communities have transformed their bookstalls into full-fledged bookstores specializing in pentecostal and evangelical titles. But specialized charismatic renewal bookstores, independent of any particular neopentecostal group, also arose, for books and pamphlets on the topic in question were marketed easily, and not infrequently became religious best-sellers.

In the course of the movement's development, specialized charismatic renewal publishers emerged to supply even secular bookstores with their increasingly marketable book and cassette tape titles. Of these publishing houses, the largest and most famous was Logos International, Plainfield, New Jersey, founded by Dan Malachuk.

Malachuk, a high school dropout and jeweler in Plainfield, New Jersey, had long been active in the FGBMFI. During the 1960s, he decided to set up a publishing house. An old work by Rafael Gasson on his conversion from spiritualism to Christianity, *The Challenging Counterfeit,* was the first book published by Malachuk under the Logos imprint; however, his first great success was *Run Baby Run,* by Nicky Cruz, which was first published in 1968 and sold into the millions. Malachuk quickly established Logos International as the leading publisher of charismatic renewal titles, and he took over the publication and distribution of other previously published works by smaller houses. By 1972, he was forecasting sales of 5 million books a year; and his bimonthly magazine, *Logos Journal*, reached over a hundred thousand in circulation by the early 1970s.

Logos International and other neopentecostal publishers such as Bethany Fellowship and Servant Publications were a significant factor in the growth of charismatic renewal. Their early success was also an indicator of the health and strength of the movement in general. Most Logos books were action-packed adventures, often bordering on the sensational. By the end of the 1970s, Malachuk's firm seemed to be searching for financial stability and a new publishing direction in the face of the declining visibility of charismatic renewal. A national newspaper, *National Courier*, was launched by Logos in 1975, with disastrous results, and publication had to be halted already in 1977. Thereafter, Logos International declined further. And despite urgent appeals for money, the whole venture collapsed in September 1981.[9]

PREACHERS AND LECTURERS

In addition to editors and publishers, ordained ministers of the various historic denominations represented in charismatic renewal often became organizational leaders of the movement. Once a minister received the pentecostal experience and made the fact known publicly, he (or she) would probably win immediate recognition from one or more charismatic renewal organizational segments, and would most likely become associated with a neopentecostal community, possibly within his own denomination, and, perhaps, take on particular leadership responsibilities in that group. A minister's ecclesiastical standing made him a desirable lecturer within the charismatic renewal movement as a whole; for, through lecturing and/or writing, he could help recruit participants from his denomination while he added respectability to the movement more

9. William Willoughby, "How to Publish a Best Sellur," *Logos Journal* (November-December 1972), pp. 48–49 (reprinted from Washington, D.C., *Evening Star and Daily News*); "Statement of Ownership," *Logos Journal* (November-December 1973), p. 252; and Looney, pp. 27, 28.

generally. In time, the neopentecostal minister might come to "represent" his denomination within the larger charismatic renewal.

We have said that certain individuals within neopentecostalism came to be recognized as leaders simply by virtue of an easily discernible personal charisma. These persons would rise to positions of leadership without regard to bureaucratic training requirements or upward mobility through the ranks. We have also seen that some charismatic renewal leaders functioned in more strictly organizational roles (for example, in denominations or other ecclesiastical structures or the religious media). Many such leaders are, in fact, endowed with a degree of personal charisma, which helps them; but it is really their standing (ecclesiastical, intellectual, or social) that enhanced the emergence of these clergy and laypeople in organizational leadership circles. Unlike classical pentecostalism, neopentecostalism understood itself for the most part as a movement of the *respectable*—in whatever context. Hence, the respectability attached to one who had previously achieved social, intellectual, or ecclesiastical standing was a great asset to his or her participation in the movement. Certain attainments related to status were indeed desirable as prerequisites of organizational leadership.

For clergy, a college or university education, plus formal theological training, including (in the United States) a seminary degree, increased a minister's respectability in neopentecostalism. Education at "prestigious" institutions was also beneficial, since a charismatic renewal leader's academic credentials were always emphasized (if they *were* respectable). Then, clergy were also helped in this context by regular ordination and standing within a historic denomination; and it was even better if the clergy in question already attained positions of bureaucratic leadership within their denominations or within the institutional ecumenical movement. In this regard, we can also say that academics, simply by virtue of their education and resulting social status, made good organizational leaders within neopentecostalism—especially theologians who had *both* academic and ecclesiastical standing. The charismatic renewal stress on respectability of leadership was in sharp contrast to classical pentecostal requirements for ministerial organizational leadership—Spirit baptism, spiritual gifts, and "the call" (often omitting higher education as a requisite altogether). Of course, there are *some* ordained neopentecostal organizational leaders without benefit of higher education and mainline ecclesiastical standing, but their rise to the ranks of leadership often had more to do with personal charisma or previous classical pentecostal standing than anything else.

For laypeople, other criteria were also beneficial in the context of desirable "requisites" for charismatic renewal organizational leadership. These included formal higher education (as in the case of clergy), but also public esteem, participant lay membership in one of the historic denominations, and financial success. For especially wealthy neopentecostals (such as Full Gospel Business Men), leadership in one or more of the charismatic renewal organizational segments was predicated on the degree of generosity they exhibited toward the movement's sometimes very ambitious activities and projects (pentecostals, like other evangelicals, are admonished to tithe—at least). Rich lay leaders of the various neopentecostal organizations were often called on to help support the evangelistic efforts of charismatic renewal minister-lecturers-become-world-travelers who could not finance such trips themselves. Within neopentecostalism, laypeople did rise both to charismatic and organizational leadership; but their active participation was more often "in the background" and quieter than that of ordained ministers, whose vocal leadership in preaching and teaching was *expected* by virtue not only of their recognized spiritual gifts, but also because of their training and ecclesiastical standing.

IMPORTANT EARLY LEADERS

During the course of nearly two decades of development as a movement, charismatic renewal did produce a number of highly visible leaders who, individually and together, shaped the movement's identity as an ecumenical force for religious revival in the modern world. Most important among them were the late Kathryn Kuhlman, Oral Roberts, David du Plessis, Michael Harper, Demos Shakarian, Jean Stone, and Pat Robertson.

Kathryn Kuhlman

With the rise of Kathryn Kuhlman, divine healing (or "faith healing") in Christian orthodoxy increased in respectability. By 1970, even *Time* magazine could say,

> Joyfully middle-class, fiftyish, a lady who likes fine clothes, Kathryn Kuhlman looks for all the world like dozens of the women in her audience. But hidden underneath the 1945 Shirley Temple hairdo is one of the most remarkable Christian charismatics in the U.S. She is, in fact, a veritable one-woman shrine of Lourdes. In each of her ... services ... miraculous cures seem to occur.[10]

It was only since the mid-1960s or thereabouts that Kuhlman had been identified with the pentecostal movement at all. Previously, she was very much an "independent" phenomenon—an ordained Baptist minister through whom, her fans believed, God worked to perform miraculous healings. We have already said that Kuhlman's identification with charismatic renewal enhanced her popularity as well as the fortunes of the movement she supported. In 1972, Oral Roberts himself invited her to speak to the graduating class of Oral Roberts University and receive the institution's first honorary doctorate.[11]

Kathryn Kuhlman's style contrasted sharply with that of the stereotyped American revivalist faith healer. There were no healing lines, prayer cards to be completed beforehand (alleged to sort out "hopeless" cases), prayer cloths, or special talismans; nor was there the traditional "miracle touch" ("point of contact," as Oral Roberts called it, between the faith healers and their subjects).[12] Kuhlman held her miracle services in numerous places in the

---

10. "Miracle Woman," *Time* (September 14, 1970), p. 62.

11. James Morris, *The Preachers* (New York: St. Martin's Press, 1973), p. 252.

12. Ibid., pp. 237, 240.

United States (rarely elsewhere)—regularly at the First Presbyterian Church, Pittsburgh; Stambaugh Auditorium, Youngstown, Ohio; and the Shrine Auditorium, Los Angeles. Chartered buses (offering guaranteed reserved seats) made the trip to these locations whenever services were held. Once the buses emptied into a given auditorium, people outside who may have waited several hours were allowed inside until the hall was filled—just a few minutes after the doors were opened. Hundreds, even thousands, were regularly turned away or forced into "overflow" space connected to the live service by closed-circuit television. Kuhlman seemed to prefer "limited access" to her meetings, for she *could* have rented larger facilities.

Kuhlman's services, as James Morris describes them, were "folksy, friendly, and charming."[13] There was often musical entertainment at the beginning, followed very frequently by a sermon. Charismatic activity was noticeably curtailed, although participants practiced the pentecostal (and very ancient) *orans* prayer posture (hands uplifted), and were almost always "slain in the Spirit" (falling backward into an usher's arms) when Kuhlman touched them *after* their testimonies to an alleged or verified healing. At the conclusion of her sermon (if there was one), the charismatic leader would point to various places in the audience where she discerned healings had already occurred prior to that moment. She would cite the ailment—everything from terminal cancer to allergies (although amputated limbs never reappeared, teeth were not miraculously filled with gold)—and ask those who felt they were healed to come forward to the platform to testify about what had happened. (Trained ushers tried to screen cases and verify healings as much as possible beforehand.) Quite often there were physicians on the platform who themselves could be asked for confirmation, and everyone was urged to confirm an apparent cure with his or her own doctor. Some individuals, of course, testified, but were not healed; others seemed to get better, but later regressed; probably most in attendance were not cured at

---

13. Ibid., p. 239.

all. Nevertheless, the media and various respected authorities attested that a small number of people, at least, did receive an apparently miraculous cure. Some of these appeared on Kuhlman's daily radio and weekly half-hour television programs, which spanned the country.[14] Other spectacular cases were "documented" in her three books.[15] Unlike most traditional faith healers, people who experienced healing in the Kuhlman services were generally mainline Protestants and (increasingly) Roman Catholics—not classical pentecostals. In addition, even "nonbelievers" (Jews, agnostics, and atheists) were healed ("mercy healings," according to Kuhlman), while highly committed Christians might continue to suffer.[16] Yet, Kathryn Kuhlman refused to take the credit for any of the healings that took place in her presence. She often said, "I have nothing to do with these miracles."[17]

Born in 1907 in Concordia, Missouri, the daughter of a Methodist mother and Baptist father, Kuhlman underwent an evangelical conversion during her early teens. She dropped out of high school after her sophomore year to take up preaching (Kuhlman was sensitive about her lack of education[18]) and was ordained by the Evangelical Church Alliance (Missouri) after two years of informal Bible study.[19] Four years after an unhappy marriage, Kuhlman was divorced,[20] and spent over two decades as an itinerant preacher in Idaho and the Midwest. After her Spirit baptism in 1946, a woman claimed to be cured of an ailment during a Kuhlman service in Franklin, Pennsylvania. In 1947, the

---

14. Ibid., p. 252.

15. *I Believe in Miracles* (Englewood Cliffs, N.J.: Prentice-Hall, 1962); *God Can Do It Again* (Englewood Cliffs, N.J.: Prentice-Hall, 1969); and *Nothing Is Impossible with God* (Englewood Cliffs, N.J.: Prentice-Hall, 1974).

16. Steve Durasoff, *Bright Wind of the Spirit: Pentecostalism Today* (Englewood Cliffs, N.J.: Prentice-Hall, 1972), p. 185.

17. Quoted in Morris, p. 239.

18. Ibid., p. 247.

19. Ibid., p. 241.

20. Durasoff, pp. 184–185.

charismatic leader moved to Pittsburgh, and the healing aspect of her ministry began to grow. She had no membership organization, no magazine or newsletter; and of course, she urged people healed in her services to remain in their own churches. Kuhlman traveled 500,000 miles annually;[21] and, in 1970, she drew a salary of $25,000 from her foundation (but with considerable "fringe benefits").[22]

In 1972, 2,200 people gathered at the Pittsburgh Hilton Hotel to help Kathryn Kuhlman celebrate the twenty-fifth anniversary of her ministry in that city. Dan Malachuk of Logos International was there; and Carl Albert, Speaker of the House of Representatives, sent special congratulations.[23] Kuhlman earned the respect of city leaders of Pittsburgh as well.[24] Robert Lamont, former pastor of Pittsburgh's prestigious First Presbyterian Church, where the Kathryn Kuhlman Foundation held meetings every Friday, insisted that he examine the charismatic leader's finances before granting her permission to use his church sanctuary for services. Having scrutinized her financial records closely, he stated in 1972, "I've been doing this for the last four years and can report that her finances are cleaner than the United Presbyterian Church."[25] On October 11, 1972, Kuhlman was invited by Pope Paul VI to a private audience with him in the Vatican—during which time he assured her of his personal blessing on her work and his continual prayers[26]—thus guaranteeing an even larger Roman Catholic

---

21. Morris, p. 252.

22. "Miracle Woman," *Time* (September 14, 1970), p. 62.

23. "Kathryn Kuhlman: 25 Years in Pittsburgh," *Logos Journal* (November–December 1972), p. 33–36.

24. Morris, p. 243.

25. Quoted in "Kathryn Kuhlman: 25 Years in Pittsburgh," p. 35.

26. *Logos Journal* (January–February 1973), p. 32. See also the sympathetic and folksy, but important, biography by Jamie Buckingham, *Daughter of Destiny* (Plainfield, N.J.: Logos International, 1976). For a parapsychological interpretation of Kuhlman, see Allen Spraggett, *Kathryn Kuhlman: The Woman Who Believes in Miracles* (New York: New American Library, 1971). A less positive assessment of her ministry is offered by William A. Nolen, *Healing* (New York: Random House, 1974), pp. 41–102.

following for this remarkable woman, who died of heart failure and overwork early in 1976.

Within neopentecostalism, Kathryn Kuhlman was clearly a prominent charismatic leader. She was *the* representative of the movement's healing ministry; but more than that, as we have said, Kuhlman's miracle services greatly increased the respectability of divine healing in Christian orthodoxy.

Oral Roberts

For three decades, Oral Roberts has been the most prominent pentecostal in the United States. Pentecostal preachers were proud to have him as a champion, and the popular faith healing evangelist's crusades attracted as many as 25,000 people at a time in America, and up to 60,000 in other countries.[27] Unlike Kathryn Kuhlman, Roberts always had a significant ministry abroad. His healing crusades took place under the great "cathedral tent," where services were conducted in the American revivalistic tradition—with the focus on prayer for the sick who generally stood in "healing lines" waiting for the evangelist to "touch" them and pray for them. But Roberts's style was never so sensational as many of his pentecostal counterparts, his financial dealings were apparently more open to inspection and honest, and he integrated his crusades early.[28] Oral Roberts's personal charisma and success as a faith healer (he disliked the term[29]) made him classical pentecostalism's most prominent leader long before he identified with charismatic renewal.

The faith healing evangelist's parents dedicated Roberts to the service of God while he was a young child. His father was a Pentecostal Holiness minister, and the family was very poor. Roberts played basketball in high school (one reason why Oral Roberts University has had one of the best basketball teams in that colle-

---

27. Durasoff, pp. 113, 126.

28. See Oral Roberts, *The Call: An Autobiography* (Old Tappan, N.J.: Spire Books, 1971), pp. 93–112.

29. Durasoff, p. 119.

giate sport); but, during tournament play, at the age of sixteen, he collapsed on the court, and was later diagnosed as having tuberculosis in both lungs. Defeat turned into victory, however, for Oral Roberts's family took him to a pentecostal faith healer in his native Oklahoma, and young Roberts experienced a dramatic healing that changed the course of his life. Two months after his miraculous cure, Oral Roberts began preaching—an unusual feat for someone who had once been extremely fearful of crowds and a chronic stutterer. Like his father, Roberts became a Pentecostal Holiness pastor, first in Georgia and then in Oklahoma. In the course of time, his own gift of healing became manifestly apparent to many who attended his services. While pastoring, Oral Roberts spent several semesters at Oklahoma Baptist University and Phillips University, but never graduated. In 1947, a highly successful evangelistic effort in Tulsa, Oklahoma, led the faith healing evangelist to make that city his headquarters. A year later, in Durham, North Carolina, Roberts began his healing crusades in earnest; and it was only a matter of time before pentecostalism, divine healing, and Oral Roberts became synonymous.[30]

After two decades of healing ministry both in the United States and abroad, Roberts pulled down the big tent permanently in 1967. An unsuccessful crusade in Anaheim, California, that year had been the final blow. He says, "I could see that the tent was ceasing to be an asset. People were no longer attracted by its novelty. They had become used to cushioned chairs and air-conditioning and to watching television."[31] The day of preaching from a platform with a backdrop of pastors followed by a healing line had come and gone. The day of the gospel tent was over.

But Oral Roberts had already been moving in another direction. By the early 1960s, the Oral Roberts Evangelistic Association held substantial assets—chiefly in real estate (Roberts himself forsook "love offerings" for a regular salary paid by the association in

---

30. Ibid., pp. 114–126; and Roberts, pp. 93–96.
31. Roberts, p. 175.

1960).[32] With the additional help of numerous pentecostal supporters and Full Gospel Business Men,[33] the faith healing evangelist realized his long-standing dream in 1965—to found a distinctively Christian university with high academic standards. Oral Roberts University (ORU) officially opened in 1965, and some 300 students comprised the first class of undergraduate first-year and transfer students. By 1981, the university's student body had grown to 4,000 full-time students representing every state, every race, more than 40 denominations, and many countries. The total investment of the university, including campus facilities and endowment, stood at more than $250 million. The academic programs are fully accredited, and ORU has a faculty of more than 300. Graduate education began in 1975, with schools of theology and business, and graduate and professional programs in medicine, dentistry, nursing, law, and education have since been implemented.

At the center of campus stands a twenty-story "prayer tower," which is staffed twenty-four hours a day by people who take telephone calls from all over the world (Roberts started his telephone prayer-request ministry in 1958). ORU was formally dedicated in 1967, with Billy Graham as featured speaker; and it won full regional accreditation in 1971—only the second private college or university to receive this distinction so soon after its opening. It had been a long way for Oral Roberts from Pentecostal Holiness faith healer to president of his own university.[34]

In 1968, Oral Roberts left the Pentecostal Holiness Church, joined Boston Avenue United Methodist Church in Tulsa, and was received as an ordained minister (through transfer of credentials) by the Oklahoma Conference of the United Methodist Church. Although the university president had been a Methodist as a young child and had numerous friends and colleagues in that denomination (including several faculty members and the chaplain of ORU),

---

32. Ibid., p. 158.

33. Hollenweger, *The Pentecostals,* p. 365.

34. Durasoff, pp. 135–137.

Roberts's sudden change of ecclesiastical affiliation seemed dramatic at the time. It was something a pentecostal leader "just didn't do." He says, "I was charged with having gone liberal, turning Communist, and being a backslider."[35] From April to December 1968, income received by the Oral Roberts Evangelistic Association and ORU decreased by more than one-third. His classical pentecostal supporters thought Roberts had left the faith.[36]

The prominent charismatic leader never intended to change his basic theology—only his style. As a respectable United Methodist university president who was deeply involved in the transdenominational charismatic renewal, Oral Roberts would have a much broader appeal to mainline Christian parents of prospective students and to qualified academics who were potential faculty members than he would as a classical pentecostal who was still associated with the denominational pentecostal cultural milieu. The United Methodist Church would allow Roberts to work for spiritual renewal as a neopentecostal within its ranks. Thus, he declares,

> I began to feel that God was leading me to transfer to the Methodist Church. To my mind, the Methodist Church was more than a denomination. It represented all the diverse elements of historic Christianity. In its membership and ministry were deeply committed evangelicals. Yet it had radical liberals, too. More importantly, it had maintained a free pulpit; Methodist ministers could preach their convictions.[37]

Oral Roberts had explicitly rejected the sectarian notion of a "pure church" in favor of a very inclusive ecclesiastical structure that could embrace lay members and ministers of considerable theological diversity. His "conversion" to the United Methodist Church— from leadership within classical pentecostalism to leadership in

---

35. Roberts, p. 134.
36. Ibid., p. 137.
37. Ibid., p. 131.

charismatic renewal—almost signaled the "conversion" of pentecostalism itself. James Dunn, writing in the *Scottish Journal of Theology* in 1970, suggested, "The fact that the well-known Pentecostal evangelist Oral Roberts joined the Methodist Church in 1968 is a significant indicator of the new direction of Pentecostalism, and may mark a turning point for the whole movement, old and new."[38]

By projecting a new radio and television image, Roberts had also forsaken classical pentecostal's rejection of the wider society and culture. The faith healing evangelist first appeared on television in 1954[39] with a traditional pentecostal image, and continued successful programming until 1967, when he dropped the use of this medium. In 1969, however, he returned to the air with a very different format. Roberts's television sermons took on an "existential" character—*focusing* on "the now" more than on the hereafter; but more important than that, talented and carefully selected students at ORU (where the weekly half-hour shows are taped) began to offer regular musical entertainment and highly sophisticated choreography. These "World Action Singers" now offer both religious and secular popular music—from gospel to folk to rock—and interracial coupling (with handholding, even) is a notable characteristic of the show. The university produces two nationally televised programs: a weekly half-hour show, "Oral Roberts and You," and "Sunday Night Live with Oral Roberts," a one-hour prime-time series. The programs are taped at the Television Production Center on campus, using university-owned equipment. "Oral Roberts and You," viewed by weekly audiences of up to 4 million people on more than 350 stations across the United States and Canada, is the most popular Sunday morning syndicated religious program on television today. And "Sunday Night Live with Oral Roberts" is broadcast every Sunday evening

---

38. James Dunn, "Spirit Baptism and Pentecostalism," *Scottish Journal of Theology* (November 1970), p. 403. See "Oral Roberts Joins the Methodists," *Renewal* (August–September 1968), pp. 4–5; and Jeanne Hinton, "Oral Roberts and the Heart of British Methodism," *Renewal* (April–May 1970), pp. 7, 9–10.

39. Roberts, p. 177.

before a live audience by means of ORU's earth station beamed to a satellite 22,300 miles away. The inclusion in his television programming of celebrities from the "worldly" show business industry, together with a culture-affirming interracial group of student entertainers from his own university who dance as well as sing, is another mark of the new Oral Roberts and a new style of ministry within the so-called electronic church, the conglomerate of television and radio evangelists, networks, satellites, viewers, and listeners, which together form a new religious movement transmitted and shaped almost entirely by the mass media. Indeed, among all the "televangelists," Roberts has been the most important pioneer of the whole contemporary electronic church phenomenon.[40]

But in addition to ORU and his television ministry, Oral Roberts has also established—not without controversy—the ultra-modern, patient-centered "City of Faith" medical and research center, a facility adjacent to and associated with the university, which opened in 1981, and focuses on the causes and treatment of cancer, heart disease, and problems related to aging. Facilities include a sixty-story diagnostic clinic, a thirty-story hospital, and a twenty-story research and continuing education center, with 2.2 million square feet of floor space. At full operation (projected for 1988), the City of Faith will have 4,000 full-time employees, with 300 physicians and 750 nurses.

Over the course of his ministry, Oral Roberts has led both classical pentecostalism and charismatic renewal along the course of upward mobility, trying hard to integrate theology and culture in his television programming and faith and reason in his university and City of Faith, where faith in God and medical science are seen to work hand in hand.[41]

---

40. Ibid., pp. 185–196. See David Edwin Harrell, Jr., *All Things Are Possible: The Healing and Charismatic Revivals in Modern America* (Bloomington, Ind.: Indiana University Press, 1975), pp. 41–52, 150–159; and Richard Quebedeaux, *By What Authority: The Rise of Personality Cults in American Christianity* (San Francisco: Harper & Row, 1982), pp. 33–35, 63, 95–98, especially.

41. For a less positive treatment of Roberts and his career, see Morris, pp. 57–126.

David du Plessis

No single person is more responsible for neopentecostal growth throughout the world than David du Plessis, whose rise to leadership within the pentecostal movement came about largely through his own organizational ability. Speaking for neopentecostals in general, Michael Harper calls him "our pentecostal father-in-God."[42] Du Plessis terms himself a pentecostal "ecumaniac," and he is widely known in charismatic renewal circles simply as "Mr. Pentecost."[43] Although David du Plessis still considers himself a classical pentecostal, there is good reason for all these titles.

Born in South Africa of French Huguenot stock in 1905, du Plessis experienced an evangelical conversion in 1916, and received baptism in the Holy Spirit in 1918. He describes himself as "a little white heathen saved by the life and ministry of black Christians."[44] In 1927, du Plessis was married, and the following year was ordained to the ministry of the Apostolic Faith Mission of South Africa.[45] Like most pentecostals of the time, he had no formal theological education.[46] Reared in the typically sectarian pentecostal tradition, du Plessis related how his parents were turned out of the Dutch Reformed Church for their pentecostal activity. This fact, of course, shaped the course of his early ministry:

> I began preaching at a very youthful age. In those days there was much preaching against the Pentecostals. I used to listen to Dutch Reformed ministers preach against us and call us false prophets standing on street corners. Then I would promptly go back to the

---

42. Harper, *None Can Guess,* p. 6.

43. Ibid., pp. 44, 58.

44. David du Plessis, *The Spirit Bade Me Go,* rev. ed. (Plainfield, N.J.: Logos International, 1970), p. 10.

45. Ibid., p. 122.

46. Hollenweger, *The Pentecostals,* p. 7.

street corner and preach against "these blind leaders of the blind." How we attacked one another.[47]

From 1928 to 1949, David du Plessis gradually emerged into bureaucratic leadership within the Apostolic Faith Mission—from evangelist, pastor, youth leader, Sunday school director, and chief editor, to general secretary of the denomination.[48]

As we have seen, after World War II, the characteristically sectarian traits of pentecostalism began slowly to abate. In 1947, the first Pentecostal World Conference was called in Zurich. Du Plessis attended this meeting as a delegate from his denomination; and in 1948, he was asked to convene a second such conference in Paris and to serve as its secretary—an office he held also at the third and fifth Pentecostal World conferences, in London (1952) and Toronto (1958), respectively.[49] His position as an important organizational leader of world pentecostalism was now firm. In 1949, du Plessis became a permanent resident of the United States, and in 1955 gained ministerial standing in the Assemblies of God.[50]

The "ecumenical odyssey of Mr. Pentecost" began in 1951. Du Plessis says, "In 1951 the Lord spoke to me and clearly told me to go and witness to the leaders of the World Council of Churches."[51] Introducing himself as "world secretary" of the pentecostal movement, he was warmly received by members of the WCC New York office.[52] In 1952, du Plessis was invited to the International Missionary Council assembly at Willengen, Germany—his first experience as a pentecostal at an ecumenical convention. As the guest of John Mackay, then president of Princeton Theological Seminary and an eminent leader in the ecumenical movement, du Plessis talked about the dramatic success of pentecostalism on the

---

47. Du Plessis, *The Spirit Bade Me Go,* p. 11.

48. Ibid., p. 122.

49. Ibid., pp. 12, 122.

50. Ibid., p. 122.

51. Ibid., p. 13.

52. Ibid.

mission field and related the pentecostal message to numerous WCC officials in attendance. Then, in 1954, "Mr. Pentecost" attended the second WCC assembly in Evanston, Illinois, at the invitation of General Secretary Willem Visser 't Hooft (the former also held staff status). This was followed in 1961 by his participation as a pentecostal observer at the third WCC assembly in New Delhi.[53] Du Plessis's once-sectarian attitudes had now changed dramatically: "Instead of the old harsh spirit of criticism and condemnation in my heart, I now felt such love and compassion for these ecclesiastical leaders that I would rather have died for them than pass sentence upon them.[54]

As a result of his new ecumenical contacts and the recognition he was accorded in the ecumenical movement, David du Plessis lectured at Princeton Theological Seminary, Yale Divinity School, Union Theological Seminary (New York), and at other mainline Christian theological schools in the years just before neopentecostalism emerged as a movement in 1960.[55] Since then, "Mr. Pentecost" has continued his strong ecumenical ties. He was pentecostal observer at Vatican II,[56] and was co-chairman of the first five-year "dialogue" between the Secretariat for Promoting Christian Unity of the Roman Catholic Church and leaders of classical pentecostalism (a few of them at least) and charismatic renewal.[57] Du Plessis has lectured and preached in more than forty-five countries,[58] and he travels throughout the world almost without a break.

But "Mr. Pentecost's" ecumenism cost him his standing in the Assemblies of God. In 1962, he was "disfellowshiped" by the governing board for his fraternal contacts with the WCC (although

---

53. Ibid., pp. 15, 122.

54. Ibid., p. 16.

55. Ibid., p. 122.

56. Hollenweger, *The Pentecostals*, p. 7.

57. "Early Stages of Agreement in Roman Catholic/Pentecostal Dialogue," *Renewal* (August–September 1972), p. 2.

58. Du Plessis, *The Spirit Bade Me Go*, p. 122.

Donald Gee continued to back his efforts).[59] Du Plessis is supported by no denomination and admits that he now has no "official" standing in the worldwide pentecostal movement (although he obviously remains an "organizational" leader):

> Recently a group of Episcopal ministers in America asked me who sponsored me in this work and what my position was now in the Pentecostal Movement. I had to explain that this was a faith venture. No one hired me and no one can fire me. I have resigned from every position I held, and so I have become just a great "has been" insofar as positions are concerned. I am a good will ambassador for Christ.[60]

Because of his ecumenical ties, David du Plessis encountered much opposition both from classical pentecostals and from fundamentalists and evangelicals more generally. Yet he continues to act as a neopentecostal facilitator and liaison between classical pentecostalism and charismatic renewal—again, still calling himself a classical pentecostal. Responding to his critics, du Plessis declares,

> There are many today who make a study of the Ecumenical Movement to find out what is wrong with it. Diligently they seek out men and statements that appear liberal and socialistic, and then seek to blanket the whole Movement with the few "exceptions" that they have discovered. On this basis I have every reason to blanket the Ecumenical Movement with a "conclusion" that they are Pentecostal. Not only does their published literature propagate strong Pentecostal teachings, but there are now many Spirit-filled, yes indeed, "tongues-speaking" ministers in the National and World Council of Churches. I shall not be surprised when our fundamentalist friends who attack the Pentecostals as severely as they do the World Council, begin to "expose" the Pentecostal trend with the ranks of the Ecumenical Movement.
>
> The Holy Spirit has never recognized barriers.[61]

---

59. Hollenweger, *The Pentecostals*, p. 7.

60. Du Plessis, *The Spirit Bade Me Go*, p. 20.

61. Ibid., p. 27. See also Hollenweger, "Handbuch der Pfingstbewegung" (08.137.002).

Du Plessis did not speak publicly about the action taken against him by the Assemblies of God in 1962 until his bold interview in 1978 in the pentecostal journal, *Agora*.[62] But, given the increased level of communication and fellowship between classical pentecostals and neopentecostals in recent years, he was restored to fellowship as an ordained minister in the Assemblies of God in 1980. In 1974, du Plessis was listed among "the eleven most influential Christian thinkers of today" by Interchurch Features (an advisory group of editors of various religious magazines in the United States and Canada.)[63]

Michael Harper

As editor of *Renewal*, Michael Harper has been the foremost organizational leader of charismatic renewal in Great Britain. His numerous books—dealing not only with the pentecostal experience itself, but also with its function as a force of Christian renewal more generally—put Harper in the position of one of neopentecostalism's leading theoreticians as well.

Unlike Dennis Bennett, another Anglican, Michael Harper came out of a strong evangelical rather than Catholic tradition. In 1950, he took up residence at Emmanuel College, Cambridge, as a law student. Later that year, Harper experienced an evangelical conversion at a very unlikely place—Sunday morning communion at King's College Chapel—and thereafter affiliated with Cambridge's evangelical establishment, the Cambridge Inter-Collegiate Christian Union (CICCU).[64] He says,

I became deeply affected by the ethos of evangelicalism. Most of my friends came from this "set." My books were "sound." My vacations were patterned for me by my friends. There was little time for "cultural" education. Nearly all the vacations were taken up with

---

62. "*Agora* Talks to David du Plessis," *Agora* (Summer 1978), pp. 8–13.

63. See James A. Taylor, "A Search for Giants," *A.D.* (September 1974), pp. 20–23. See also David du Plessis (with Bob Slosser), *A Man Called Mr. Pentecost* (Plainfield, N.J.: Logos International, 1977).

64. Harper, *None Can Guess*, pp. 12–14.

conferences, house parties, missions and camps. The first flush of inspiration, when I really did know the imprint of the Holy Spirit was upon my life, was gradually lost.[65]

In 1952, Harper changed his course from law to theology, became a candidate for Holy Orders, and, in 1953, entered (the strictly Evangelical) Ridley Hall Theological College in Cambridge. He was ordained in 1955, married in 1956, and assigned as a curate of All Souls Church, Langham Place, London, in 1958, under its rector, John R. W. Stott. (Stott and All Souls Church have been synonymous with established evangelicalism in Great Britain.) Harper's specific responsibility during his six-year curacy there was chaplain to the Oxford Street department stores; he was only one of six curates assisting Stott at the prestigious church in London.[66] All seemed settled—until 1962.

While preparing to speak at a weekend parish conference at St. Luke's Church, Hampstead, in September, Harper experienced something that changed his life dramatically. He felt liberated from his "legalistic" background, discovered a new sense of freedom in preaching, and his attitude toward *people* was transformed.[67] Shortly thereafter, Harper's wife, Jeanne, had the same experience (thus remedying the dilemma of a "distracted wife" and an "impossibly enthusiastic husband").[68] But neither of them knew exactly *what* had happened—or what to call it. At first, Jeanne and Michael Harper appeared to equate their recent experience with a "second blessing" or entire sanctification made popular by the holiness movement. As yet, neither had spoken in tongues.[69]

During 1963 an architect, a member of Michael Harper's "lunch-hour congregation" of London business people, related his

---

65. Ibid., p. 14.
66. Ibid., pp. 17–19.
67. Ibid., pp. 20–28.
68. Ibid., p. 33.
69. Ibid., p. 39–41.

recent Spirit baptism to the department store chaplain, how he had suddenly spoken in tongues—while in the bath one evening.[70] The architect had become interested in the emerging charismatic renewal in the United States, and had heard David du Plessis talk about the experience behind it at a meeting in the City of London. Harper was willing to accept everything but glossolalia. The architect gave him a copy of *Trinity,* which deeply impressed the All Souls curate, since the magazine described the same experience he and Jeanne shared at a recent occurrence among Episcopalians in the United States. Priests and laypeople had become loving and caring, and were worshiping with new enthusiasm; there was a new freedom to express the faith, a new conviction of truth. Even more important, these Episcopalians were staying in their own churches. Yet, the Harpers were troubled, because this was an experience that, except for glossolalia, was entirely similar to the one that they had had.[71] Gradually, they came in contact with others who were involved in charismatic renewal.

In May 1963, Michael and Jeanne Harper met with Frank Maguire (Dennis Bennett's colleague) in London. A private gathering was arranged at All Souls Church, and Maguire told the Harpers that Larry Christenson would be visiting London later that year. As it happened, Christenson and his wife stayed with the department store chaplain during their visit to London, and the Harpers first spoke in tongues at that time.[72] The latter were pleased that their neopentecostal friends had not doubted the authenticity of their previous experience because they had not yet spoken in tongues (in the typical white classical pentecostal fashion)—but had still encouraged them to seek this gift also.[73]

In October 1963, David du Plessis came to London again, and Michael and Jeanne Harper were able to meet him personally then. Harper himself arranged to have Larry Christenson's booklet,

---

70. Ibid., p. 43.

71. Ibid., pp. 44–47.

72. Ibid., pp. 54–57.

73. Ibid., p. 54.

Speaking in Tongues: A Gift for the Body of Christ, printed privately at about the same time. Two thousand copies were quickly distributed throughout the British Isles.[74] The All Souls curate had natural organizing ability. Soon his flat at the corner of Harley Street became the center of charismatic renewal activity in Great Britain. The phone rang continually. A bookroom from which tapes could also be borrowed was started. Letters arrived at an increasing rate, and the Harpers' dining room became an office. One publication had already come off the press, and a neopentecostal conference was planned for early 1964.[75]

It is not surprising that Michael Harper's new activities would conflict with his parish duties—especially since John R. W. Stott himself did not share the pentecostal experience, and was rather unhappy with what was happening in his church.[76] Thus, Harper resigned from his post, effective June 1964 (without pressure to do so), in order to pursue his charismatic renewal interests on a full-time basis. From the beginning, it was recognized that some kind of organization would be necessary to facilitate further publication of books (and, beginning in 1966, *Renewal* magazine). Hence, the Fountain Trust was established by a group of neopentecostals in October 1964 as a registered charity. Harper was immediately appointed secretary on an agreed salary, and he directed the Fountain Trust's publications, regional, national, and international conferences, and other fellowship activities. Although finances posed a difficulty at first, funds gradually began to flow in as charismatic renewal continued to grow, and Michael Harper came to be recognized as its foremost leader in Great Britain.[77]

From 1964 to 1970, the Harpers traveled over a hundred thousand miles in the British Isles alone and made their first overseas

---

74. Ibid., pp. 58–60.

75. Ibid., p. 60.

76. See John R. W. Stott, *The Baptism and Fullness of the Holy Spirit* (Downers Grove, Ill.: InterVarsity Press, 1964).

77. Harper, *None Can Guess,* p. 63.

visit in 1965—to the United States as guests of the Full Gospel Business Men's Fellowship International.[78] During 1967, the then secretary of the Fountain Trust traveled around the world, speaking in New Zealand, Australia, and South Africa.[79] After that, international travel became an integral part of Michael Harper's neopentecostal ministry, for he was soon to be regarded throughout the world as charismatic renewal's most articulate British spokesperson and as a leading theoretician of the movement as a whole. Like David du Plessis, Harper was a member of the first international dialogue between classical pentecostals and neopentecostals and the Roman Catholic Church, sponsored by the latter's Secretariat for Promoting Christian Unity.[80] The world scope of his charismatic renewal ministry finally forced the former chaplain to Oxford Street's department stores to curtail his Fountain Trust duties. A new secretary was appointed in 1972, but Michael Harper remained editor of *Renewal* and chairman of the executive board (as "director" of the trust)[81] until 1975, when he resigned these posts to write and travel more extensively. By the late 1970s, the pentecostal experience had gained the respectability within mainline Christianity in Britain that Harper had hoped for in the beginning. And charismatic renewal fellowship and prayer groups could be identified easily in a large number of locations in the British Isles. Thus, the Fountain Trust—which never sought to compete with the institutional church—was quietly disbanded in 1981, because, very simply, it was no longer necessary. And in the same year, Michael Harper returned as editor of *Renewal,* now a successful popular Christian magazine within the broader charismatic-evangelical milieu.[82]

---

78. Ibid., pp. 90–93.

79. Ibid., pp. 108–118.

80. "Early Stages of Agreement in Roman Catholic/Pentecostal Dialogue," *Renewal* (August–September 1972), p. 4.

81. "Fountain Trust Gets New General Secretary," *Logos Journal* (September–October 1972), p. 60.

82. *New Covenant* (August 1975), p. 23.

Demos Shakarian

We have already observed the extent to which the Full Gospel Business Men's Fellowship International has contributed to the growth of charismatic renewal in the United States and in other countries throughout the world. Demos Shakarian, a wealthy Armenian-American one-time dairyman in California, is the leading figure behind the FGBMFI organization, which is based in Costa Mesa, California.

The Shakarian family left Armenia for the United States (California, ultimately) in 1905 as a result of prophetic warnings (during World War I, every person in their village was slaughtered when the Turks overran Armenia).[83] Having settled in Los Angeles, the Shakarians witnessed the Azusa Street revival in 1906 firsthand (they had been among those Presbyterians in Armenia who were practicing glossolalia long before the beginnings of the pentecostal movement[84]), and became pentecostals. Demos's father, a dairy farmer, started his business with three cows, but by 1943 owned a herd of 3,000.[85]

Demos Shakarian himself did not feel called to the ministry, although he began sponsoring pentecostal evangelists in 1940. At a 1951 Oral Roberts campaign, Shakarian shared his idea concerning the establishment of a pentecostal layman's organization for evangelism with the faith healing evangelist who later publicized the fellowship in the course of his crusades.[86] (Walter Hollenweger maintains that Shakarian's idea arose because of the Assemblies of God's decision not to accept into their leadership those who were not full-time pastors.[87]) Later, in 1951, the wealthy dairyman called an initial meeting of pentecostal laymen to the "upper room" of Clifton's Cafeteria in Los Angeles (twenty-one at-

---

83. Durasoff, p. 145. See Nickel.

84. See Kelsey, pp. 65–68.

85. Durasoff, p. 146.

86. Ibid., p. 147.

87. Hollenweger, *The Pentecostals*, p. 6.

tended[88]); that was the beginning of the Los Angeles chapter. In 1953, five directors were appointed (including Lee Braxton, first chairman of the Board of Regents of Oral Roberts University), and articles of incorporation were drawn up. That year, the FGBMFI also published the first issue of *Full Gospel Business Men's Voice* magazine (5,000 copies), which was intended to be distributed throughout the world.[89]

Begun by and for denominational pentecostals, the FGBMFI never had any official ties with pentecostal ecclesiastical structures. Thus it became a natural vehicle to facilitate the growth of charismatic renewal. Mainline Christian ministers and laymen from the historic denominations who identified with the Full Gospel Business Men were not pressured to leave their churches; they could enjoy expressive pentecostal fellowship (without formal membership) at the regularly scheduled and relaxed breakfast and dinner meetings of the FGBMFI in downtown restaurants and prestigious hotels.[90] David du Plessis calls the organization truly ecumenical in that the "Full Gospel Business Men's Fellowship has been bridging the gap between Pentecostals and 'mainliners.' "[91] This fact is especially true with respect to Roman Catholics, who are particularly responsible for the FGBMFI's dramatic growth in recent years.[92] Discussing opposition to his organization, Shakarian once said that it "comes mainly from those we believe should support us [that is, fundamentalists, evangelicals, and many classical pentecostals]. None from liberal Christians."[93] Of those who attend FGBMFI gatherings in some American cities, as many as 80 percent are nonclassical pentecostal (women and young people are now invited, too, but do not share organizational leadership.)[94]

---

88. See William C. Armstrong, "Demos Shakarian: A Man and His Message," *Logos Journal* (September–October 1971), pp. 13–14.

89. Durasoff, pp. 148–149.

90. Ibid., p. 150.

91. Quoted in ibid.

92. See Kevin and Dorothy Ranaghan, *As the Spirit Leads Us,* pp. 118–125.

93. Quoted in Durasoff, p. 150.

Demos Shakarian, FGBMFI president, is in his late sixties. Seven thousand people attended the nightly meetings of the twenty-eighth world convention of the FGBMFI in Philadelphia in 1981, and there are now over twenty-four hundred active chapters of the organization worldwide—more than eighteen hundred of them in the United States and Canada. *Full Gospel Business Men's Voice* magazine presently has a monthly circulation of 700,000 and is translated into seven languages.[95] International directors include corporation presidents, attorneys, distributors, surgeons, real estate developers, building contractors, owners of insurance agencies, and retailers[96] (hence the predominant FGBMFI philosophy that God "prospers" people [financially] who are committed to him).[97]

Organization is highly decentralized, and kept to an absolute minimum. The executive committee approves applications for affiliation submitted by a prospective FGBMFI local chapter. Apart from the fact that the same committee also has the power to "disfellowship" a local chapter (it rarely exercises that authority), most organizational authority rests with the individual chapters themselves and their own officers. Steve Durasoff says that "a great stress is placed upon love as the true basis of unity, rather than doctrinal agreement"[98] —while the organization's chief purposes are (1) evangelism (especially the spread of the pentecostal message) and (2) interdenominational fellowship for classical pentecostals and neopentecostals. FGBMFI regional, national, and international conventions offer an important platform to eminent charismatic and organizational leaders of charismatic renewal—Oral Roberts, David du Plessis, Michael Harper, and the

---

94. Ibid., p. 151.

95. For information on the FGBMFI until the early 1970s, see "Pentecostal Unit Gains Followers," *Full Gospel Business Men's Voice* (October 1972), pp. 2–3, 26 (reprinted from *New York Times*, July 16, 1972).

96. Durasoff, p. 155.

97. Ibid., pp. 151–155.

98. Ibid., p. 156.

like. Thus we can discern the degree to which the Full Gospel Business Men's Fellowship International provides evidence of the prominent role of laymen in the emergence and growth of charismatic renewal as a movement in various parts of the world.[99]

Jean Stone

The Blessed Trinity Society (so named to reemphasize the work of the third person of the Trinity in a "high church" context) was founded in 1961 by Jean Stone, a well-to-do Episcopal laywoman and communicant of St. Mark's Episcopal Church, Van Nuys, California, while Dennis Bennett was its rector. Walter Hollenweger says of this affluent housewife and mother (whose husband, Donald, was a corporate director of Lockheed Aircraft),

> Though she assiduously prayed in the way that is required in the Anglican church, went to all the services and gave a good deal of money to the church, she "felt a void in my life, which nothing but more of him could fill." Because she was a woman she could not be ordained in the Anglican church, because she was a mother she could not become an Anglican nun and because her husband had no vocation on the mission field, she could not become a missionary. So she saw no possibility of active work in the church. But when she was filled with the Holy Spirit, she saw that it was not her destiny to waste her life with aimless conversations at parties with the "high society" of California. Her home became a meeting place for clergy and laity from the upper levels of society who sought the baptism of the Spirit.[100]

Thus, the Blessed Trinity Society was organized in Jean Stone's living room as the first distinctively neopentecostal organizational structure for fellowship, teaching, evangelism, and, most of all, publication. (Although the Full Gospel Business Men's Fellowship International welcomed and encouraged Mrs. Stone,[101] she could

---

99. Ibid. See also Demos and Sherrill Shakarian, *The Happiest People on Earth* (Lincoln, Va.: Chosen Books, 1975).

100. Hollenweger, *The Pentecostals*, p. 5.

101. See Jean Stone, "A High Church Episcopalian Becomes Pentecostal," *Full*

never have assumed leadership in that men's organization.) Fellowship and teaching *were* important functions of the society (for example, the "Christian Advance" seminars to acquaint people with Spirit baptism[102]), but it was formed primarily to publish *Trinity* magazine (1961–1966), a charismatic renewal quarterly aimed at "the well-educated conservative suburbanite from the denominational church."[103] Her editorship of *Trinity* made Jean Stone one of the first organizational leaders of neopentecostalism (and by 1963 the Blessed Trinity Society had enrolled fifty-nine "patrons" who had each contributed at least $100 for its support).[104] With the magazine's increased circulation, Mrs. Stone became a recognized authority and lecturer on charismatic renewal.[105] Writing in 1965, Michael Harper said of *Trinity,*

> It seems to find its way sooner or later on to the desks of most ministers in the Western Hemisphere and seldom ends up in the wastepaper basket. It gets more and more dog-eared as it passes from vicarage to manse, and usually dies of sheer exhaustion at a ripe old age. Anglican bishops (publish it not in Gath) have surreptitiously read it and passed it on to their chaplains.[106]

Until 1966, the Blessed Trinity Society in Van Nuys was the unofficial "headquarters" of neopentecostalism; *Trinity,* its leading periodical voice; and Jean Stone, its most important spokeswoman. But Mrs. Stone's travels and organizational leadership in the movement destroyed her marriage that year. The divorce was quiet and unpublicized; the Blessed Trinity Society and its maga-

---

Gospel Business Men's Voice (October 1960), pp. 9–10 (reprinted from *The Living Church*).

102. See *Trinity* (Christmastide 1961–1962), p. 49.

103. John L. Sherrill, *They Speak with Other Tongues* (New York: Pyramid Books, 1964), p. 122.

104. *Trinity* (Transfiguration 1963), p. 50.

105. See, for instance, *Trinity* (Transfiguration 1963), pp. 28–39.

106. Harper, *As at the Beginning*, p. 72.

zine suddenly ceased to exist; and Jean Stone disappeared from the charismatic renewal scene for almost a decade.[107] She subsequently married her associate editor, Richard Willans, and together they went to Hong Kong as independent "faith missionaries" for the movement.[108] Melodyland Christian Center, Anaheim, California, later become one of neopentecostalism's new American "headquarters" for a number of years, until the late 1970s; Christian Advance reemerged as Melodyland's "charismatic clinics" (which included such speakers and teachers as Dennis Bennett, Herald Bredesen, Larry Christenson, David du Plessis, Michael Harper, Kathryn Kuhlman, Kevin Ranaghan, and Oral Roberts); and in 1971, *Logos Journal* (Plainfield, New Jersey) and *New Covenant* (Ann Arbor, Michigan) succeeded *Trinity* as the leading charismatic renewal periodicals published in America.

Pat Robertson

Charismatic renewal's leaders made extensive use of the mass media, but no one (including Oral Roberts himself) did so more effectively, or with more innovation, than Pat Robertson. He has been the foremost innovator in adapting the format and style of religious television to the popular tastes of middle-class culture and its need for entertainment, even in the realm of religion. At first glance, Robertson's "700 Club" might appear to be a Christian version of the "Tonight Show," with a sophisticated camera setup and stage props decorated with potted plants, a walnut desk, and comfortable chairs against a fake-skyline background, all in living color. There is an enthusiastic, cheering audience and an in-house band. Celebrity guests appearing on the show might include a bestselling author, a gold-record singer, and the wife of a troubled politician, all Christians.

Robertson wears a pin-striped, three-piece suit, reminiscent, perhaps, of his days at Yale Law School (he is also a Phi Beta Kappa

---

107. Walter Hollenweger, personal communication, January 1970.

108. See Jean Stone Willans, *The Acts of the Green Apples* (Altadena, Calif.: Society of Stephen, 1973), a spiritual autobiography.

graduate of the University of Virginia, and studied at New York Theological Seminary in Manhattan), and he was an early participant in charismatic renewal. This prominent television evangelist and business entrepreneur of the electronic church is handsome, articulate, charming, and *very* middle class. He is able, on a moment's notice, to change the subject from "Bible prophecy" and Armageddon to the current economic crisis and the "perils of big government" without losing his audience's attention for a minute. And the "700 Club" provides at least as much sheer entertainment for its viewers as content-oriented teaching by the host or his guests.

On October 1, 1961, Robertson began his television ministry with one small UHF station, WYAH, in Portsmouth, Virginia, broadcasting three hours a day. In 1963, the "700 Club" was born when the television evangelist asked 700 viewers to pledge $10 a month for the station's continued operation. The first successful "700 Club" telethon was in 1965, and after the second Christian Broadcasting Network telethon a year later (CBN was a full-fledged network by 1974), the "700 Club" turned into the popular daily television program it is today. Robertson's early broadcasts were flawed by regular technical difficulties. Furthermore, a rather freewheeling pentecostal flavor prevailed on the show, with impromptu healing services, "praise" sessions, and calls to the program's "telephone volunteers" for salvation or Spirit baptism. However, CBN slowly gained technical expertise and hired several people from the major networks to further improve its quality. By the mid-1970s, the distinctive "pentecostalism" of the early days of "700 Club" programming had gradually given way to a more sedate style and a more broadly "evangelical" theological emphasis, more compatible with the times (Gallup proclaimed 1976 "the year of the evangelical"). Today the format of the "700 Club" has been tightened up and toned down even more. In fact, several program features are in the "general interest" rather than purely "religious" category (such as news and drama).

Pat Robertson's "700 Club" is carried in major television markets across America; however, it is usually aired during marginal time slots. A 24-hour satellite network (which broadcasts the show several times a day) is on several cable systems, and a new venture emphasizing traditional "family programming" has recently entered the cable market. Then, at the close of the 1970s, as a result of Robertson's overall television successes, he founded CBN University, an institution that specializes in electronic media studies.

Pat Robertson and Oral Roberts were joined by other pentecostals and charismatics, such as Jim and Tammy Bakker ("PTL Club"), Rex Humbard ("Cathedral of Tomorrow"), and Paul and Jan Crouch (Trinity Broadcasting Network), as leaders of the electronic church. In earlier years, they stimulated interest in charismatic renewal specifically and increased the movement's visibility. This was their major contribution to neopentecostalism. More recently, however, their interests have accommodated to those of their more broadly evangelical and fundamentalist viewers, making it difficult (as noted earlier) to discern any major difference in theology between these charismatic television evangelists and the noncharismatic fundamentalist and evangelical preachers of equal prominence. All of them, obviously, are great entertainers for the born-again in the 1980s.[109]

We have now discussed some of the most important charismatic renewal organizations and leaders in the context of a fully decentralized, segmentary, and weblike pentecostal movement. Charismatic and organizational leadership have facilitated neopentecostal growth; but it was a personal *experience* rather than leadership per se that held the movement together. We shall now consider charismatic renewal faith and practice as it developed from that experience.

---

109. Looney, pp. 25–27; Pat Robertson and Jamie Buckingham, *Shout It from the Housetops: The Story of the Christian Broadcasting Network* (Plainfield, N.J.: Logos International, 1972); Ben Armstrong, *The Electric Church* (Nashville, Tenn.: Nelson, 1979), pp. 101–107; and Quebedeaux, *By What Authority*, pp. 56–58, especially.

Chapter Five

Faith and Practice

Given the heterogeneous character of neopentecostalism with respect to issues of faith and practice, we must be content to speak of observable tendencies rather than *all-pervasive features*. Apart from specific theological and behavioral expectations a given church or fellowship group *may* impose on its own adherents, charismatic renewal as such has no mandatory or even optional statements of faith, and does not require compliance with any set code of conduct. Neopentecostal unity has been unity in a great deal of diversity.

In the pentecostal movement as a whole, ministry has been democratized. Kilian McDonnell suggests that although classical pentecostal groups tend to be "minister oriented" and often "leader dominated," ministry itself is conceived as "body ministry"—the whole body of Christ witnessing. This is true in worship, evangelism, and service. Ideally, what distinguishes a minister from a layman or laywoman is a specific charism—a special gift and call of the Holy Spirit. Rather than thinking of the priesthood of all believers, classical pentecostals focus on a related concept—gifts of the Spirit. Laypeople have their own gifts, their ministries. Gifts and ministries differ, but all have received one Spirit, and all have a voice in witnessing. Everyone is a speaker; everyone has a message. Everyone is involved in worship, evangelism, and service.[1]

In charismatic renewal, as in classical pentecostalism, each denomination or independent congregation sets its own require-

---

1. Kilian McDonnell, "The Ideology of Pentecostal Conversion," *Journal of Ecumenical Studies* (Winter 1968), pp. 114–115.

ments and standards for ordination. For example, Melodyland Christian Center has on its staff duly ordained ministers with standing in a historic denomination, but it ordains ministers independently as well.[2] Neopentecostalism as a movement cannot of itself ordain and sanction clergy. Yet all ministries are recognized. Thus, Michael Harper declares "that this movement is the most unifying in Christendom.... [For] *only in this movement are all streams uniting, and all ministries being accepted and practised.*"[3]

PROMINENCE OF THE LAITY

Even though, as has been noted, the laity have been prominent at all levels of charismatic renewal participation and leadership from its beginnings,[4] the distinctive (for example, sacramental) functions of ordained ministers and priests—and their special "calling"—are nevertheless clearly recognized. Throughout the movement in general priests and ministers predominate in leadership, and they are almost always referred to by their ecclesiastical titles (for example, "the Reverend" or "Father"). Furthermore, laypeople who rise to leadership in charismatic renewal but who are not educationally or otherwise qualified for ordination in the historic denominations *may* be ordained by a local, independent neopentecostal congregation such as Melodyland Christian Center.

Perhaps the best expression of the cooperative role of clergy and laity in the movement has been articulated by George Martin, a Catholic pentecostal layman. Although Martin speaks of the specific situation in the Roman Catholic Church, his comments reflect a widespread feeling within charismatic renewal more generally:

2. See *Melodyland Messenger* (September 1969), p. 6.

3. Harper, *None Can Guess,* pp. 149, 153.

4. See, for instance, Ralph Martin, "Life in Community," pp. 145–163; and Bertil W. Ghezzi, "Three Charismatic Communities," in Kevin and Dorothy Ranaghan, eds., *As the Spirit Leads Us,* pp. 164–186.

It is clear that the charismatic ministers do not replace the ordained ministry; priests need not worry about becoming obsolete . . . Christian communities cannot be formed by the work of either clergy or laity alone. . . .

The charismatic renewal of the Church holds promise for a much more balanced state of affairs. The maturing of the charismatic ministries holds a promise of a fuller involvement of every member of the Church in building up the body of Christ without jeopardizing anyone's role. It holds this promise because its primary focus is not on the differences between clergy and laity, but on the gifts of service that every follower of Christ receives.[5]

YOUNG PEOPLE AND WOMEN

The "outburst of tongues" within the Inter-Varsity Christian Fellowship at Yale University in 1962 heralded the beginning of visible participation of young people (that is, students) in neopentacostalism.[6] Accounts of similar events in other colleges and universities in the United States followed shortly thereafter.[7] As we have seen, Catholic pentecostalism first emerged among academics and students at Duquesne, Notre Dame, and Michigan State Universities, and at the University of Michigan in 1967. Today, some of the most vigorous communities of Catholic pentecostals are still centered in the university environment.[8] For a while, even the Full Gospel Business Men's Fellowship International tried to encourage youthful involvement in charismatic renewal by instituting teaching seminars by and for young people—students and academics[9]—and by publishing a scholarly

5. George Martin, "Charismatic Renewal and the Church of Tomorrow," in Kevin and Dorothy Ranaghan, eds., As the Spirit Leads Us, p. 242.

6. See Trinity (Christmastide 1963), pp. 2–17.

7. See, for instance, Trinity (Eastertide 1963), pp. 4–25; and Trinity (Transfiguration 1963), pp. 6–9, 20–21.

8. See Ghezzi, "Three Charismatic Communities," in Kevin and Dorothy Ranaghan, eds., As the Spirit Leads Us, pp. 164–186.

9. See, for instance, Jerry Jensen, "Charismata in the Twentieth Century," Full Gospel Business Men's Voice (June 1965), pp. 3–21.

journal appealing to serious thinkers (first called *View*, then *Charisma Digest*, in 1966–1969). The businessmen soon tired of catering to the intellectual interests of scholars and students, yet they continued to welcome student participation in the movement.[10] With the advent of the "Jesus People" movement in 1969, it became clear that many American young people had embraced the pentecostal experience, for most of the Jesus People (and their various groups) stressed—or at least tolerated—pentecostal phenomena (especially glossolalia and divine healing) within their ranks. Although neopentecostalism has been a movement largely within the institutional church, and the Jesus People movement was not, most neopentecostals were quick to affirm and support the Jesus People anyway simply because of the latter's pentecostal leanings and practices.[11] By the mid-1970s, many of the Jesus People had joined existing classical pentecostal or neopentecostal churches or had established similar structures of their own.[12] In any case, although the active participation of young people in Protestant and Catholic charismatic renewal has continued, their numbers have decreased since the late 1970s.

Women also were prominent participants (active ones) in neopentecostalism. But they generally have not risen to prominent leadership in the movement. Among the exceptions were a few highly respected "healers" such as the late Kathryn Kuhlman and Ruth Carter Stapleton and, to a lesser degree, Agnes Sanford[13] in the United States, and Jean Darnall[14] in England. There was Jean

---

10. Jerry Jensen, former editor of *Full Gospel Business Men's Voice*, personal communication, Autumn 1970.

11. See, for instance, Pat King, "The Jesus People Are Coming," *Logos Journal* (September–October 1971), pp. 6–7; J. Rodman Williams, "Charismatic Journey" (November–December 1971), pp. 13–15, and "Adventure into Faith," *Full Gospel Business Men's Voice* (October 1972), pp. 39–42.

12. Ronald M. Enroth, "Where Have All the Jesus People Gone?" *Eternity* (October 1973), pp. 14–15, 17, 28, 30.

13. See her spiritual autobiography, *Sealed Orders* (Plainfield, N.J.: Logos International, 1972).

14. See Jeanne Hinton, "Breakfast with the Darnalls," *Renewal* (December 1969–January 1970), pp. 9, 11–12.

Stone, of course, a notable exception. And one may also mention Catherine Marshall, the novelist, who is a Presbyterian lay-woman.[15] Unlike some classical pentecostal denominations (for example, Assemblies of God, International Church of Foursquare Gospel, and Pentecostal Holiness Church), Melodyland Christian Center, for instance, neither ordains women nor permits them membership on its governing board.[16] One of the most prominent women within Catholic pentecostalism, Josephine Ford, an eminent New Testament scholar at Notre Dame University, has been especially vocal in recent years criticizing the "sexist" character of the pentecostal movement in the Roman Catholic Church.[17]

SPIRITUAL AUTHORITY

In fundamentalism and evangelicalism as a whole, Scripture *itself* functions as the final authority in matters of faith and conduct. Generally speaking, biblical "inerrancy" as a doctrine has been the "test" of fellowship whereby individuals and groups are either accepted as "true believers" or rejected as heterodox or heretical. Thus, liberals (who may not accept the full and final authority of Scripture) and Roman Catholics (who accept the authority of tradition as well) have rarely been admitted into fellowship with evangelicals and fundamentalists. For the latter, there can usually be no (institutional or even "spiritual") Christian unity apart from doctrinal agreement (on certain essential "truths"—or "fundamentals") based on the propositional authority of the Bible.[18] In

---

15. See Catherine Marshall, *Something More* (New York: McGraw-Hill, 1974).

16. This fact is well known but not widely publicized by the church.

17. Ford, *The Pentecostal Experience*, p. 37. See also her book, *Which Way for Catholic Pentecostals?* Ford's criticism of male domination in Catholic pentecostalism caused her to break with the Notre Dame community. See her article, "Biblical Material Relevant to the Ordination of Women," *Journal of Ecumenical Studies* (Fall 1973), pp. 669–699. On the role of women in Catholic pentecostalism, see Joseph H. Fichter, "How It Looks to a Social Scientist," *New Catholic World* (November–December 1974), pp. 244–248.

18. See Gerald T. Sheppard, "Biblical Hermeneutics: The Academic Language of

charismatic renewal, however, it is felt that the truth of Scripture is available to the reader or hearer *only* through the power of the Holy Spirit, who himself is understood as the (experiential) source of all Christian unity. Neopentecostal intellectuals maintain that biblical authority (the Word written) must always be subservient to the authority of the *living*, "dynamic" Word of God made known through the present activity of the Spirit itself. Michael Harper says,

> Christians are finding in their experience of the Holy Spirit a new unity in Christ, and that is exactly what Christ prayed for.
>
> But there are some who, while agreeing with the doctrine of the baptism of the Spirit, are looking askance at this. They cannot yet accept the movement among Roman Catholics, for example, as being a genuine work of the Holy Spirit. They are suspicious of liberals, who now speak hopefully of a revival of the Holy Spirit. They stress the need for unity in truth rather than unity in experience. . . .
>
> It is of the greatest significance that in the Acts of the Apostles Jesus gave the experience of the Holy Spirit to men as a uniting factor *before* they were united in truth. Christians then, as now, made the mistake of thinking that men had to believe as they did before they could experience the Holy Spirit. . . . Complete unity and agreement in the truth is impossible in this life and age. In this life "we see through a glass darkly." We live in a fallen creation, and our mental processes are not infallible. But we can trust the Holy Spirit to lead us all immeasurably closer to one another in the truth.[19]

This stance, whereby the Holy Spirit is seen to lead people to theological truth *following* (rather than prerequisite to) a common experience, has generally been ascendant among theologians in neopentecostalism; it is one reason why evangelicals, liberals, and Roman Catholics have been joined together (spiritually, at least) for the first time.

Evangelical Identity," *Union Seminary Quarterly Review* (Winter 1977), pp. 81–94.

19. Michael Harper, "Christian Unity—the Growing Fact," *Renewal* (December 1970–January 1971), pp. 4–5.

The subordination of Scripture—the Word written—to the Holy Spirit's authority is also illustrated by the acceptance in charismatic renewal of the validity of the gift of prophecy in the life of the contemporary church. For neopentecostals (no less than for their classical counterparts), God speaks today just as authoritatively as he spoke to the authors of the Bible. This existential understanding of the Word of God (in which revelation did not cease with the closing of the canon) is articulated by J. Rodman Williams:

> The Bible truly has become a fellow witness to God's present activity. What happens today in the fellowship and in individual lives also happened then, and there is the joy of knowing that *our* world was also *their* world. If someone today perhaps has a vision of God, of Christ, it is good to know that it has happened before; if one has a revelation from God, to know that for the early Christians revelation also occurred in the community; if one speaks a "Thus says the Lord," and dares to address the fellowship in the first person—even going beyond the words of Scripture—that this was happening long ago. . . . If one speaks in the fellowship of the Spirit of the Word of truth, it is neither his own thoughts and reflections . . . nor simply some exposition of Scripture, for the Spirit transcends personal observations, however interesting or profound they may be. The Spirit as the living God moves through and beyond the records of past witness, however valuable such records are as a model for what happens today. For in the Spirit the present fellowship is as much the arena of God's vital presence as anything in the Biblical account.[20]

Catherine Marshall puts it another way:

> Jesus' promise of "further truth" gives us clear reason to believe that not all the truth and instruction Christ has to give us is contained in the canon of the Old and New Testaments. . . . He who *is* Truth will never find the people of any given century able to receive

---

20. J. Rodman Williams, *The Era of the Spirit* (Plainfield, N.J.: Logos International, 1971), p. 16.

everything He wants to give. Because the Holy Spirit is a living, always-contemporary Personality, down all the centuries there must be an ever-unfolding manifestation of Jesus, His personality, His ways of dealing with us along with new, fresh disclosures of the mind of the Father.[21]

However, it should not be thought that pentecostalism—as a movement—old or new, ever capitalized on "new revelation" as extrabiblical doctrine per se. The use of prophecy in pentecostal worship is natural, nonsystematic, and usually in the form of an assurance of God's presence with the group, or a summons by God for the group to prepare itself for worship or for the reception of some manifestation of the miraculous. In other words, the prophecies are part of worship, not additional revelation in the form of doctrine or new theological knowledge. Sometimes, however, prophecy does appear almost like clairvoyance, by which individuals or the group as a whole are given a "word of knowledge" (compare with 1 Cor. 12:8). This Spirit-generated insight could point out a special problem, declare that a healing is taking place (as in the late Kathryn Kuhlman's services), or delineate other spiritually related matters of a purely transitory nature. Rarely have classical pentecostals or new charismatics written down prophecies for fear that they could become permanent additions to the biblical canon. Thus, for instance, the prophecies included in the appendix to Aimee Semple McPherson's autobiography (*This Is That*) were removed in later editions of the book. And this is one reason why the early fascination with tapes of leaders' prophecies (and the interpretation of tongues) within charismatic renewal abated quickly.[22]

Nevertheless, in neopentecostalism, spiritual authority rests ultimately in the present activity and teaching of the Holy Spirit at least as much in the Bible itself, whose essential truth is made known to individuals only by the power of the Spirit.[23]

---

21. Marshall, p. 270.

22. Sheppard, "Commentary."

23. For a contrary evangelical view, see Palmer Robertson, "Neo-Pentecostalism

HUMAN AUTHORITY

The belief that the Holy Spirit speaks and acts today in the same way he did in biblical times (as recorded in Scripture)—through the charismata—obviously sanctions a widespread diffusion of gifts (and related authority) in the local church. As we have seen, all Christians who are baptized in the Spirit see themselves and each other as endowed with certain gifts and ministries for worship, evangelism, and service. Ideally, the "charismatic congregation" functions as the primary human authority base in neopentecostalism. Here, God does not restrict his revelation to the Bible (that is, a closed canon) or to an ordained ministry. Anyone with an authentic gift of prophecy may speak the very word of God (accepted or rejected as such by the given community of faith in which it is spoken, however). Thus, in charismatic renewal as a whole there have been few leaders holding *absolute* authority. Submission to authority, ideally, was to be *mutual* submission, although individuals differing in recognized charismatic endowment also differed with respect to the degree of "actual" authority they wielded (or following they had) in a specific segment of the movement or in the movement as a whole. For instance, within a given local church, prayer group, or wider segment of the movement, a leader might well demand submission to his or her authority as the chief "discerner of the Spirit" and teacher of theology, without allowing much—if any—theological "negotiation" among participants in or members of the group (especially in matters of eschatology). But this has not been the movement's normative method of operating.

The charismatic congregation itself is a reflection of the widespread diffusion of charisma in the wider society today. It is almost a truism to say that traditional patterns of absolute or "legitimate" authority in every quarter of contemporary society are increasingly questioned and rejected. Furthermore, the consequent alternative stress on "reasonable" authority has been reinforced both by the secular human potential movement and by the various social "lib-

---

and the Freedom of the Christian," *Presbyterian Guardian* (January 1975), pp. 18–19.

eration" movements focusing on personal freedom and fulfillment, self-worth, and "growth" (discovering and developing inherent abilities, talents, and "gifts"). Thus it is only logical that this trend toward charismatic diffusion in the wider society should itself enhance the general attractiveness of a religious movement motivated and led by the charismatic congregation in which every participant, ideally, has a vital function—a unique ministry.

As normative as the ideal of the charismatic congregation has been in the course of neopentecostal development, it has not gone unchallenged. The issue of human authority was, in fact, the focal point of two of the most important controversies in the movement's brief history. The first, initiated by Josephine Ford, the feminist New Testament scholar and theologian, affected mainly Catholic pentecostalism; but the second, the growth of "non-denominational charismatic churches" (led by "shepherds") had an impact on the movement as a whole.

Catholic pentecostalism's development has centered on strong "core groups" that vary considerably in their internal structure and in their relationship with the wider prayer group. The most common situation is an ordinary prayer group with a highly committed core of member leaders. Whether or not they are formally organized into "ministry teams," these core members are extremely active in prayer group activities (especially in such elite activities as teaching "Life in the Spirit" seminars—based on materials published by Charismatic Renewal Services—organizing conferences, giving theological instruction, and running prayer meetings). They spend sizable amounts of time with each other, not only in accomplishing leadership tasks, but also in providing much mutual support for their extreme level of commitment. But even more visible than *this* common mode of organization within Catholic charismatic renewal is the "covenanted community" (such as Ann Arbor/South Bend). Groups of this type are typically, but not necessarily, residential communities organized into households and often economically communal as well. They resemble the communes that were established by the countercultural Jesus People. Although it is surely possible for an entire prayer group to constitute a covenanted community, often the covenanted body is the core or sponsor of a larger prayer group.

In the course of the emergence and development of Catholic pentecostalism, these core groups have tended to move in one of two different directions—"traditionalist" or "modernist"—with respect to their attitudes toward authority and other issues. The vast majority, so it would seem, moved in a generally traditionalist direction, emphasizing internal doctrinal orthodoxy, male "headship" and female "submission" to that authority, and a measure of "separation from the world" when it comes to participation in certain "worldly" activities. And although modernist critics of this traditionalist mode accuse it of "fundamentalism" and "sectarianism," Catholic pentecostals here *are* consciously prochurch, ecumenical, and intellectually sophisticated (unlike the typical sectarians and fundamentalists). They are simply more conservative than their critics in doctrinal matters, favoring, for instance, the dictums of Pope John Paul II over the teachings of the controversial liberal theologian, Hans Küng. The modernist direction was followed by a much smaller number of Catholic pentecostals, led, in the beginning, by Josephine Ford. They stressed pluralistic, flexible, and eclectic group expressions of religiosity and patterns of authority.

THE JOSEPHINE FORD CONTROVERSY

Until 1971, Ford had been a member of the South Bend community (which aligned itself with the Ann Arbor Word of God community and its magazine, *New Covenant*). She accused the group of modeling its mode of operation after sectarian Anabaptist patterns rather than on churchly Catholic tradition, and was expelled from the community for her strong manner of dissent. In *Which Way for Catholic Pentecostals?* the Notre Dame professor elaborated on this critique, suggesting that the dominant Ann Arbor/South Bend covenanted community approach had adopted a rigid hierarchy of men to whom obedience is required, a nonprofessional (and traditionalist) teaching body that purports to speak directly through the inspiration of the Spirit, a complicated exclusion system (by which she herself was excluded), the general subordination of women to men (in its "headship" doctrine), and withdrawal from the world in a fundamentalist and sectarian fashion.

Josephine Ford's well-articulated, but highly controversial, complaints were published in 1976, the same year an assortment of like-minded Catholic pentecostal intellectuals (including Donald Gelpi) started a new magazine to develop her critique further and launch out in their own nontraditionalist direction. *Catholic Charismatic* pursued a more modernist course as an alternative to *New Covenant* until 1980, when lack of sufficient circulation resulted in its collapse that year.

For seven years the leaders of the Ann Arbor and South Bend communities did not respond publicly to Ford's accusations. But in the April 1978 issue of *New Covenant,* Steve Clark repudiated them and defended the teaching and practice of the communities she critiqued and of which he was a core leader. (Interestingly enough, Ford's character as a controversialist among Catholic pentecostals was enhanced further the same month with her appearance in a *Penthouse* symposium on evangelical Christianity, a gathering at which she astonished her fellow participants by singing in tongues.)[24]

THE RISE OF "SHEPHERDING"

The Ford controversy rocked the Catholic pentecostal intelligentsia during the 1970s, but the rise of nondenominational charismatic churches—and their shepherding leaders—resulted in schisms *throughout* charismatic renewal in the same decade. The issue, again, was human authority in the lives of charismatic believers. During the first decade of the movement, charismatic renewal gatherings usually consisted of rather spontaneous wor-

---

24. McGuire, pp. 191, 192; Ford, *Which Way for Catholic Pentecostals?;* Clark, "Response to Dr. J. Massyngberde Ford," *New Covenant* (April 1978), pp. 14–20; see also Steve Clark's book, *Man and Woman in Christ,* and "Symposium: The Evangelical Movement," *Penthouse* (April 1978), pp. 70–72, 74, 82, 90.

ship, testimonies, messages in tongues, prophecies, and general teaching on Spirit baptism. At their close, participants could request prayer for healing, personal problems, or the pentecostal experience itself. But by the end of the 1960s, it was clear that many of those who had received baptism in the Spirit within charismatic renewal and the Jesus People movement had lost interest after the initial excitement had worn off. In a word, there was a widespread felt need among new charismatics for deeper teaching and more discipline for their lives of faith. This need was met for more than a few of them by the emergence of what became Christian Growth Ministries, by its own teachers, and by those in other segments of the movement who sympathized with them.

Christian Growth Ministries (named as such in the early 1970s) was founded in 1968 as the Holy Spirit Teaching Mission. Based in Ft. Lauderdale, Florida, it organized frequent conferences (mainly in Miami) and published *New Wine,* an unpretentious magazine sent free to all who requested it. The four men who emerged as its leaders (and for a time, the sole contributors to the magazine) were Derek Prince, Don Basham, Charles Simpson, and Bob Mumford (in 1975, Ern Baxter, a Canadian classical pentecostal, also joined the group). The four new charismatics represented a curious blend of rather different backgrounds, talents, and temperaments. Mumford and Simpson (a Southern Baptist minister) possessed ongoing, enthusiastic personalities and were extremely effective speakers. Basham's talents (he was a Disciples of Christ minister) lay in journalism, as was evident in the increasingly professional format of *New Wine* after he became editor. Prince, an Englishman and one-time fellow of King's College, Cambridge (in philosophy), was the most scholarly. His message was carefully prepared, reasoned, and laden with Scripture. And *his* presence, especially, gave the organization's outreach a measure of credibility.

In the early 1970s, the leaders of Christian Growth Ministries made an effort to broaden their influence and the scope of the ministry, and *New Wine* was transformed accordingly at this time. The April 1971 issue contained eleven articles with such titles as

"A Biblical Look at the Holy Spirit Baptism," "How to Judge Prophecy," and "How to Start a Home Prayer Group"—typical neopentecostal literature. Two years later, however, the May 1973 issue contained only six articles, with such titles as "God Doesn't Make Mistakes" and "Communication Comes First," representing discussion of broader issues than had been the center of concern within charismatic renewal until that time. In fact, after 1973, there were fewer and fewer references to Spirit baptism, speaking in tongues, and exercising spiritual gifts in *New Wine*. The emphasis turned, instead, to issues of authority, discipline, and community, with topics such as "The Government of God," "Christian Community," and "The Ministry of a Shepherd." Along with such articles were published large doses of personal advice on such concerns as parenting and financial responsibility.

Soon conferences were halted, and the leaders began billing themselves as teachers to the body of Christ at large. Each of them traveled widely and ministered to very diverse groups of people (they were among the first Protestant charismatics to welcome and encourage the fledgling Ann Arbor/South Bend Catholic pentecostals). Their tapes and books multiplied their influence within charismatic renewal, and the circulation of *New Wine* reached more than 100,000, surpassing that of *New Covenant*.

Christian Growth Ministries (and its sympathizers) became the target of criticism by other leaders of charismatic renewal by the mid-1970s over the group's seemingly "authoritarian" dominance over the members of their nondenominational charismatic congregations. (These critics included Dennis Bennett, David du Plessis, Kathryn Kuhlman, Pat Robertson, Demos Shakarian, and Ralph Wilkerson—whose own nondenominational church, Melodyland Christian Center, took on the characteristics of a typical independent evangelical congregation rather than those espoused by the Florida-based organization.) Baxter, Mumford, Simpson, Basham, and Prince were emphasizing Christian growth and behavioral change through the teachings of a God-commissioned elder (or "shepherd")—always male—who has authority over the spiritual and personal growth of his disciples. Critics alleged that the elders were taking "unscriptural control" of others' day-to-day lives, even to the point of usurping Christ's authority. But more than that, the leaders of Christian Growth Ministries were accused of promoting "extralocal submission"—a move to build a chain of command linking many sympathetic local groups around the United States to themselves. The critics feared that these teachers, in reality, were forming a new sectarian denomination. (The essence of the group's stress on discipleship and shepherding was popularized by the Argentinian pentecostal evangelist, Juan Carlos Ortiz, whose book, *Call to Discipleship*, also influenced the South Bend and Ann Arbor covenanted communities.)

Two "summit meetings," one in 1975, and the other in 1980, were called by the critics of Christian Growth Ministries and included some, but not all, of the prominent leaders from both sides of the controversy. Little was accomplished at the first meeting, but the second did result in a measure of accommodation and reconciliation among the warring parties. Leaders of the non-denominational charismatic churches admitted *some* "doctrinal excesses," blamed the religious and secular news media for "misrepresenting" their teaching, disclaimed any intention to become sectarian, and some of them began spending an increased amount of time in ecumenical dialogue. In the words of Charles Simpson, "We're trying to make a statement to the rest of the [charismatic renewal] leaders about our interest in Christian unity."[25]

Another point of contention lay in the Christian Growth Ministries' belief in "demon possession," of even Spirit-filled believers, and in the need for exorcism of such people (that is, a "deliverance ministry," long practiced in classical pentecostalism). Other neo-pentecostals, like Ralph Wilkerson, admitted the possibility of non-Christians being possessed, but *not* believers. A measure of accommodation took place here, too, when those engaged in the dispute began to refer to believers with this problem as "demon *obsessed*" and to only nonbelievers as "demon *possessed*."

---

25. Quoted in John Maust, "Charismatic Leaders Seeking Faith for Their Own Healing," *Christianity Today* (April 4, 1980), p. 44.

The rise of nondenominational charismatic churches has centered on Christian Growth Ministries (now based in Mobile, Alabama), but other prominent groups moved in a similar direction during the late 1970s. Foremost among these is the International Convention of Faith Churches and Ministries in Tulsa, Oklahoma, led by Kenneth Hagen, Sr., of Tulsa, and Kenneth Copeland of Fort Worth, Texas. These "faith confessionalists," as they are called, have been criticized by fellow charismatics as preaching and teaching materialism, and for "laying guilt trips" on their followers, whom, they insist, believe that unanswered prayers for healing or material goods are due *entirely* to their own lack of faith.

Obviously, both the Ford dispute and the shepherding controversy over the issue of human authority in the lives of the Spirit-filled were a challenge to the unity of charismatics and other Christians that charismatic renewal had always insisted on. And although neither conflict was ever resolved entirely, neither one brought about the enduring, major schisms that were once feared —at least not yet. They did, however, underscore the growing heterogeneity of authority patterns within the movement.[26]

EVANGELISM

Gerlach and Hine suggest that a major factor in explaining the spread of a modern religious movement is face-to-face recruitment along lines of preexisting significant social relationships. Whatever motivation for "joining" that is verbalized by the participant or imputed by the social scientist using deprivation, disorganization, or maladjustment models, they declare, it cannot occur without the catalytic agent—another human being.

In classical pentecostalism (until the 1970s), Gerlach and Hine say, recruitment was most successful among relatives. But kinship ties are apparently more important at lower socioeconomic levels; hence, in neopentecostalism recruitment is most often undertaken

---

26. Looney, pp. 24, 25, 33, 34, especially; Maust; and Edward E. Plowman, "The Deepening Rift in the Charismatic Movement," *Christianity Today* (October 10, 1975), pp. 52–54.

among close friends, especially fellow church members, and among neighbors, business associates, fellow students, and the like, where previous significant interaction has already occurred. Furthermore, these anthropologists stress the fact that pentecostals in general do not do well by recruiting loners or drifters who would have difficulty in bringing in others; they fare much better recruiting those who have an "automatic" influence over friends, family, associates, or admirers and fans (thus we can understand why neopentecostals emphasize and affirm as leaders prominent denominational pastors and ecclesiastical officials, academics, celebrities, and wealthy businessmen).

Gerlach and Hine also tend to reject the sociological notion that "deprivation" of some kind is the prime reason individuals join sectarian or enthusiastic churches or movements.[27] They found in their research repeated examples (both among classical pentecostals and neopentecostals, for instance) where economic or social status deprivation is clearly nonexistent, and disorganization or maladjustment simply is not observable.[28] John Kildahl, however, in his ten-year study of neopentecostal speakers in tongues, concludes "that a personal crisis of some kind preceded the initial experience of speaking in tongues in 87 percent of the cases examined."[29]

In charismatic renewal, the sociological concept of recruitment is expressed by the theological word *evangelism*—the proclamation (and demonstration) of the good news, the *full* gospel. Rooted in Baptist and holiness piety, evangelism here means proclaiming (1) the necessity of a *personal* commitment to Jesus Christ as Savior and Lord (conversion), plus (2) the *subsequent* (but related) need for Spirit baptism or infilling. There can be no Spirit baptism *prior* to conversion. In this respect, it is likely that many seemingly

---

27. For one important example of "deprivation theory" in this context, see Charles Y. Glock and Rodney Stark, *Religion and Society in Tension* (Chicago: Rand McNally, 1965), pp. 242–259.

28. Gerlach and Hine, "Five Factors Crucial to the Growth and Spread of a Modern Religious Movement," pp. 30–31.

29. Kildahl, p. 78.

nonevangelical neopentecostals (such as Catholics and "liberals") actually have experienced an evangelical conversion closely linked to their Spirit baptism. Such is particularly apparent in testimonies of Catholic pentecostals who try to integrate the "saving efficacy" of the sacraments with their new "personal relationship with Jesus."[30]

Most neopentecostal fellowship organizations are also evangelistic. Charismatic renewal participants often invite their nonpentecostal friends to FGBMFI gatherings, for example, where specially gifted speakers and others tell of their own pentecostal experience in such a way as to attract the interest of prospective candidates for Spirit baptism. This evangelism is usually very "low key" in character, and *emphatically* does not require a convert to leave his or her present church. And, although literature published by these organizations advertises charismatic renewal meetings, face-to-face recruitment is still the most important factor in attracting converts. Kildahl says of the neopentecostal evangelistic zeal,

> The happy effects of this phenomena [glossolalia] were testified to by tongue-speakers from coast to coast of the United States. . . . The glossolalist noted first that there had been a maturing of his own religious life, which then expressed itself through an intense concern that one's friends and fellow church members should share the same experience.[31]

Again, new participants in charismatic renewal are urged by the movement's leaders not only to remain in their churches, but also to become *better* church members as a result of their experience. In the very early years of the movement, they were told to expect at least *some* opposition, but to avoid all "spiritual pride" that might develop as a result of this opposition. The hope, obviously, was to

---

30. See, for instance, Leon and Virginia Kortenkamp, "Power to Witness," in Kevin and Dorothy Ranaghan, eds., *As the Spirit Leads Us*, pp. 103–113.

31. Kildahl, p. 84.

attract recruits by a changed life and "a gentle witness, filled with love."[32] Don Basham writes,

> Let your experience of the Holy Spirit draw you into deeper and more loving participation in the life of your church, not only with some charismatic group you may join, but in the church's worship and service as well. Other church members having heard your testimony, will be waiting—and rightly so—to see the fruit of your experience in your actions, and they will be far more impressed with what you share if the experience leads you into a deeper love for the church and its people, than if they see you deserting the church to start off on some tangent of your own.[33]

At first, many neopentecostals called their emerging movement a "charismatic revival"—heralding the restoration of the charismata to the life of the contemporary church.[34] Soon, however, the term *revival* was generally replaced with *renewal* to (1) dissociate the movement from revivalistic fundamentalism, and to (2) link it with a larger goal of not only reintroducing spiritual gifts to the historic denominations, but also of relating the charismata to spiritual and institutional Christian renewal more inclusively and comprehensively.

Renewal here, however, has never been an hysterical reassertion of religious truth by investment in strong emotions. Although a case can be made that charismatic renewal does provide some evidence of the power of emotion in a highly routinized society in which technology seems to dominate, it is also true that—in contrast to much of (especially black and Latino) classical pentecostalism—emotional expression in neopentecostalism (a predominantly white, middle-class movement) has been greatly subdued. Michael Harper argues that the "present-day charismatic movement, generally speaking, is not . . . a movement of unthinking fools floating

32. Don Basham, *A Handbook on Holy Spirit Baptism* (Monroeville, Pa.: Whitaker Books, 1969), p. 85.

33. Ibid., p. 114.

34. See Blessed Trinity Society, *Return to the Charismata* (Van Nuys, Calif.: Blessed Trinity Society, 1962), p. 8.

on a wave of emotional experience."[35] Nor has charismatic renewal necessarily been a sidestepping of critical theological onslaught, or the alternative legitimation of religious truth from Scripture to *experience* confirmation alone (although experiential validation *has* been a frequent tendency, especially among Protestant neopentecostal laypeople). Harper goes on to castigate unequivocally the antiintellectualism of white classical pentecostalism and to declare that an "unthinking old-fashioned fundamentalism will always be a hindrance to the forward surge of the Holy Spirit."[36]

In neopentecostalism, renewal has been a positive concept related to Christian unity and "wholeness" (the full gospel) more generally, and is linked to the present operation of the Holy Spirit in the church. To quote Harper again,

> Our aim has been to be positive. The Church needs restoration, not demolition. It needs encouragement, not condemnation. It needs divine inspiration, not a new set of human instructions. Many Christians are battered and bruised. Others are disheartened. Is this the time to draw attention to their faults and failings, which they are all too well aware of, or is it not time to point them to the Lord Jesus Christ, who is ready to forgive, and to fill them with the Holy Spirit?[37]

Furthermore, going beyond mere *Christian* renewal, J. Rodman Williams envisioned charismatic renewal as ultimately "a renewal and advancement of the whole human situation." His understanding of the renewal marks the most comprehensive and idealistic expressed by any neopentecostal theologian:

> Again, this new world of the interpenetration of the spiritual and the natural not only brings into play spiritual powers but also enhances natural capacities and functions. By no means does the natu-

---

35. Michael Harper, "On to Maturity," *Renewal* (December 1972–January 1973), p. 34.

36. Ibid.

37. Harper, *None Can Guess,* pp. 158–159.

ral become less important, but it is given fuller power and direction under the impact of the Holy Spirit. The mind takes on keener awareness of the true shape of reality; the feelings become more sensitive to the moods, the concerns, the hopes of the world and of people; the will finds itself strengthened to execute with more faithfulness and determination those ethical actions to which it gives itself. Thus through the conjoining of the spiritual and the natural, in which strange powers penetrate and invigorate the natural realm (the vast area of the intellectual, the aesthetic, the moral), there is a renewal and advancement of the whole human situation.[38]

FELLOWSHIP

The small group has been the center of charismatic renewal life. Even in churches where the minister or priest and majority of members are neopentecostal participants, charismatic activity is most often confined to small prayer groups in which members reinforce each other in their faith and experience. Formal services of worship tend to remain rather untouched.

PRAYER MEETINGS

Although charismatic renewal groups have been of different kinds (for example, study, fellowship, or testimony), prayer with charismatic expressions tended to be the central feature of any given group. By 1969, Basham could say,

In every town of any size there is at least one charismatic prayer group—usually interdenominational [sponsoring church members bring friends from other churches]—meeting in a home or church. Such groups not only offer inspiration and fellowship, they also help keep us "aglow with the Spirit,"[39] giving us confidence to speak the quiet word of witness where we work or in our own church and among our friends and neighbors.[40]

---

38. J. Rodman Williams, *The Era of the Spirit*, p. 58.

39. See Frost, *Aglow with the Spirit*.

40. Basham, p. 115.

At the same time, it was recognized early by neopentecostal leaders that such small groups easily become "in-groups," and thus have a divisive function in the more inclusive congregation. Larry Christenson, a Lutheran pastor, speaks about the small-group principle in general, and the tendency toward divisiveness or fragmentation in particular:

> We do not encourage speaking in tongues during the regular Sunday worship service.... It seems more appropriate ... at an informal meeting or a prayer group.
> We prefer to have these prayer groups meet either in the church, or in the home of one who is clearly recognized as a responsible leader in the congregation.[41]
> Seek fellowship with others who share your joy and enthusiasm in this blessing. But guard against any "cliques" within the congregation. Prayer meetings and group get-togethers should generally be open to any member of the congregation. Beware of spiritual pride.[42]

Harper elaborates further on the problem of divisiveness, and the related issue of the charismatic fellowship group becoming a "substitute" for parish church membership and participation (something the Fountain Trust prevented by irregular scheduling of its own events):

> It is an almost universal feature of the present wave of new blessing coming to God's people that there is an intense longing for deeper fellowship than is sometimes possible in our churches.... There is surely no harm in such meetings, as long as the dangers of divisiveness are remembered. If such a group develops in a local church, it should do so with the knowledge and permission of the minister and elders. There are few things more dangerous in a church than a secret society.... Sometimes people may meet together who are members of different local churches. Again, there is nothing wrong, and indeed much blessing can flow from these meetings. But the dangers should not be forgotten. This kind of group can become a

---

41. Christenson, *Speaking in Tongues and Its Significance for the Church*, p. 107.
42. Ibid., pp. 105–106.

substitute for a local church, and would, therefore, sap rather than strengthen the churches. They can easily develop into "holy huddles," concerned only with a narrow aspect of truth, instead of fellowships where Christians can rekindle the gift of the Spirit within them, and go back to their local church with greater strength than they had before.[43]

Although small groups have constituted an important feature of Protestant and Anglican charismatic renewal, they have taken on an even greater significance within Catholic pentecostalism. Of prayer meetings among Roman Catholic pentecostals, Edward O'Connor says,

When the Pentecostal movement began at Duquesne and Notre Dame, it took root first among people who already belonged to prayer groups, and the prayer meeting was spontaneously and unquestionably adopted as the natural vehicle of the movement. In fact, it has proved to be an ideal vehicle, to such an extent that wherever the movement has spread, the prayer meetings have gone with it.[44]

In such prayer meetings (not unlike those conducted by Protestant neopentacostals), someone is called on to be a leader. Each member, in the context of a set *order,* is free to pray in any manner he or she wishes (respecting the demands of "love and faith"). The focus is on people praying *together,* not simultaneously. Content of the meetings may include, in addition to prayer, Scripture readings, testimonies, hymns, and various charismatic expressions (for example, glossolalia, prophecy, and divine healing). Participants commonly gather together for long periods of time at regular intervals (four to five hours not being uncommon), but informality is a key feature; coffee breaks are part of the general practice of such fellowship gatherings.[45]

---

43. Michael Harper, *Walk in the Spirit* (Plainfield, N.J.: Logos International, 1968), pp. 88–89.

44. O'Connor, *The Pentecostal Movement in the Catholic Church,* p. 112.

45. Ibid., pp. 112–117. Also see Jim Cavnar, *Prayer Meetings* (Pecos, N.M.: Dove Publications, 1969).

Out of Catholic pentecostal prayer meetings, again, emerged strong covenanted communities (as well as distinctively charismatic parishes)[46] focusing on every aspect of life as it pertains to Christian "renewal" in the charismatic context. One of the strongest of these communities has been the Word of God in Ann Arbor, near the University of Michigan. It had over a thousand members by the mid-1970s. Corporate prayer meetings attract hundreds of people at a time, and these gatherings are supplemented by numerous well-attended teaching seminars. Membership in the community requires a high degree of commitment to its purposes and goals, and a willingness to submit to the discipline it imposes. By 1970, the Ann Arbor community also consisted of nine subcommittees, including living groups. Each living group has a "head" or coordinator who directs activities, and each also conforms to its own statement of purpose. One subcommunity, for instance, functioned as a guest house for women visitors to the larger community. Another engaged in evangelism of the campus and its environment. A third focused primarily on the life of prayer and sharing of the various responsibilities of Christian community life. All groups meet regularly for worship, retreats, and social activities. It is clearly apparent, moreover, that members of Catholic pentecostal covenanted communities in general—because of the rather strict (but not necessarily ascetic) discipline they follow—do separate themselves to a large degree from the everyday concerns of the wider society. In fact, one sees in this covenanted community phenomenon a concrete expression of the typically Catholic notion that to really be *religious,* one must set himself apart with others having the same goal in an "order" (which, in this case, however, may include married as well as celibate members).[47]

---

46. See John Randall, *In God's Providence: The Birth of a Catholic Charismatic Parish* (Plainfield, N.J.: Logos International, 1973).

47. Ghezzi, "Three Charismatic Communities," pp. 179–186. See, for instance, Steven B. Clark, *Building Christian Communities* (Notre Dame, Ind.: Ave Maria Press, 1971); and *New Covenant* (February 1975).

UNITY IN DIVERSITY

The foundation of charismatic renewal theology and ethics is the experience of baptism in the Holy Spirit, however interpreted. We have seen that neopentecostals accept as normative for the Christian church in every age the historic narratives of the Book of Acts—which, in the words of Michael Harper, relate how "Jesus gave the experience of the Holy Spirit to men as a uniting factor *before* they were united in truth."[48] Thus, close doctrinal agreement is not a prerequisite for unity or "fellowship."

"Feeling" is an important part of the pentecostal experience. Theologically, biblical doctrine becomes almost existential, as Leonard Evans, writing in *View* magazine, suggests,

> So speak a growing host of people today, Pentecostal and denominational, of a God we not only "think" but a God whom we can "feel," as a wonderful child of God put it. Then we discover that God not only loved us in the past, in the provision of a marvelous atonement for our sins, but loves us today in His desire to minister directly to our person and corporate hunger for Him and His real presence.[49]

Although neopentecostalism *has* placed its chief emphasis on experience, Harper warns that, taken in isolation—apart from Scripture, the sacraments, and the church—experience alone is dangerously subjective and tends to cause division and breakdown. It must be "harnessed properly" to the point where Spirit baptism allows Christians to discern the reality and vitality of the sacraments and Scripture in the context of their experience.[50]

Steve Clark praises the pentecostal movement for having brought Catholics into contact with other Christians "through a

---

48. Michael Harper, "Christian Unity—the Growing Fact," *Renewal* (December 1970–January 1971), pp. 4–5.

49. Leonard Evans, "A Personal Itinerary in the Charismata," *View*, no. 2 (1964), p. 14.

50. Harper, *None Can Guess*, pp. 154–155.

sense of common sharing in the life of the Spirit" and into communication with "a group of Christians who never spoke with Catholics on a Christian level before—members of the pentecostal denominations."[51] Donald Gelpi, a Jesuit theologian, considers this Roman Catholic classical pentecostal rapprochement especially remarkable in view of the fact that so many of the pentecostal churches embody "just about all the enthusiastic tendencies that the Catholic Church over the centuries has judged to be heretical and divisive."[52] He then accounts for such an unlikely feeling of oneness among one-time belligerents by his understanding of the qualitative unity and diversity of the charismatic experience:

> The charismatic experience is an experience which from generation to generation admits a wide variety of historical expressions. The experience, therefore, has both qualitative unity and diversity. Moreover, both the qualitative unity and the qualitative diversity of the experience possess a discernible historical background. The qualitative unity of the charismatic experience is grounded in the normative character of Jesus' own charismatic experience of divine sonship. Since his charismatic experience was a human experience of what it means to be by nature the Son of God, his charismatic experience of divine sonship is the limit toward which the charismatic experience of those who share his Spirit by adoption must converge. Hence, the qualitative unity of the charismatic experience is teleological. It is produced by the convergence of a variety of charismatic experiences toward the same normative limit.[53]

So intense has been the unity in diversity felt in charismatic renewal that even those ministers and laypeople who had been pressured or forced to leave their own churches because of their pentecostal experience were encouraged by the movement's leadership to be reconciled. David du Plessis insists, "Nothing formulates error as fast as isolationism. . . . I am praying desperately that we

---

51. Steve Clark, "Charismatic Renewal in the Church," in Kevin and Dorothy Ranaghan, eds., *As the Spirit Leads Us,* pp. 24–25.

52. Gelpi, *Pentecostalism: A Theological Viewpoint,* p. 35.

53. Ibid., p. 99.

will not do anything to stop the move of God by our lack of love or harsh criticism of those who have hurt us in the past."[54]

GENERAL THEOLOGICAL ORIENTATION

Edward J. Carnell, the second president of Fuller Theological Seminary, Pasadena, California, defined historic orthodoxy as "that branch of Christendom which limits the ground of religious authority to the Bible."[55] By and large, charismatic renewal has been orthodox in that sense of the word. Of course, there is in neopentecostalism a dynamic, rather than static, understanding of the Word of God; and, among Catholic pentecostals, Scripture stands as authoritative only in the context of the whole Christian tradition, as stated by Kevin Ranaghan:

> There is no question that the Bible is affirmed to be the inspired Word of God. As it has been given by the Holy Spirit to the people of God . . . it is a testimony to the authentic faith and a primary source of spiritual direction and nourishment. Scripture, however, from a Catholic point of view stands at the heart of, or at the core of, the whole Christian tradition. It stands very much *within* the Church; it was inspired and written within the Church, is proclaimed in the Church. . . .
>
> To the Catholic mind, since it is believed that the inspiration of the Holy Spirit is operative in the life of the Church as a whole as well as in Scripture (which is nevertheless uniquely inspired), the Holy Spirit acts authentically in a variety of ways: in teaching, in sacramental celebration, in prayer, and in the ordinary life of the Catholic people.[56]

Neopentecostalism also has tended to be evangelical—aggressively concerned with the proclamation of the gospel to bring nonbeliev-

---

54. Quoted in Jamie Buckingham, "Breakthrough in Unity," *Logos Journal* (September–October 1972), p. 39.

55. E. J. Carnell, *The Case for Biblical Christianity*, ed. Ronald H. Nash (Grand Rapids, Mich.: Eerdmans, 1969), p. 168.

56. Kevin Ranaghan, "Catholics and Pentecostals Meet in the Spirit," in Kevin and Dorothy Ranaghan, eds., *As the Spirit Leads Us*, pp. 138–139.

ers into the Christian faith and Spirit baptism. It has been re-formist in its desire to *renew* existing ecclesiastical structures rather than to build new ones, and ecumenical in its search for Christian unity across denominational lines. Speaking of neopen-tecostals, Walter Hollenweger, the eminent authority on pentecos-talism, describes these people as follows: "Most of them, but not all, are rather evangelical. But all of them want to stay within their churches and try very hard to remain faithful to their liturgy and theology."[57] (Pat Robertson, Jim Bakker, Dan Malachuk, and Ralph Wilkerson have been especially prominent in aligning themselves with "conservative" evangelicals and their insistence on the doctrine of biblical errancy and, for the most part, a dispensational view of the Second Coming.) Most notable among charismatic renewal leaders who do not portray themselves as traditional evangelicals (in the American revivalistic sense) is Arnold Bittlinger of Germany, a Reformed theologian, very active in World Council of Churches concerns.[58] Indeed, there are now even a few Unitarian-Universalist charismatics.[59]

Howard Ervin, an early theological spokesman for neopentecos-talism, saw charismatic renewal as an alternative to both an-tisupernaturalist ("liberal") theology on the one hand, and to doctrinaire orthodoxy on the other:

> An anti-supernaturalist "theology" has no solution, only theories, for the human predicament, which is basically man's alienation from God. Instead, it acknowledges its redemptive sterility by its unabashed capitulation to the human predicament, and by its fre-netic pursuit of "relevance" to the contemporary mood.... It is captive by consent to modern society's ego-centric humanism....
>
> On the other hand, a doctrinaire theological orthodoxy is not a serious option. It is essentially a refurbished scholasticism whose

---

57. Walter Hollenweger, "Charismatic and Pentecostal Movements: A Challenge to the Churches," in Dow Kirkpatrick, ed., *The Holy Spirit* (Nashville, Tenn.: Tidings, 1974), p. 214.

58. Ibid., p. 215. See, especially, Arnold Bittlinger, ed., *The Church Is Charismatic* (Geneva: World Council of Churches, 1981).

59. See Robert Doolittle, "Denominational Renewal," *Unitarian Universalist World* (May 1, 1975), p. 3.

concept of metaphysical reality has congealed in abstract definitions and propositions. It is too prone to confound definition with essence. . . . Its continuing strategy is largely retrenchment, rather than dynamic involvement. Intimidated by apostasy, it has largely surrendered all hope of revival, charismatic or otherwise. Characteristically, its ethic is a platitudinous legalism. . . . Its strategy is fundamentally "trench warfare" waged from dogmatic bastions. . . .

If the book of Acts bears witness to normative Christian experience—and it undubitably does—then by every Biblical standard of measurement contemporary Churchlife is subnormal. As a consequence, it does not speak meaningfully, much less authoritatively, to our fragmented modern world. . . .

It is precisely at this point that the Holy Spirit through the present charismatic awakening of the fragmented Christian Community, speaks urgently to the whole Church on the ecumenical, the denominational, the congregational, and the personal levels of a unity of Spirit and of Life. Only out of the plenitude of its own charismatic "fullness" can the modern Church plunge into redemptive confrontation with an alienated world.[60]

BAPTISM IN THE HOLY SPIRIT

Central to pentecostal theology is the doctrine of Spirit baptism. Don Basham describes baptism in the Holy Spirit as a *second* encounter with God (after conversion) in which the Christian begins to receive the supernatural power of the Holy Spirit into his life.[61] Walter Hollenweger defines Spirit baptism as a "religious crisis experience subsequent to and different from conversion."[62] Hollenweger goes on to say that baptism in the Holy Spirit has been "generally but not always identified with speaking in tongues."[63] With respect to this issue, Basham declares,

What is significant for us to remember is that the baptism in the

60. Ervin, *These Are Not Drunken, As Ye Suppose* (Plainfield, N.J.: Logos International, 1968), pp. 225–226.

61. Basham, p. 10.

62. Hollenweger, "Charismatic and Pentecostal Movements," p. 225n.

63. Ibid.

Holy Spirit, which Jesus Himself bestows, includes speaking in tongues. . . .

The baptism in the Holy Spirit with speaking in tongues was normative in the early church. We pray it will become normative in the church today.[64]

In classical pentecostal theology, the distinction was made between Spirit baptism with the *initial* evidence of speaking in tongues, and the *gift* of tongues (*continuing* glossolalia). And for Dennis and Rita Bennett—like most white pentecostals—the initial experience of glossolalia is not enough. It should be cultivated so that the first "utterances" grow, ultimately, into a "language" for prayer:

> If it were true that most believers only prayed in tongues once, at the time of receiving the Holy Spirit, and perhaps never again, or very rarely, it would be of paramount importance to be sure that those first "utterances" were totally inspired by the Spirit, and not human effort. We are teaching, however, what we know to be true, that these first efforts at obeying the Spirit are only the beginning. It doesn't matter if the first sounds are just "priming the pump," for the real flow will assuredly come. . . .
>
> Keep on with those sounds. Offer them to God. . . . As you do, they will develop and grow into a fully developed language.[65]

The Bennetts feel that there are two ways speaking in tongues may be manifested. The most common, in their view, is glossolalia as a devotional language for private edification, needing no interpretation. Less common, but still important, is the *public* manifestation of tongues—always with interpretation—in which it is felt that God is speaking to the unbeliever (as a "sign" to him or her), or to the believer, or in which the speaker is offering a public prayer to God.[66]

---

64. Basham, p. 26.

65. Dennis and Rita Bennett, *The Holy Spirit and You* (Plainfield, N.J.: Logos International, 1971), pp. 71–72.

66. Ibid., pp. 84–88.

Exactly what *is* glossolalia? William Samarin, a prominent linguistics scholar, suggests that glossolalia consists of strings of generally simple syllables that are not matched systematically with a semantic system. Moreover, it is clearly "learned behavior"—a linguistic phenomenon that can occur independently of any participating psychological or emotional state. Then, speaking in a religious context, Samarin goes on to say that for neopentecostals glossolalia both signals and symbolizes transition (similar in character to an evangelical conversion). It is a "linguistic symbol of the sacred—a symbolic, pleasureful, expressive, and therapeutic experience." He concludes his argument (which runs counter to the older notions that speaking in tongues indicates psychological pathology, suggestibility, or hypnosis, or is the result of social disorganization and deprivation)[67] by declaring that people practice glossolalia because it offers them the fulfillment of aspirations their previous religious experience created in them.[68]

Hollenweger defines speaking in tongues as a "meditative nonrational form of prayer, wrongly confused by non-specialists with ecstatic experiences [as commonly defined]; highly valued by Paul for private prayer (1 Cor. 14:4, 39) but regulated for liturgical use (1 Cor. 14:27)."[69] Pentecostals often insist that glossolalia is a "real language" in the linguistic sense. Although not denying this notion, Larry Christenson attempts a more adequate definition in the face of various linguistic evidence to the contrary: "Speaking in tongues is ... speaking in a language [not "gibberish"]—a language which expresses the deep feelings and thoughts of the speaker, a language which God understands."[70] If speaking in tongues expresses the meaning of the speaker, then, for Christenson, it is a language.

For most Protestant neopentecostal leaders, Spirit baptism has

---

67. See, especially, George B. Cutten, *Speaking in Tongues: Historically and Psychologically Considered* (New Haven, Conn.: Yale University Press, 1927).

68. Samarin, pp. 199, 231, 235.

69. Hollenweger, "Charismatic and Pentecostal Movements," p. 225n.

70. Christenson, *Speaking in Tongues and Its Significance for the Church*, pp. 25–27.

been linked directly to the glossolalia phenomenon. Basham, as we have seen, described the dual experience as "normative," and Christenson affirmed that the "baptism with the Holy Spirit, with the manifestation of speaking in tongues, was for *all* believers (Acts 2:4, 10:44–46, 19:6)."[71] Among Catholic pentecostal leaders, however, there was a greater openness to the possibility of Spirit baptism *without* the gift of speaking in tongues. Thus, Edward O'Connor could say, "Some people begin speaking in tongues at the moment of baptism. Others do not begin until hours, days, or even weeks later, and some never do."[72]

Finally, we should also be reminded that glossolalia is not the *only* gift of the Spirit in charismatic renewal theology. Other spiritual gifts most often mentioned by neopentecostals are those listed in 1 Cor. 12, for instance, and categorized by Dennis and Rita Bennett as follows: (1) inspirational or fellowship gifts: tongues, and interpretation of tongues and prophecy; (2) gifts of power (power to *do*): healings, working of miracles, and the gift of faith; and (3) gifts of revelation: discernment of spirits, the "word of knowledge," and the "word of wisdom."[73] Arnold Bittlinger, however, has insisted on a much broader understanding of the charismata:

> To *each* one gifts are given. The possession of spiritual gifts is therefore in no sense a measure of Christian maturity. Spiritual gifts are received as presents from God by every Christian who will accept them in childlike faith. The sinner who comes before God in his helplessness with the words 'God have mercy on me a sinner' receives, to begin with, the *charisma* of eternal life (Rom. 6:23).
>
> There are a number of places in the New Testament where the gifts of divine grace are listed (e.g., Rom. 12:5–8; 1 Cor. 12:8–10; 1 Cor. 14:26f; Eph. 4:11). The great multiplicity of gifts makes it clear that the activity of Jesus extends to the whole range of human experience. The list of gifts in 1 Corinthians 2:8–10 is concerned

71. Christenson, *Speaking in Tongues and Its Significance for the Church*, pp. 25–27.

72. O'Connor, *The Pentecostal Movement in the Catholic Church*, p. 134.

73. Dennis and Rita Bennett, p. 83.

especially with the controversial gifts, those that were often misused or misunderstood.[74]

WATER BAPTISM AND CONFIRMATION

One of the most difficult problems in neopentecostalism (especially in Catholic pentecostalism) is the relationship between Spirit baptism (or infilling) and water baptism (as well as conversion and confirmation). For the evangelical Protestant, a second definite "work of grace" after conversion—Spirit baptism—does not pose great theological difficulties except with respect to the question of whether the Holy Spirit enters a person at the time of conversion (or water baptism, in Catholic theology) or only in the *experience* of the Holy Spirit itself. This problem, then, is also related to the exact nature of Spirit baptism. Are receiving the Spirit and becoming a Christian identical?

Pentecostals base their doctrine of two steps to the "fullness of the Spirit" on Luke-Acts (Hollenweger, contrary to Dale Bruner and James Dunn,[75] both evangelical New Testament scholars, feels that they are right in doing so). Following the argument of Eduard Schweizer, a New Testament scholar, Hollenweger maintains that Luke does in fact favor the two-stage approach—first, water baptism or becoming a Christian, and second, baptism in the Spirit with recognizable signs—while Paul appears to have a different understanding of the Holy Spirit. For Paul, it would seem that becoming a Christian and receiving the Spirit are identical. Although much has been written about the Pauline and Lukan views of the Spirit—and how to reconcile them—Hollenweger, believing that the Bible is not necessarily a "unified system," is

---

74. Bittlinger, *Gifts and Graces*, pp. 26–27. Important recent studies of glossolalia include Cyril G. Williams, *Tongues of the Spirit*, and D. Christie-Murray, *Voices from the Gods: Speaking with Tongues* (London: Routledge & Kegan Paul, 1978).

75. See Frederick Dale Bruner, *A Theology of the Holy Spirit: The Pentecostal Experience and the New Testament Witness* (Grand Rapids, Mich.: Eerdmans, 1970); and James Dunn, *Baptism in the Holy Spirit* (Naperville, Ill.: Allenson, 1970).

prepared to accept *both* the Lukan and Pauline doctrines as not fundamentally contradictory. (Pentecostals, however, try to solve the problem by positing two modes of the Holy Spirit's operation—a primary mode, essential for regeneration [Paul], and a secondary mode, providing additional equipment for service [Luke]. Salvation is seen by them as being baptized by God in Christ and in the Spirit, while the second work has the Holy Spirit as the agent of baptism.)[76]

Catholics understand Spirit baptism differently from Protestant pentecostals. Edward O'Connor accepts the reception of the Spirit as a twofold experience, but in a sacramental context. In the first stage, at the moment of water baptism, the Holy Spirit comes to dwell in a person's life; but his presence there remains "hidden" until the second stage of reception occurs. This stage is baptism in the Holy Spirit by which the Holy Spirit becomes "manifest" in an individual.[77] Kevin and Dorothy Ranaghan compare the Catholic and Protestant pentecostal views as follows:

> To evangelical pentecostals, baptism in the Holy Spirit is a "new" work of grace. In the life of a Catholic it is an "old" work, yet practically "new" because the phrase as used by Catholic pentecostals is a prayer of renewal for everything that Christian initiation is and is meant to be. In practice it has come to be an experience of reaffirmation rather than of initiation. Among Catholic pentecostals this baptism is neither a new sacrament nor a substitute sacrament. Like the renewal of baptismal promises, it is a renewal in faith of the desire to be everything that Christ wants us to be. . . . For Catholics this experience is a renewal, making our initiation [into the church] as children concrete and explicit on a mature level.[78]

Thus, for Protestant neopentecostals, baptism in the Holy Spirit is a second work of grace (after conversion) in which the Spirit is actually "received" for the first time *or* in which the Spirit's super-

---

76. Hollenweger, "Charismatic and Pentecostal Movements," pp. 231–233, n. 52.

77. O'Connor, *The Pentecostal Movement in the Catholic Church*, pp. 132–135.

78. Kevin and Dorothy Ranaghan, *Catholic Pentecostals*, p. 142.

natural *power* is initially received (for example, Basham). For Catholic pentecostals, Spirit baptism is nonsacramental. In it, the Holy Spirit, present in an individual (in a hidden state) since water baptism, becomes manifest. Here baptism in the Holy Spirit functions as a *renewal* of water baptismal initiation rather than as a second, literal baptism. This renewal, moreover, is similar to (but not identical with) the renewal of baptismal vows in confirmation, and is a spiritual renewal that, in the words of J. Rodman Williams, "seems to have little or no relation to . . . [a person's] confirmation—or lack of it."[79]

SACRAMENTAL INTERCOMMUNION

In charismatic renewal, celebration of the sacraments (or ordinances) has been most often confined to the formal services of worship of whatever denominations and churches are represented. Ecumenical conferences, however, may include an interdenominational service of communion—particularly at their conclusion. As in the ecumenical movement more generally, some neopentecostal ecclesiastical leaders do occasionally participate together in sacramental celebration (or "concelebration"). In this regard, Williams relates a few of his experiences:

> I can look back over the past several months and recall occasions of *full* participation at the Lord's supper in traditions as widely different as Roman Catholic and Assembly of God, Episcopal and Church of Christ. As a Presbyterian minister it has been my privilege to concelebrate Mass, jointly to officiate at the Eucharist with an Episcopal priest, and perhaps the most amazing of all, to participate in a service of Holy Communion presided over by an Assembly of God minister assisted by a Roman Catholic priest and myself![80]

---

79. J. Rodman Williams, *The Era of the Spirit*, p. 41n. On the relationship of Spirit baptism to sacramental life, see Kilian McDonnell and Arnold Bittlinger, *The Baptism in the Holy Spirit as an Ecumenical Problem* (Notre Dame, Ind.: Charismatic Renewal Services, 1972).

80. J. Rodman Williams, *The Era of the Spirit*, p. 45n.

NEOPENTECOSTAL CULTURE: ACCOMMODATION OF HOLINESS TO THE MIDDLE CLASS

Classical pentecostal culture is rooted in American revivalism, which emerged in the late eighteenth century, became a major national religious movement during the first two-thirds of the nineteenth century, and was radicalized in the holiness movement of the last third of the nineteenth century. Although the "cultural baggage" of revivalism in general and classical pentecostalism in particular certainly did find its way into the pentecostal movement in the historic denominations, it was largely resisted—especially by those churches (for example, Roman Catholic, Episcopal, Lutheran, and Presbyterian) that are not grounded in the revivalist-fundamentalist tradition. One result of this rejection of cultural traditions in large segments of neopentecostalism has been the accommodation of holiness to the middle class and the values of upward mobility more generally. In charismatic renewal, it is increasingly the case that holiness has more to do with a positive attitude of the heart and good interpersonal relationships than it does with the traditional moral rigorism and negativism. Thus, Robert Frost could say,

> True holiness can never be cataloged as a list of do's and don'ts. Rather it is an attitude of the heart that lovingly recognizes the Lordship of Jesus Christ. . . .
>
> So often we have a tendency to logically construct an artificial list of worldly do's and don'ts as if holiness of heart could be measured by men's minds.[81]

Kevin Ranaghan is particularly firm about his rejection of classical pentecostal cultural baggage:

> Often with the revivals came a simplistic and individualistic Christian ethic. The righteous life [holiness] was characterized by clean living; therefore no smoking, drinking, dancing, makeup, theatre-

---

81. Robert Frost, *Overflowing Life* (Plainfield, N.J.: Logos International, 1971), p. 115.

going or other amusements were allowed. While it was considerably tempered over the last several decades, the revivalistic culture continues to pervade denominational pentecostalism. . . . In its own cultural setting and development, this religious style is quite beautiful, meaningful and relevant. But it is not essential to or desirable for the baptism of the Holy Spirit, especially among people of far different religious backgrounds.[82]

In Catholic pentecostalism especially, but also in neopentecostalism more generally, there has been very little desire to forsake the affirmation of the wider culture for the culture rejection that was characteristic of classical pentecostalism and sectarian religion as a whole. The accommodation of holiness—of sanctification—to middle-class values in charismatic renewal and, increasingly, in classical pentecostalism as well has blurred the traditional revivalistic distinctions between the "sacred" and the "secular." To quote Kevin and Dorothy Ranaghan again,

The men and women, clerics and lay people who have sought and received the baptism in the Holy Spirit, are by and large ordinary Catholic people from every walk of life, profession and socio-economic bracket. . . . Serious about their religion, concerned for the spiritual welfare of others, anxious for constructive renewal in the Church, they have been equally involved in their civic communities and employment, entering fully into all the normal activities which mark this period of our national life—human rights, law, justice, good government, peace.[83]

This culture affirmation in Catholic pentecostalism is also described in Hollenweger's account of the prayer meetings typical of the pentecostal movement in the Roman Catholic Church:

It was not the uneducated but the intellectuals, not the uncritical but the critical exegetes, not frustrated Puritans, but quite normal Christians who took part in the meetings. There is not only speak-

---

82. Kevin Ranaghan, "Catholics and Pentecostals Meet in the Spirit," in Kevin and Dorothy Ranaghan, eds., *As the Spirit Leads Us*, p. 129.

83. Kevin and Dorothy Ranaghan, *Catholic Pentecostals*, pp. 142–143.

ing in tongues but critical discussion of theological and social problems; not only the singing of hymns but the composition of new hymns, not only praying, but eating, drinking and smoking.[84]

We have already mentioned the new television image of Oral Roberts since he joined the United Methodist Church and the rise to religious stardom of Pat Robertson and his Johnny Carson–like "700 Club." Another pentecostal celebrity who became well known in the entertainment industry years ago is Pat Boone. Boone's popularity as a vocalist during the late 1950s and early 1960s rivaled that of Elvis Presley. Formerly an active Church of Christ layman, Boone was always regarded as "the nice clean all-American boy who lived next door and wore white buck shoes"[85] —but his singing and acting career was also the target of criticism by fellow American fundamentalists and evangelicals. After a family and business crisis experience in 1969, and through the influence of Oral Roberts, Harald Bredesen, David Wilkerson, and George Otis, a millionaire businessman, Pat Boone (and his wife and four daughters) were baptized in the Holy Spirit. Having been "disfellowshiped" by his Church of Christ congregation as a result, he identified with the emerging Jesus People movement, but finally joined the International Church of the Foursquare Gospel (specifically "The Church on the Way," Van Nuys, California), and became active in charismatic renewal leadership circles. Boone's religiosity is well known in the entertainment industry, where he has many "secular" friends. As long ago as 1970, he wrote,

> Dean Martin and I have hacked up some songs and golf courses together. Not long ago, in his mock-serious 100 proof way, Dino cracked a new one.
> "That's Pat Boone! He's so religious! Y'know, I shook hands with him the other day and my whole right side sobered up!"

---

84. Hollenweger, *The Pentecostals*, p. 8.
85. Boone, p. 46.

My friends in the entertainment profession are colorful, vital people! We have a great time together.[86]

Pat Boone clearly does not believe in "separation from the world" in the traditional pentecostal sense; he does not reject the wider culture per se. The entertainer has appeared on a Dick Clark rock-and-roll television special (Clark was a leading rock promoter for many years) in which Boone sang a number of his hit records and discussed his positive view of rock music with Clark. When his business schedule permits (he is now a multimillionaire and lives in Beverly Hills, California), Boone travels extensively to keep concert engagements with his wife and daughters, who together sing both secular and religious songs—even at the major hotels in Las Vegas.[87]

If the spiritualization of holiness allows culture affirmation, its socialization (from a rigorous personal moral negativism to a concern for the healing of interpersonal relationships and humanity as a whole) represents a departure from the focus on "pious words and practices" typical of fundamentalism to a newer interest in social morality. Hence, Kevin and Dorothy Ranaghan express their hope for a "humanly concerned" Christian witness within charismatic renewal:

Men today are not interested in pious practices or abstract virtue. Where Christianity is part of the fiber of the society as an establishment, where the nation goes to church but the Sunday dose of spiritual medicine wears off in Monday's marketplace, faith is dead. A God may indeed be worshipped here, but he is faceless and abstract. He is not the Father of our Lord, Jesus Christ.

The idealistic young, the "secular" theologians ... the "man in the street" all seem to be crying out: "Down with pretty music and pious preaching; let us love one another right now!" Christian witness if it is to survive, if it is to be Christian, must be humanly concerned. It must be truly loving. It must be Christ.[88]

---

86. Ibid., pp. 5–6.

87. Ibid.

88. Kevin and Dorothy Ranaghan, *Catholic Pentecostals*, pp. 188–189.

SPIRIT BAPTISM AND SOCIAL CHANGE

To what degree, we might ask at this point, has there been an interest within the pentecostal movement in working for social change? Kilian McDonnell suggests that white classical pentecostalism has most often been associated with indifference to social conditions and political issues—until World War II, a reflection, in part, of the political and social apathy common to the lower socio-economic levels[89] (although black pentecostals gave a broad measure of support to Martin Luther King, Jr., and *some* white classical pentecostals had been pacifists during World War II—the Assemblies of God once had a statement affirming pacifism in its by-laws, but later rescinded it). This apathy was reinforced by the sociopolitical conservatism inherent in American fundamentalism that influenced white pentecostalism deeply.[90] McDonnell also insisted, already in 1970, that there is nothing innate in the pentecostal experience to change a person's political and social attitudes. He says that although

> The Pentecostal experience does seem to elicit a new openness and generosity toward others it does not endow people with a new passion for political and social justice. If socio-political awareness were present before one became involved in Pentecostalism, the Pentecostal experience supports and reinforces it. But the Pentecostal experience will not, by and of itself, supply one with socio-political awareness.[91]

In other words, Spirit baptism is what sociologists call an "independent variable." If the newly baptized pentecostal believer is socialized (that is, taught and "discipled") in a group committed to social change, he, too, will probably move in that direction. (In the Third World and Europe, especially, there are even *Marxist* pen-

---

89. Kilian McDonnell, "Catholic Pentecostalism: Problems in Evaluation," *Dialog* (Winter 1970), p. 51.

90. See Quebedeaux, *The Young Evangelicals.*

91. Kilian McDonnell, "Catholic Pentecostalism: Problems in Evaluation," *Dialog* (Winter 1970), p. 51.

tecostals.) But if the new pentecostal is socialized in a conservative community of faith, he or she will most likely come to share *its* position here.

Nevertheless, among the leadership of charismatic renewal there has been at least a measure of interest in social concern, which is sometimes felt to be an appropriate consequence of Spirit baptism. For instance, Michael Harper discusses this issue:

> True pietism ... has in the past been deeply concerned with social matters, and ... its prophets have attacked social injustice and exalted social righteousness. The roots of modern British Socialism stretch down to the seedbeds of Methodism, for instance.
>
> Every one of us should be passionately concerned about justice, public morality, and the plight of the under-nourished and under-privileged, and a balanced spirituality should reflect really deep commitment to the cause of man's physical as well as spiritual well-being. The Holy Spirit in the Acts of the Apostles was constantly destroying racial barriers, and reconciling deeply entrenched prejudices. It is important to notice too that in 1 Cor. 12:13 the baptism in the Spirit is seen in this context.[92]

Given the fact that Catholic pentecostalism emerged within the liberal academic community itself and within a church that, compared to its evangelical and fundamentalist Protestant counterparts, is not inherently "middle-class" nor associated with the social and political status quo, it should not be surprising that Catholic pentecostals seem to have a greater social conscience than most Protestant neopentecostals. Yet, according to Edward O'Connor, there has been a strong feeling within *some* quarters of Catholic pentecostalism, at least, that *more* corporate interest and involvement in social change is desirable. He speaks of the early Notre Dame community:

> The members of the Notre Dame community are involved in many different forms of social action.... A group of young families on

---

92. Harper, *Walk in the Spirit,* pp. 59–60.

the West Side of South Bend are actively working to improve race relations between black and whites. . . .

While the members of the community are . . . active in a multitude of ways, there is no . . . work proper to the whole community. . . . This has disturbed some, who feel that the community as such ought to have a ministry. "God does not form a Christian community just to hold prayer meeting," they sometimes declare.[93]

Already in 1969, Kevin and Dorothy Ranaghan addressed the issue of social change with a sense of urgency:

We have before us the task of being Christ in the world. That means that in, with, and through him, by the power of the Spirit we are to worship, love, and adore our Father, just as Jesus did. It also means that we, the corporate Body of Christ, must communicate the experience of the saving love of Jesus to the world. To the world means to mankind; not to men's feelings or emotions, not to men's disembodied spirits, but to human people in human societies and man-made institutions. The world that needs Jesus' love is shackled with poverty and disease, with racism and war, with lust for power and just plain indifference to the "other guy." This is the world we are sent to transform with Jesus' love, not so the world will be condemned but that it will be saved.[94]

In the course of its development as a movement, charismatic renewal did provide an innovative context for those new pentecostals committed to social change in general—its intentional communities which were set up to model the transforming love of God the Ranaghans describe. Some of these groups became heavily involved in social service. Others engaged in more direct political action as well. Most notable among these intentional communities centered on social change has been the Episcopal Church of the Redeemer, Houston, Texas, a once-dying inner-city parish whose rector, Graham Pulkingham, was baptized in the Holy Spirit in 1964. In 1963, parish enrollment stood at 900, with one-third of that number inactive (most had moved to the local suburbs). But

93. O'Connor, *The Pentecostal Movement in the Catholic Church,* p. 106.
94. Kevin and Dorothy Ranaghan, *Catholic Pentecostals,* pp. 211–212.

by 1971, parish enrollment had risen to 1,400, average weekly attendance had reached 2,200, and "pledging" to meet the church budget was discontinued. As an experiment, Pulkingham and thirty parishioners (all neopentecostal) established a residential community, in the inner city near the church, that was patterned after the second chapter of Acts. The rector describes that initial community as follows:

> For six months thirty-one people all but lived together. In order to include wives and children in this fellowship, husbands continued [to meet] at the early morning hour and returned at 7:30 in the evening for a family gathering. All day Saturday, and Sunday after church, were spent together in one of the member's homes. Although nothing formal was put forward and no covenants were signed, each family let me know that everything they had or could command was at the disposal of the ministry [the community]—savings, insurance, earnings, possessions, borrowing power, themselves; we relinquished everything in a literal way. It was made available to help the needy.[95]

Somewhat similar to the Catholic pentecostal covenanted communities, numerous other communes were founded within the Church of the Redeemer parish. Suburbanites returned to the inner city until, by 1972, there were 40 communities with 350 people—ranging from groups of working people to homes for parentless children. The success of this ministry in Houston in the 1960s and early 1970s took Pulkingham to Scotland, where he spent several years facilitating the work of other intentional charismatic renewal communities before returning to the Church of the Redeemer in 1980. In describing the impact of his church, the rector *underscores* the commitment of his neopentecostal parishioners to social change:

> The fellowship members have not turned their backs on society. On the contrary, they are trying to make changes in society at large and

---

95. Pulkingham, *Gathered for Power: Charisma, Communalism, Christian Witness*, p. 128.

particularly in the Houston area by setting an example for others to follow.[96]

PATTERNS OF WORSHIP

Set largely in the context of middle-class Christianity—and in historic ecclesiastical structures where liturgy is highly regulated—the pentecostal experience of worship has been "subdued" in charismatic renewal. Kilian McDonnell describes classical pentecostal speech patterns, prayer postures, mental processes, and expectations as part of the cultural heritage of marginalized Afro-Americans and whites that need not be accepted and used in neopentecostalism. Although these practices may have validity in one religious culture, they do not in another, since such traditions (or "cultural baggage") are culturally determined and not transferable.[97] In this regard, David du Plessis advises middle-class neopentecostals,

Do not conform to Pentecostal patterns, for example, clapping one's

---

96. Ibid., p. 135; also see this book as a whole. In addition, see W. Graham Pulkingham, *They Left Their Nets: A Vision for Community Ministry* (New York: Morehouse-Barlow, 1973); Michael Harper, *A New Way of Living* (Plainfield, N.J.: Logos International, 1973); and Walter Hollenweger, *New Wine in Old Wineskins* (Gloucester, England: Fellowship Press, 1973), pp. 27–28. A conservative work on social concern in charismatic renewal was written by Larry Christenson, *A Charismatic Approach to Social Action* (Minneapolis, Minn.: Bethany Fellowship, 1974). On social concern within Catholic pentecostalism, specifically, see *New Covenant* (June 1974); Joseph H. Fichter, "Liberal and Conservative Catholic Pentecostals," *Social Compass* 21 (1974), 303–310; and his book *The Catholic Cult of the Paraclete* (New York: Sheed & Ward, 1975); Ford, *Which Way for Catholic Pentecostals?;* Sheila M. Fahey, *Charismatic Social Action* (New York: Paulist Press, 1977); and Léon Joseph Suenens and Dom Helder Camara, *Charismatic Renewal and Social Action* (Ann Arbor, Mich.: Servant Publications, 1979). Finally, for an interesting discussion of politically radical tendencies among *some* pentecostal groups, see Walter Hollenweger, *Pentecostal Between Black and White: Five Case Studies on Pentecost and Politics* (Belfast: Christian Journals, 1974). And, on the social change issue more generally, see "Charismatic and Socio-Political Movements," *Social Compass* 25 (1978), 1–163.

97. Kilian McDonnell, "Catholic Pentecostalism: Problems in Evaluation," *Dialog* (Winter 1970), pp. 41–42.

hands out of imitation of the [classical] Pentecostals, or raising one's arms in prayer.[98]

He also says,

Let me say right here that I consider it heresy to speak of shaking, trembling, falling, dancing, clapping, shouting, and such actions as manifestations of the Holy Spirit. These are purely human reactions to the power of the Holy Spirit and frequently hinder more than help to bring forth genuine manifestations.[99]

Nowhere has the "routinization"—and suppression—of the original African liturgical forms of movement, vocalization, and spiritual communication been more apparent than in contemporary Protestant and Catholic charismatic healing services. The "giant" independent pentecostal faith healers of the 1940s, 1950s, and 1960s all practiced those Africanisms in their campaigns. Services were marked by the holy dance, shouts and responses at appropriate times during the sermon, and dramatic exorcisms. This is one reason blacks felt at home in the healing revivals of white evangelists like Jack Coe (1918–1957) and A. A. Allen (1911–1970), and why middle-class whites criticized their meetings so much.

We have already seen the routinization of pentecostal divine healing in the ministry of Kathryn Kuhlman in the 1960s and early 1970s. But the subduing of charismatic manifestations in worship was even more apparent in the services of Ruth Carter Stapleton in the late 1970s, in which she preached her own brand of "inner healing," a religious style of "wholeness" development, heavily informed by modern psychology in general and by the human potential movement in particular. Also in the mid to late 1970s, there arose a Catholic faith healer, Francis MacNutt, who accommodated the ministry of divine healing to even intellectually oriented Catholics by integrating the practice of spiritual healing (from

---

98. Quoted in ibid., p. 41.

99. Du Plessis, *The Spirit Bade Me Go*, p. 93.

their own long tradition) with modern psychology in his services. But the handsome, Harvard-educated priest lost popularity within charismatic renewal as a whole when he was married without the Pope's permission in 1980.

Neopentecostal charismatic activity has tended to be relegated to small prayer groups of believers only, so as not to "frighten" and thus deter middle-class newcomers who are present during formal worship; it is always highly regulated. Addressing the matter in question, Larry Christenson speaks of charismatic activity in his Lutheran congregation:

> We do not encourage speaking in tongues during the regular Sunday worship service, although it surely is not forbidden. It seems more appropriate, however, at an informal evening meeting or a prayer group. . . .
>
> We discourage the copying of any set of traditions, customs, or mannerisms in our prayer groups. We have nothing against these traditions from other Christian groups, but we do not feel that they are essential to the manifestations of the gifts of the Spirit in our setting. It is unnatural for our people to pray in loud voices, or to intersperse another person's prayer with frequent "Amen's" or "Hallelujah's."[100]

Michael Harper, likewise, is explicit about the regulation of charismata in the context of neopentecostal worship:

> Just as we hand presents graciously to those we love . . . and do not thrust them rudely at them, so we should manifest spiritual gifts "decently." This means we shall not shout unnaturally words of prophecy, nor speak so quietly that no one can properly hear us. It means we will not lay hands violently on people for healing, but gently and reverently . . . and the laying-on-of-hands should be carefully ordered in the churches. The minister and other leaders in each church should specify who should have this ministry. . . .
>
> We should also observe the principle of orderliness. "God is not a God of confusion but of peace," Paul reminds the Corinthians (1

---

100. Christenson, *Speaking in Tongues and Its Significance for the Church,* pp. 107–108.

Cor. 14:33). We may receive, for example, an anointing to manifest a gift during a service, but that does not mean that we have to do so there and then. We can wait until an appropriate opportunity presents itself.

In some churches it is customary to punctuate prayers or sermons with loud "amens" and "hallelujahs," etc. This can be very distracting to the one who is leading in prayer or exhortation, as well as to the congregation, each member of which should be following what the one leading is saying. . . . Another tradition to avoid is the practice of speaking in tongues during a meeting, without interpretation and in concert. This contradicts the command of Paul in 1 Cor. 14:28.[101]

(Harper's critique here is, obviously, a reflection of his own Anglican religious style. In black pentecostalism, "amens" and shouts are an expected, almost musical, punctuation of the sermon. Without them, a preacher would feel like a failure.)[102]

We shall now delineate the specific differences between the development of classical pentecostalism and charismatic renewal that have already been briefly mentioned—cultural and social differences, and differences in theological belief and practice.

---

101. Harper, *Walk in the Spirit,* pp. 74–75, 77–78.

102. Sheppard, "Commentary."

Chapter Six

The Development of Classical Pentecostalism and Charismatic Renewal in Contrast

In contrasting the development of classical pentecostalism with charismatic renewal or neopentecostalism, we are immediately reminded of the characteristic pattern of sect development into a church or denomination. Classical pentecostalism has usually been regarded as illustrative of the sect-type religious organization in sociological typologies. Charismatic renewal, because of its nature as a movement largely *within* the historic Protestant, Anglican, and Eastern Orthodox denominations and the Roman Catholic Church, has been identified with the church- or denomination-type religious organization.

Bryan Wilson, reader in sociology at Oxford University, suggests the following as typical characteristics of a *sect:* (1) a voluntary association; (2) membership by proof to sect authorities of some claim to personal merit such as knowledge of doctrine, affirmation of a conversion experience, or recommendation of members in good standing; (3) exclusiveness, and expulsion against those who dispute doctrinal, ethical, or organizational precepts; (4) self-conception of a special elect; (5) personal perfection (however this is judged) as the expected standard of aspiration; (6) belief (at least as an ideal) in the priesthood of all believers; (7) high level of lay participation; (8) opportunity for spontaneous expression of commitment by members; and (9) hostility, or indifference, to secular society and the state. By way of elaboration on these points, Wilson then goes on to say that the commitment of the sectarian is more total and well-defined than that of the denominational or churchly believer. Sect ideology is clearer than that of church or denomination, and behavioral expectations serve to keep sect members apart from the wider society—"the world."[1]

In Wilson's typology of religious sects, classical pentecostalism is described as reflective of the "conversionist" sect model. A conversionist sect centers its teaching and activity on evangelism or recruitment. It is typified by biblical literalism and the demand for conversion as the test of fellowship. Much emphasis is placed on individual guilt for sin, and the need for redemption through Christ. The conversionist sect precludes no one, and revivalist techniques are employed in evangelism. It is distrustful of denominations and churches it feels have diluted or betrayed "authentic" Christianity. This sect is hostile to clerical learning, and especially to liberalism. It is opposed to modern science, particularly to geology and theories of evolution. And finally, the conversionist sect disdains culture and the artistic values accepted in the wider society.[2]

In the course of the decades following 1906 (more so since the end of World War II, and especially since the 1970s), however, classical pentecostalism as a whole has undergone a transformation that has caused it to lose many of its sect characteristics and to take on various traits of the church or denomination type of religious organization. By the mid-1960s, classical pentecostalism could no longer be *uniformly* identified with the disadvantaged and deprived often associated with sect membership. John Nichol makes the point well:

---

1. Bryan R. Wilson, "Sect Development," in Bryan R. Wilson, ed., *Patterns of Sectarianism* (London: Heinemann, 1967), pp. 23–24.

2. Ibid., p. 27.

Pentecostals have become property owners rather than being property-less. They have risen economically, and their churches have become more elaborate, their worship more dignified. There is a greater demand for music of a professional quality and for an educated ministry. The groups have grown in influence and numbers, and, in the process, they have developed an increasing amount of ecclesiastical "machinery." Prior concerns of meeting the needs of an adult membership have been subordinated to a stress on the religious education of the young. Those cultural standards which the fathers condemned, the children have embraced. The stress on the future, on preparing for the next world, have given way very largely to a principle of accommodation to the surrounding culture.[3]

In a sense, the likelihood of classical pentecostalism being denominationalized was always high, because in so many ways it came out of a tradition that was in direct continuity with evangelical Protestantism. Only Spirit baptism and the charismata (speaking in tongues, particularly) stood out as *manifestly* separatist and sectarian; they were the *raison d'etre* of the movement's separate existence. This element of what Max Weber would call the ecstatic was clearly not part of the old Protestantism as received through the historic denominations, and it was in some ways a threat to the old ascetic—a type of spiritual indulgence. Hence, classical pentecostalism was sectarian because it pitched the balance of ascetic and ecstatic at a different point and sought scriptural warrant for so doing. (It was the doctrinal underpinning and strict scriptural basis, of course, that made pentecostalism so much more respectable than earlier glossolalic movements, and it could fit the spiritual gifts into a received ecclesiology, too.)

Neopentecostalism, as we have said, has been a movement of spiritual renewal mainly within the historic denominations identified with the denomination- or church-type of religious organization. Wilson characterizes the *denomination* as follows: (1) formally, a voluntary association; (2) acceptance of adherents

---

3. Nichol, pp. 236–237.

without imposition of traditional prerequisites of entry and with purely formalized admission procedures; (3) stress on breadth and tolerance; (4) laxity of enrollment, leading to a lack of interest in the expulsion of the apathetic and wayward; (5) unclear self-understanding, and deemphasis of doctrine; (6) satisfaction of being one movement among others; (7) acceptance of the values and standards of the prevailing culture and conventional morality; (8) an educated professional ministry; (9) restricted lay participation; (10) formalized services without spontaneity; (11) more concern for education of the young than for evangelism; (12) nonreligious character of additional activities (apart from worship); (13) weak individual commitment; (14) acceptance of the values of the secular society and the state; and (15) membership drawn from any section of the community.[4]

Since charismatic renewal has been a decentralized movement, there could be no "real" members—only participants. But when the pentecostal experience becomes *dominant* in a given local church which is part of a historic denomination, certain traits inherent in the denomination-type religious organization are often transformed into attributes more typical of the sect type. For instance, "first-class" membership requires evidence of the pentecostal experience, which is certainly a prerequisite for leadership in the church. The congregation's self-conception is very clear, and doctrinal issues become relatively more important (especially those relating to the Holy Spirit). The congregation sees itself as more generally a part of charismatic renewal, which it does not regard as merely one movement among others. It espouses more transcendent values and a "higher" sense of personal morality than does the prevailing culture. Lay participation is greater and less restricted than in the denominational model. Spontaneity does, at times, occur in services of worship—and more often during meetings of prayer groups. Evangelism (particularly as it relates to the pentecostal experience) is at least as important as religious education of the young. Finally, most additional activities do tend to be

---

4. Wilson, *Patterns of Sectarianism*, p. 25.

religious in nature, and individual commitment is very intense indeed.

Charismatic renewal has been primarily an upper-middle-class movement within the "respectable," white historic denominations. Already in 1964, Stanley Plog, then a psychologist at University of California at Los Angeles (UCLA), said of the neopentecostals he interviewed that "they're determined to fit the gift of tongues—and the gift of healing, too—into a 'normal,' calm, middle-class way of life, and that's definitely something new."[5]

THEOLOGY

As already noted, pentecostal theology emerged among working-class and marginalized whites and blacks, in the context of their own holiness and Baptist backgrounds. In the early years of classical pentecostalism, the "breakthrough" experience of Spirit baptism—evidenced by speaking in tongues—was first testified to, then fitted into a variety of received Christian traditions. And this experience, which gained worldwide visibility at Azusa Street in 1906, remained the hallmark of the pentecostal movement to the present day.

Classical pentecostal theology emerged and developed in a far more heterogeneous manner than is usually supposed. Pentecostal believers looked to numerous leaders who came from a wide range of ecclesiastical backgrounds, inherited views, and theological preferences. As in charismatic renewal, no one person—however popular—could ever speak for classical pentecostals as a whole. Within a decade, in typical sectarian fashion, the original unitative movement had fragmented into many factions with major doctrinal segments—"second-work trinitarians" (stressing sanctification as a distinct, second work of grace), "finished-work trinitarians" (emphasizing sanctification as an ongoing process), and "unitarians" (the "oneness" or "Jesus only" groups). Other diver-

---

5. Quoted in Dean, "Strange Tongues: A Psychologist Studies Glossolalia," *Trinity* (Trinitytide 1964), p. 39.

gences included the use of wine rather than unfermented grape juice in communion, the practice of foot washing as an ordinance, and baptism by sprinkling instead of immersion. These were serious issues of theological conflict.

Because of doctrinal variations, cultural and regional differences, and clashing personalities, by 1914, theological unity (as well as racial integration) was but a memory. And by 1920, as noted earlier, the major doctrinal battles within pentecostalism were over. About even proportions of all trinitarian pentecostals in the United States identified with the second-work position on sanctification, on the one side, and with the finished-work view on the other. About a quarter of all pentecostals eventually joined the oneness faction in the matter of christology. These proportions have remained fairly constant since then.

In the decades following, white pentecostalism gradually built an (albeit shaky) alliance with fundamentalism—despite the latter's belittling attitude toward the movement. First, especially after the *Scofield Reference Bible* appeared in 1909, there was an increasing interest among Spirit-filled whites in the dispensational premillennialism promulgated by fundamentalists.[6] Later, then, after prominent white pentecostal denominations joined the National Association of Evangelicals in the early 1940s, they, too, began emphasizing the doctrine of biblical inerrancy, which was the hallmark of the NAE. Although literalism in the interpretation of the Bible characterized both white and black classical pentecostalism from the start, inerrancy—as a central point of dogma and test of faith—did not take root in the black segments of the movement.

Because of its distinctively white, middle-class, denominational origins, charismatic renewal theology emerged and, in the main,

---

6. The best works on dispensationalism as a doctrinal system are Charles Ryrie, *Dispensationalism Today* (Chicago: Moody Press, 1965), a favorable view; and Clarence B. Bass, *Backgrounds to Dispensationalism* (Grand Rapids, Mich.: Eerdmans, 1960), a critical assessment. On the diffusion of dispensational expectations in pentecostal theology, see Dwight Wilson, *Armageddon Now! The Premillenarian Response to Russia and Israel Since 1917* (Grand Rapids, Mich.: Baker Book House, 1977).

developed quite differently—combining *some* aspects of modern evangelical theology (the born-again experience and a "high" view of scriptural authority) with the various received traditions from the churches of the movement's leaders. Despite the fundamentalist leanings of a few of the nondenominational charismatic churches, and despite the rise of biblical inerrancy as a test of faith here and there, charismatic renewal has pursued a generally nonsectarian (and quite moderate) theological course. It has affirmed the authority of Scripture, the necessity of a personal commitment to Christ as Savior and Lord, and the mandate for evangelism, while rejecting fundamentalist cultural "excesses" and theological "extremes."[7] Although dispensational expectations are still widespread among neopentecostals, a number of prominent charismatic renewal leaders such as Howard Ervin, Josephine Ford, Donald Gelpi, Michael Harper, Edward O'Connor, Kevin and Dorothy Ranaghan, and J. Rodman Williams (as we have seen) have been quite firm in their disavowal of dispensationalism and most other fundamentalist tenets. Michael Harper summarizes the characteristic charismatic renewal stance on this key issue as follows:

> Pentecostalism in some people's minds is equated with a belief in the verbal inspiration of Scripture (usually the King James version only), a kind of proof textualism, whereby chapter and verse answers every question irrespective of context. It seems to require a belief in the pre-millennial view of the Second Coming, and an almost complete distrust in theology. . . . An unthinking old-fashioned fundamentalism will always be a hindrance to the forward surge of the Holy Spirit.[8]

WORSHIP

Influenced deeply by the black religious experience, worship in classical pentecostalism has been noted for its enthusiasm and

---

7. For a discussion of the specific differences between fundamentalism and evangelicalism, see Quebedeaux, *The Young Evangelicals*, pp. 1–45.

8. Michael Harper, "On to Maturity," *Renewal* (December 1972–January 1973), p. 34.

spontaneity (which includes the exercise of charismata), on the one hand, and its well-orchestrated "liturgical order"—built on the long tradition of slave religion and black spirituality as a whole—on the other hand (less so in Great Britain than in the United States, however, and increasingly less so with the passage of time and the greater upward mobility in pentecostal denominations).[9] This liturgical orchestration, however, was deliberately constructed to allow a great deal of congregational participation and to prohibit any "quenching" of the Spirit. "A pentecostal meeting where you know what is going to happen next is backslidden," Donald Gee declares.[10] Typical of a Church of God (Cleveland, Tennessee) service—until the late 1960s—for instance, might be the following:

> 7:40 P.M.—Our Annual Saturday Evening Testimony and Praise Service, V. R. Sherill in charge. Charles, Harper, Davis and Ted sang, "I Shall Ride on the Cloud." Brother Sherill called on the different sections in the balcony to praise the Lord, starting on one side and going all around. This ended in a shout of praise on the platform. The quartet sang, "I See the Lighthouse." The congregation stood and clapped hands. A march was started on the platform and continued on the main floor of the building. The blessings of the Lord were upon the people and they danced, shouted and rejoiced in the Lord. One clerk described the outpouring thus: "A march of victory is started on the large platform with leaping, shouting and praising the Lord. Now they move down and make their way through the shouting congregation. Such unity of the spirit I have never felt. The large congregation is aflame with the fire and power of the Holy Ghost and almost everyone is shouting. The large platform is quaking from the impact of hundreds of feet striking the surface as God continues to shower blessing after blessing upon His people. The people on the main floor testified by sections, one after the other. The praises rang out around the balconies again and then all praised the Lord together. At the close of this praise

---

9. See Bloch-Hoell, pp. 161–164.

10. Quoted in ibid., p. 161.

service, Clayton Sherill, his wife and Louise Sherill sang, 'I'm So Glad He Found Me.' "[11]

The progression of services of this kind followed certain oral liturgical "rules," characteristic of black revivalism more generally, where it still takes place. A quartet's singing leads to shouts of praise in the congregation, which the pastors orchestrate in different sections, concluded by those on the platform. Then another quartet sings, leading to yet another praise response, but this one (again with pastoral direction) is conducted with standing and clapping (often called a "clap offering"), during which a variety of shouts, prayers, and holy dance manifestations occur. Then the familiar "victory march" or "Jericho march" takes place, starting from the platform and moving around the tiers of pews. Subsequently, testimonies are given—section by section—followed by a final response of praise, and the typical concluding hymn, which can be used by the pastor in charge to cut off the praises and bring the meeting to a somber finale. The whole process, led by the pastors—but with significant congregational participation—follows repeated patterns of familiar conduct, and is in no way *purely* spontaneous or mere "emotionalism."[12] Like many other scholars, Walter Hollenweger associates this general form of worship with liberation from psychological stress caused by various kinds of deprivation.[13]

As late as 1966, Wade Horton, a Church of God (Cleveland, Tennessee) overseer, criticized the more middle-class charismatic renewal for subduing the classical pentecostal manner of enthusiastic worship. He spoke against the voice that

accepts the mechanical, quiet, sophisticated tongues speaking, but rejects the emotional, unspeakable joy, spiritually intoxicated, rushing-mighty-wind kind of Pentecostal experience. This group wants

11. Quoted in ibid., pp. 161–162.

12. Sheppard, "Commentary."

13. Hollenweger, *The Pentecostals*, pp. 53–59.

to be sure that the multitudes are not confounded and amazed at their actions, and most certainly that they are not accused of being drunk as were the first Pentecostal believers. They want to steer their ship clear of the Pentecostal pattern as recorded in Acts 2. This voice says, "I will accept glossolalia, but, please, not as the Pentecostals do."[14]

Neopentecostals, as we have seen, have always viewed the (non-middle-class) Africanisms, typical of traditional pentecostal worship and part of classical pentecostalism's "cultural baggage," as *not* essential to the pentecostal experience. They tend, rather, to stress "the quiet Spirit," in Kathryn Kuhlman's words, within formal services of worship. Although uplifted hands in prayer and being "slain in the Spirit" are generally permitted in such services —at appropriate times—most charismatic activity is relegated to small prayer groups of *believers* (and others seriously interested in Spirit baptism) so as not to "frighten" and deter middle-class newcomers attending worship. Furthermore, exercise of the spiritual gifts is always regulated according to white, middle-class liturgical rules (such as speaking in tongues only with interpretation, and one person at a time—although "unison prayer" in tongues does sometimes occur, anyway). Again, charismatic renewal has adopted the charismata to a framework of "ordered respectability" suitable for educated middle-class Christians who are members of the historic denominations. In 1964, Jean Stone suggested the following rules of conduct for glossolalia and related phenomena in a group context. Her words reflect the normative neopentecostal position today:

Speaking in tongues is not spooky; it's wholesome, good, clean, beautiful. We use no weird positions, no peculiar gymnastics. Don't add your own little goodies to it. If you make it sound peculiar, you'll scare people pea-green. I remember one pastor's wife moaned, and it scared my husband to death! Don't moan or shriek. Remember, the gift is to edify and shrieking isn't edifying. And

14. Wade H. Horton, "Introduction," in Wade H. Horton, ed., *The Glossolalia Phenomenon*, p. 17.

beware of personal prophecy, or prophecy about catastrophic happenings. If we seem too strange to outsiders, we're not going to get many outsiders to become insiders. You'll only attract desperate people. Don't develop separatist tendencies. Instead we are trying to save souls and be witnesses for Christ in what we say and in the way we live. And don't make the Bible a magical thing; be grounded in the Bible, but don't be a Bible thumper.[15]

ECCLESIASTICAL STANCE

With their new experience, the first classical pentecostals were not welcomed in their own "respectable" churches. Like the original new charismatics, the early pentecostals did *not* intend to form a new denomination, but rather, a nonsectarian movement that could unify Christians. The Azusa Street revival attracted a wide variety of people, including many from the historic churches. Because of external opposition and internal conflicts, however, classical pentecostalism did divide into new denominations, separating black from white, trinitarians from Jesus-only unitarians, gradualists from perfectionists, and all pentecostals from the Christian mainstream. But by the early 1940s, some influential pentecostal leaders began to question the isolationist stance their movement had taken during the preceding three decades. So, in 1943, a number of the major white pentecostal denominations in the United States joined the National Association of Evangelicals (NAE). The Pentecostal Fellowship of North America (PFNA) was then founded in 1948–1949, an umbrella organization that incorporated the NAE's doctrinal positions—including the affirmation of inerrancy —into its own stance. These two events set the course for the total accommodation of white American pentecostals (the trinitarians, at least) to evangelicalism by the late 1970s. (Black pentecostal denominations stayed out of both the NAE and the PFNA.)

At the same time, however, classical pentecostalism also began to move in a more generally intercultural and "ecumenical" direc-

---

15. Quoted in Dean, "Strange Tongues: A Psychologist Studies Glossolalia," *Trinity* (Trinitytide 1964), p. 39.

tion. In 1947, the first Pentecostal World Conference was held in Zurich. North American white pentecostals wanted this organization to align itself with evangelical doctrinal distinctives in the same manner the PFNA was destined to do, but they met stiff opposition from Scandinavian and other European delegates. Thus, the Pentecostal World Conferences have continued to assemble without doctrinal consensus, but, unlike the PFNA, *with* the participation of black pentecostal denominations.[16]

Then, in the early 1960s, a few South American pentecostal denominations took the "ultimate" step by becoming the first pentecostal churches to join the World Council of Churches (an action vigorously denounced by American pentecostals).[17] And since the advent of charismatic renewal in 1969, it has become increasingly difficult for classical pentecostals as a whole to continue separating themselves altogether from the historic denominations, many of which include large numbers of neopentecostals within their ranks who share the same experience.

As we have seen, when Dennis Bennett, the charismatic renewal pioneer, then rector of St. Mark's Episcopal Church, Van Nuys, California, was put under pressure to resign from his pastorate in 1960 as a result of his recent pentecostal experience, he told his parishioners that he was *not* leaving the Episcopal Church—that "no one needs to leave the Episcopal Church [or any other church] in order to have the fullness of the Spirit."[18] Among pentecostals, that nonsectarian position was at the time revolutionary and still prevails today in neopentecostalism.

As already noted, most charismatic renewal leaders understand the pentecostal experience as transcending denominational and ideological walls while it clarifies and underscores what is authentically Christian in each tradition without demanding structural or

---

16. Sheppard, "Commentary."

17. See Hollenweger, *The Pentecostals,* pp. 438–451. Also see Roberto Barbosa, "Bread and Gospel: Affirming a Total Faith—An Interview with Brazilian Pentecostal Manoel de Mello," *Christian Century* (December 25, 1974), pp. 1223–1226.

18. Quoted in Hollenweger, "Handbuch der Pfingstbewegung," p. 825 (02a.02.206); and Harper, *As at the Beginning,* p. 63.

even doctrinal changes in any church body. They are often friendly in their attitude toward the World Council of Churches, its regional counterparts, and other ecumenical structures. Furthermore, the Protestant-Catholic encounter within charismatic renewal has been so intense and heartfelt that it is probably unparalleled in contemporary ecclesiastical experience. Regardless of his theological outlook, the neopentecostal *must*—ideally, at least—develop a genuine openness to other Christians and the church as a whole.

The very unconcern in neopentecostalism about precise doctrinal formulations is, in its emergence and overall development, in contrast to most sects—and in some considerable contrast to traditional Western Christianity, which has been an intensely "intellectual" (in the sense of being concerned about intellectual distinctions) and doctrinally oriented religion. Charismatic renewal reflects other currents in our times in being reluctant to create boundaries or to establish firm and objective criteria. There is a powerful subjectivist element in it all.

MIND AND SPIRIT

Classical pentecostalism was born in the Bible school tradition among people with very little formal education. In the early years of the movement, training at pentecostal Bible schools was primarily training in piety—education geared to the study of the English Bible and literalist exposition of the text. But with the increasing middle-class nature of the major pentecostal denominations, more pentecostal young people were educated in the increasingly sophisticated pentecostal and nonpentecostal church-related colleges and in purely secular colleges and universities.[19] Also, some of the one-time "Bible institutes" (of the Assemblies of God, the Church of God [Cleveland, Tennessee], and the Pentecostal Holiness Church, for example) were gradually transformed into "respectable" liberal arts colleges.[20] Both the Assemblies of God and

---

19. See, for instance, Hollenweger, *The Pentecostals*, pp. 38–40.

20. For instance, Lee College (Church of God), Cleveland, Tennessee; Emmanuel

the Church of God (Cleveland, Tennessee) had established a graduate theological seminary by the early 1980s, following the example of ORU's graduate school of theology and the C. H. Mason Theological Seminary (Church of God in Christ), which preceded ORU.

In 1971, the Society for Pentecostal Studies was formed. This professional organization of scholars is open to anyone interested in the study of pentecostalism—with or without a faith commitment—and its leadership is dominated by classical pentecostal academics including Russell Spittler (Assemblies of God), Vinson Synan (Pentecostal Holiness Church), and Ithiel Clemmons (Church of God in Christ). Participant speakers at the 1973 meeting, already, included such academically respectable luminaries as Martin E. Marty of the University of Chicago, an eminent Lutheran church historian; Basil Meeking of the Vatican's Secretariat for Promoting Christian Unity; Edward O'Connor of Notre Dame University, the early Catholic pentecostal theoretician; Timothy L. Smith of the Johns Hopkins University, a Church of the Nazarene minister and noted American historian; and Thomas Zimmerman, long-time general superintendent of the Assemblies of God (U.S.A.).[21]

Despite the lack of formal higher education of a number of neopentecostal leaders (such as Oral Roberts, the late Kathryn Kuhlman, and Demos Shakarian), charismatic renewal tried to integrate Spirit baptism and modern intellectual pursuits from the very beginning, reflecting its middle-class origins. For example, neopentecostals always *emphasized* the academic background and respectability of their educated leaders.[22] Oral Roberts University

---

College (Pentecostal Holiness Church), Franklin Springs, Georgia; Central Bible College (Assemblies of God), Springfield, Missouri; and Southern California College (Assemblies of God), Costa Mesa, California.

21. James M. Beaty, "Society for Pentecostal Studies to Meet," *Church of God Evangel* (November 12, 1973), p. 11.

22. See, for instance, *Trinity* (Christmastide 1962–1963), pp. 2–17; Harold Bredesen, "Leaves from a Campus Diary," *Trinity* (Transfiguration 1963), pp. 6–9; and Jerry Jensen, "Charismata in the Twentieth Century," *Full Gospel Business Men's Voice* (June 1965), pp. 3–21.

(its somewhat revivalistic ethos notwithstanding) boasts exceptional facilities, a reputable faculty, and the world's most complete collection of pentecostal sources in its library, and has adopted the policy of "educating the whole person for a whole life—spirit, mind, body" (not the spirit alone, as in the early Bible school tradition).[23] Finally, in this connection, since Catholic pentecostalism experienced its initial thrust within the university ethos itself, we should not be surprised that the vast majority of the most sophisticated charismatic renewal literature has been written by participant Roman Catholics. Michael Harper's assertion that neopentecostalism is *not* "a movement of unthinking fools floating on a wave of emotional experience" is, in fact, justified. It never was.

CHRIST AND CULTURE

Classical pentecostalism shared with American fundamentalism and the preceding holiness movement a rejection of participation in the wider culture—"the world." Emphasizing to an almost gnostic degree the spiritual life over against "the desires of the flesh,"[24] classical pentecostalism imposed a kind of "holiness code" on its adherents—to promote "purity"—that prohibited the (even moderate) use of alcohol and tobacco in any form, social dancing, gambling and card playing, attendance at the theater and cinema, rock music, "immodest dress," and sometimes even "mixed bathing."[25] Legitimate recreation was to be provided by the church ("in the Spirit") and, really, nowhere else. (For recreation, pentecostal churches had picnics, camps, quilting circles, "singspirations," and shows featuring traveling ventriloquists,

---

23. See, for instance, Roberts, pp. 197–216; "ORU: New Charismatic University," *Acts* (July–August 1967), pp. 17–18; and *Oral Roberts University School of Theology 1981–83* (catalogue).

24. See Michael Harper, "Are You a Gnostic?" *Renewal* (October–November 1972), pp. 28–29.

25. See Hollenweger, *The Pentecostals,* pp. 399–410; and Quebedeaux, *The Young Evangelicals,* pp. 129–134.

magicians, and vaudeville entertainers, missionary films of head-hunters, and the like—in the characteristic style of revivalism.) But since this holiness code and the lifestyle it permitted were part of the nontransferable baggage of revivalism and have been traditionally followed only within those churches deeply rooted in revivalistic culture (such as Baptist and Methodist churches, and their offshoots, including classical pentecostal bodies), neopentecostal Catholics, Eastern Orthodox Christians, Anglicans, Lutherans, Presbyterians, and the like were often shocked when such taboos were introduced as binding *them* after their pentecostal experience. Given the presence within charismatic renewal of former classical pentecostals and others of the fundamentalist-revivalist tradition, and the numerous fellowship contacts between neopentecostals and classical pentecostals, the nontransferable baggage of classical pentecostalism piled up in charismatic renewal and was not easily sent away.[26] It was most difficult in the early years of the movement for a typical classical pentecostal (or Baptist neopentecostal, for instance) to accept as one who shares the same experience a Catholic pentecostal who drinks, smokes, dances, and gambles—although such acceptance has become common since the mid-1970s.[27]

Holiness is still an important concept in charismatic renewal circles. But the old classical pentecostal holiness code is usually shunned. And holiness itself has been reinterpreted as an attitude of the heart, having more to do with healthy relationships with people and "the life of discipleship" and less to do with what most new charismatics would regard as moral privatism and negativism —more with what you *do* than with what you don't do.

CONSTITUENCY

Classical pentecostalism began as a movement of the poor, the uneducated, the minorities, the disenfranchised, and the socially

---

26. Kilian McDonnell, "Catholic Pentecostalism: Problems in Evaluation," *Dialog* (Winter 1970), p. 41.

27. See Wead.

and economically deprived. To a large degree—but not universally —the same kinds of people have been attracted to it in recent times as well (hence, its special strength in the American South and Midwest among rural folk, in the West among "migrants" from the South, in black and Latin ghettos in urban centers, among women, and in the Third World, in Latin America and Africa especially).[28] Yet, Hollenweger points to the relatively large proportion of pentecostal pastors with middle-class and historic-denomination backgrounds—decades ago already.[29] Furthermore, like Gerlach and Hine, Hollenweger insists that attempts to understand the classical pentecostal tradition—white or black—as "an inferior culture, as the expression solely of social, intellectual and economic deprivation" are contradicted by the most recent sociological and psychological research.[30]

Charismatic renewal, however, has always been predominantly middle-class and white in nature. It first emerged in a fashionable suburban Episcopal church in Southern California. An early sampling of monthly prayer groups that gathered at Jean Stone's home in 1964 showed about equal numbers of men and women, an average age of 42 years, a median monthly income of $630 (with people earning in excess of $1,600 also present), a large proportion of men in the "professional and technical" occupational grouping and women in the "housewife" category, and Republicans outnumbering Democrats seven to one.[31] (This is all the more striking when we note that the 1981 equivalent of the aforementioned personal incomes is $1,900 and $4,800, respectively.)

Until neopentecostalism became a force within Roman Catholicism, the movement seemed very much in continuity with the assumptions of Anglo-Saxon Protestant traditions as they are

---

28. See Mead, Damboriena, Flora, Lalive d'Epinay, Tinney, Wagner, and Barrett.

29. Hollenweger, *The Pentecostals,* pp. 474–476.

30. See ibid., pp. 489–492.

31. Stanley C. Plog, "UCLA Conducts Research on Glossolalia," *Trinity* (Whitsuntide 1964), pp. 38–39.

stereotyped.[32] Even at the present time, charismatic renewal appears chiefly among the white, middle-class, suburban populations of the Western world—North America, Great Britain (including present and former Commonwealth countries such as [white] South Africa, New Zealand, and Australia), Germany, and Scandinavia. It is classical pentecostalism, rather, that is experiencing phenomenal growth in the underdeveloped Third World.[33]

This is an appropriate place to end this discussion of the comparative development of classical pentecostalism and charismatic renewal, because, as shown, the differences in the twentieth-century emergence and development of both movements have been largely a matter of class standing. Spirit baptism is a rite of passage, the moment of initiation, into "a new way of living." But that new way of life is always worked out differently according to cultural circumstances conditioned by class. Thus, even today, the black pentecostal maid who attends a storefront church in Watts will "live in the Spirit" in ways far different from those of a charismatic heiress who attends All Saints Episcopal Church in Beverly Hills. But they are both practitioners of the full gospel and will recognize each other as such.

---

32. See Dean, "Strange Tongues: A Psychologist Studies Glossolalia," *Trinity* (Trinitytide 1964), pp. 37–39.

33. This chapter is largely a revision of my article, "The Old Pentecostalism and the New Pentecostalism," *Theology, News and Notes* (March 1974), pp. 6–8, 23. A number of differences between classical pentecostalism and charismatic renewal have also been suggested by Erling Jorstad, ed., *The Holy Spirit in Today's Church: A Handbook of the New Pentecostalism* (New York: Abingdon, 1973), pp. 22–23; and John Koenig, *Charismata* (Philadelphia: Westminster Press, 1978), pp. 167–183.

Chapter Seven

From Opposition

to Acceptance

There are a number of reasons why the pentecostal experience has tended to raise opposition. First, popular ideas of psychology lead to suspicion when any kind of pressure is put on people. Thus, when a "second encounter with God" is encouraged, fear is raised that feelings of inadequacy or deprivation will be caused without justification. Second, it is argued that the pentecostal experience disturbs the life of the church by creating a schismatic group, while the established leaders or members of a given congregation are often unwilling to concede that their own doctrine or experience is lacking in anything. Hence, the latter reject the new teaching, and the former group must either deny or "cover up" its experience or leave the church. Third, the intellectual climate of even the most "orthodox" church may encourage coldness and reject "irrational enthusiasm." The "new thing" is seemingly unmanageable, and that which may appear "supernatural" within it is reduced to whatever categories are at hand to explain it. These categories may include mental imbalance, heresy, or that such things cannot happen now (a favorite fundamentalist argument). Fourth, the churches from which (classical) pentecostalism originally emerged, as well as those which have been most bitter in their opposition to the pentecostal experience, have frequently been those which *emphasize* what they feel to be the "biblical" foundation of their doctrine and practice. This is the very charter that validates their existence. Thus, when pentecostals claim their *own* practice as the biblical pattern, it is an obvious challenge to the former (commonly fundamentalist and holiness) groups and churches. Finally, among some theological liberals (and skeptics)— not fundamentalists and evangelicals here—one finds offense that "in this modern age" even theologically educated individuals can still "take the Bible in that way" and gain public notoriety by so doing.[1]

EARLY OPPOSITION WITHIN HISTORIC DENOMINATIONS

Shortly after Dennis Bennett's forced resignation as rector of St. Mark's Episcopal Church (reported by *Newsweek,* July 4, 1960, and by *Time,* August 15, 1960), opposition within affected denominational hierarchies became apparent. Francis Bloy, then Episcopal bishop of Los Angeles, immediately banned any more speaking in tongues under church auspices.[2] In 1962 and 1963, various rather negative reports on glossolalia were prepared and circulated within the American Lutheran Church (ALC);[3] and in July 1964, Herbert Mjorud was dismissed from the ALC's denominational staff for promoting speaking in tongues.[4] Also, Everett Palmer, then Methodist bishop of the Seattle area (where Bennett had moved), called glossolalia "a perversion."[5] Such initial reactions all manifested a basic unhappiness with the appearance of the phenomenon within the churches in question. Furthermore, in the early years of charismatic renewal all negative appraisals seemed to identify pentecostalism with tongues and divine healing alone.

---

1. Greg S. Forster, "The Third Arm 2," *TSF Bulletin* (London) (Autumn 1972), pp. 19–20.

2. Harper, *As at the Beginning,* p. 56.

3. See Kilian McDonnell, "Catholic Pentecostalism: Problems in Evaluation," *Dialog* (Winter 1970), p. 52n.

4. "Taming the Tongues," *Time* (July 10, 1964), pp. 64, 66.

5. Bess, p. 173.

The late Bishop James Pike's Easter 1963 pastoral letter to the Episcopal diocese of California is the most negative of the early documents on the matter.[6] He says, in part,

> while there is no inhibition whatsoever as to devotional use of speaking with tongues, I urge that there be no services or meetings in our Churches or in homes or elsewhere for which the expression or promotion of this activity is the purpose or of which it is a part. Nor do I believe that our clergy should lead or take part in such gatherings under whatever auspices.[7]

None of the early reports *categorically* condemns the pentecostal experience (Anglicanism, of course, has a rich tradition of both divine healing and exorcism), although the formulators of these documents were profoundly disturbed by the confusion and division that seemed to attend the appearance of pentecostalism in their denominations. This concern was clearly not dictated *merely* by a reluctance to accept what was strange and new. Charismatic renewal did pose serious pastoral problems, not the least of which was the tendency of the early neopentecostals to take over uncritically the cultural practices, exegesis, and doctrine from classical pentecostalism rather than integrating the experience into their own theological traditions.[8]

With respect to the distinctively fundamentalist and evangelical denominations, opposition was initially firm (though not well formulated, and rarely published) and still continues today. This fact caused David du Plessis to remark, "I shall not be surprised when our fundamentalist friends who attack the Pentecostals as severely as they do the World Council [of Churches], begin to

---

6. On the background of Pike's pastoral letter, see *Trinity* (Transfiguration 1963), pp. 28–37. The center of pentecostal phenomena in Pike's diocese was (at that time) Holy Innocents Parish, Corte Madera, California. Its rector, Todd Ewald, an Anglo-Catholic, was a leader in charismatic renewal. He is discussed in the sources cited in Notes 5 and 6.

7. Quoted in Kilian McDonnell, "Catholic Pentecostalism: Problems in Evaluation," *Dialog* (Winter 1970), p. 52.

8. Ibid.

'expose' the Pentecostal trend within the ranks of the Ecumenical Movement."[9]

In Great Britain, however, opposition to charismatic renewal from within the historic denominations was never so strong as it was in the United States. By the time the pentecostal experience had emerged in the Church of England (and later, in the Free Churches), it no longer was a "shocking" phenomenon on the world scene. The Anglican hierarchy seemed relatively open from the beginning, while both Evangelical and Anglo-Catholic clergy became participants in the pentecostal movement without undue criticism or threats from their superiors.[10]

GRADUAL ACCEPTANCE BY ECCLESIASTICAL AUTHORITIES

In the course of the 1960s and 1970s, most of the historic denominations gradually made peace with the growing pentecostal movement within their own ranks. In 1960, the Los Angeles Episcopal diocese was the first church body to issue an official statement on charismatic renewal. Other Episcopal bodies soon did likewise. In 1962, both the American Lutheran Church and the newly organized Lutheran Church in America took a stance, followed in later years by Presbyterians,[11] Roman Catholics, Nazarenes, Baptists, United Methodists, the United Church of Christ,[12] and others.

The U.S. experience was soon paralleled in other countries. In Canada, statements on neopentecostalism were issued by Presby-

---

9. Du Plessis, *The Spirit Bade Me Go*, p. 27.

10. See *Trinity* (Whitsuntide 1964), pp. 26–31; and *Trinity* (Trinitytide 1964), pp. 28–29, 32–33.

11. *The Work of the Holy Spirit* (Philadelphia: United Presbyterian Church, U.S.A., 1970) was the first in-depth denominational assessment, and still one of the best.

12. *The Life of the Spirit in the Life of the Church* (New York: United Church of Christ Office for Church Life and Leadership, 1975) is also an important denominational evaluation, especially since the UCC is the most "liberal" Christian denomination in the United States.

terians, Roman Catholics, and the United Church of Canada. In the British Isles, Presbyterians, Methodists, the United Reformed Church, Anglicans, and Baptists made pronouncements, as did Lutherans and Catholics in Germany, the Reformed Church in Holland, Roman Catholics in Belgium, and the Evangelical Brethren in Czechoslovakia. In the South Pacific, statements were made by Presbyterians, Baptists, Methodists, and Anglicans, and in Australia by Anglicans, Methodists, Presbyterians, and Roman Catholics. In Africa, a few evaluations came out of Ghana, South Africa, and Ethiopia. In Latin America, besides two joint statements issued by Roman Catholic bishops, there were seven others by national or regional synods of bishops. Pronouncements of a more international scope came from Pope Paul VI, the Lambeth (Anglican) Conference, the Baptist World Alliance, the World Council of Churches, and Pope John Paul II during the 1970s and early 1980s.

The first Episcopal reports focused on glossolalia, and the Lutheran ones on faith healing. From then on, however, there was a progressively firmer realization that these were only superficial manifestations of a movement that was much richer and deeper. Likewise, the earlier documents tend to be more apprehensive and critical of charismatic renewal, while the later ones are more open and affirmative in their appraisal.

The most striking feature of all this literature published over the last two decades is the similarity of concerns, attitudes, and policies that run through most of the church documents, regardless of source. There is a pervasive insistence that Spirit baptism not be separated from baptism in water; that the work of the Holy Spirit in the individual cannot be separated from that which occurs in the church; that the "ordinary" fruits of the Spirit—such as love, joy, and peace—are more important than the "extraordinary" charismata such as speaking in tongues and divine healing.

One prominent question about which opinions differed markedly is whether the "spectacular" spiritual gifts were meant only for the Apostolic era or were intended to remain permanently in the church. Many Catholics recalled the teaching of Vatican II that discernment of charismata pertains chiefly to the bishops. Some Lutherans insisted that the Holy Spirit works only through the means of grace—the Word and the sacraments. And a number of Baptists were concerned that the authority structures of some charismatic communities tended to be at odds with the congregational polity of their own churches. But one has to look attentively to find any characteristically denominational divergences.

Although a few conservative denominations (notably the Missouri Synod Lutherans and the Southern Baptists) pronounced an unqualified no to the pentecostal experience, the great majority of ecclesiastical authorities have by now taken a tolerant and accepting stance on the issue. Although acknowledging the values of the neopentecostal movement, they have warned against its aberrations and offer guidelines to enable charismatic groups to fit harmoniously into their own churches. The dangers pointed out are pretty much the same throughout the literature—"emotionalism," subjectivism, spiritual pride, divisiveness, and minimalization of the institutional church. Likewise, however, the benefits seen in charismatic renewal are everywhere similar—bringing back warmth and vitality to religious life, fostering prayer and the study of Scripture, and producing a greater awareness of the presence and work of the Holy Spirit.

It was a Catholic, Kilian McDonnell, who coined the term "classical pentecostalism" as a symbol of respect for the traditional pentecostal movement. He is also the editor of a three-volume work, *Presence, Power, Praise,* published in 1981, which includes almost all of these denominational statements. Each entry is preceded by a brief introduction giving its historical background and a summary of the contents, while a general introduction sums up the main themes of the entire international collection. (McDonnell also includes the interesting exchange of letters that brought visibility to the shepherding controversy among pentecostal leaders.)

Reasons why the historic denominations have moved from opposition to acceptance of neopentecostalism are easily discerned. First, these denominations now know that the pentecostal experience is not *inherently* schismatic (nor psychologically damaging), and instead quite often tends to *increase* a person's commitment to his or her church. Second, they are convinced that, by and large, neopentecostals today have rejected the nontransferable "cultural baggage" (and doctrinal adiaphora) of classical pentecostalism. Third, the historic denominations found it impossible to effectively suppress a movement that embraces as many individuals as have been present in charismatic renewal. Finally, they have had to listen to the voices of an ever-larger number of their own theologians and other leaders who have spoken publicly in approval of the pentecostal experience and of the pentecostal movement more generally.

CHANGING ATTITUDES

Leaders of the historic denominations began to take positive notice of the pentecostal movement by the early 1950s. It is probable that this new recognition was at least partly the result of David du Plessis's contacts with the ecumenical movement since 1951.[13] Out of these contacts, du Plessis became a personal friend of John Mackay, one-time Presbyterian missionary to Latin America (where pentecostalism had already been experiencing dramatic growth), prominent ecumenical leader, and former president of Princeton Theological Seminary. This friendship developed to the point where Mackay invited du Plessis to attend the eighteenth Council of the Presbyterian World Alliance, meeting in São Paulo, Brazil, during 1959, and to give the regularly scheduled missions lectures at Princeton Seminary that same year.[14] As president of the council, John Mackay introduced the pentecostal leader to the assembly with the following words:

Whatever else history may have to say about our friend, this fact will surely be recorded. This is the first confessional body that has

---

13. See du Plessis, *The Spirit Bade Me Go* and *A Man Called Mr. Pentecost.*
14. Reprinted in ibid., pp. 35–60.

extended recognition to the Pentecostal Movement as a sound Christian Body. The records will also show that Princeton Seminary was the first institution to recognize this by inviting our friend as missions lecturer.[15]

The Presbyterian leader seems to have been impressed by pentecostalism chiefly because of its unabated growth throughout the world, and its intense spirituality. Hence, he states (referring to the pentecostals),

> Never . . . be afraid of a young fanatic or what appears to be a fanatical movement, if Jesus Christ is the supreme object of devotion. On the other hand I am terribly afraid of a cold, frigid, professionally-aired Christianity which is interested only in form. The young fanatic, if wisely dealt with, can be toned down and mellowed. However, nothing short of the sepulcher awaits those who identify conventional order and aesthetic devotion with spiritual life.[16]

In 1954 (in *The Household of God*), Lesslie Newbigin, then a bishop of the Church of South India, and later associate general secretary of the World Council of Churches, described pentecostalism as a *third* stream in contemporary Christianity— with Protestantism (emphasizing faith) and Catholicism (stressing order).[17] He suggested that pentecostalism, with its emphasis on experience and the Holy Spirit (doctrinally central to the ecumenical movement), is needed, therefore, to supplement the Protestant-Catholic ecumenical debate. In this connection, Newbigin declared,

> May it not be that the great Churches of the Catholic and Protestant traditions will have to be humble enough to receive it [that is, illumination] in fellowship with their brethren in various groups of

---

15. Quoted in ibid., p. 19.

16. Quoted in Donald Gee, *All with One Accord* (Springfield, Mo.: Gospel Publishing, 1961), pp. 9–10.

17. See Newbigin, pp. 94–122.

the Pentecostal type with whom at present they have scarcely any Christian fellowship at all?[18]

Another very positive assessment of the pentecostal movement was voiced in 1958 by Henry P. Van Dusen, a liberal Presbyterian, then president of Union Theological Seminary, and chairman of the Joint Committee of the World Council of Churches and the International Missionary Council. In an article in *Life* magazine (June 9, 1958), Van Dusen (like Newbigin) referred to pentecostalism as a "Third Force" in modern Christianity (though he also includes other distinctively fundamentalist and evangelical churches). And like Mackay, he was impressed by the Third Force's growth, deep spirituality, and sense of commitment:

> Its groups preach a direct biblical message readily understood. They commonly promise an immediate, life-transforming experience of the living God-in-Christ. . . . They directly approach people . . . anywhere—and do not wait for them to come to church. They have great spiritual ardor. . . . They shepherd their converts in an intimate, sustaining group-fellowship. . . . They place strong emphasis on the Holy Spirit . . . as the immediate potent presence of God. . . . Above all, they expect their followers to practice an active, untiring, seven-day-a-week Christianity. . . . Until lately, other Protestants regarded the movement as a temporary and passing phenomenon, not worth much attention. Now there is a growing, serious recognition of its true dimensions and probable permanence. The tendency to dismiss its Christian message as inadequate is being replaced by a chastened readiness to investigate the secrets of its mighty sweep, especially to learn if it may have importantly neglected elements in full and true Christian witness.[19]

By the end of the 1950s, it was clear that the ecumenical movement and some of its most prominent leaders had begun to take the pentecostal movement seriously as a *legitimate* Christian expression. This new positive attitude toward what is now classi-

---

18. Newbigin, p. 122.

19. Van Dusen, pp. 122, 124.

cal pentecostalism was extended toward charismatic renewal in the course of its development during the 1960s and 1970s, to the point where Krister Stendahl, then dean of Harvard Divinity School, said in his 1972 address to the Society for Pentecostal Studies,

> The "flashlight church" does not have enough to offer. The high-voltage religious experience is a breakthrough phenomenon because it is needed. If churches are not open to an infusion of high voltage, they are in real trouble. . . .
>
> God is upping the voltage in many places. He knows that it could be dangerous but he knows that it is needed, and that is the new Pentecostalism.[20]

Slower to respond were leaders of the distinctively evangelical community who, theologically, were closer to the pentecostals than were mainline ecumenical liberals. Among the first important evangelical voices to speak positively of classical pentecostalism and, later, charismatic renewal was *Eternity* magazine, published in Philadelphia. In 1958, *Eternity*'s founding editor, Donald Grey Barnhouse, announced in a major article in the journal that its editors had found themselves in "95 percent agreement" with the leaders of the Assemblies of God.[21] Later, in 1963, Russell Hitt, Barnhouse's successor, wrote a somewhat critical but still open article on neopentecostalism.[22] Then, in 1973, an unsigned editorial in *Eternity* put forward a very affirmative position on the charismata:

> More and more evangelical scholars today feel that the traditional, supposed biblical arguments for the cessation of the gifts after com-

---

20. Quoted in "High Voltage Religion," *Melodyland Messenger* (January 1973), p. 2. See also Rex Davis, "The Charismatic Renewal: Impressions from a World Survey," *Study Encounter,* 11, no. 4 (1975), 1–13.

21. Donald Grey Barnhouse, "Finding Fellowship with Pentecostals," *Eternity* (April 1958), pp. 8–10.

22. Russell T. Hitt, "The New Pentecostalism," reprinted from *Eternity* in *Trinity* (Trinitytide 1963), pp. 24–27. See also the Blessed Trinity Society's response to this article: Jean Stone and Herald Bredesen, "The Charismatic Movement in the Historical Churches," *Trinity* (Trinitytide 1963), pp. 28–35.

pletion of the New Testament, cannot be sustained by the Holy Scriptures.

The new stress is on the church as the body of Christ with its various members endowed by the Spirit with differing gifts. The gifts are 'apportioned to each of us as the Spirit chooses' (1 Cor. 12:11, Goodspeed). And who would rule out tongues as one of these gifts? Certainly Paul didn't.[23]

After a visit to California with Jean Stone in early 1962, Philip Hughes, a Church of England clergyman and then editor of the evangelical quarterly *The Churchman* (and a contributing editor to *Christianity Today*), had high praise for the emerging charismatic renewal. In an editorial in *The Churchman* later that year, Hughes made the following comments about neopentecostalism:

> It is transforming lives. It is revitalizing congregations. It is not confined to one church or to one district. Nor is it induced from without, but has the appearance of being a spontaneous movement of the Holy Spirit. Your Editor met with individuals and groups whose lives had been affected by it. He attended their prayer meetings and worshipped with them, and visited the homes of some. He heard them praying in an unknown tongue. It was all restrained and calm, and immediately someone else would interpret what had been said. . . . Much more impressive than the glossolalia were the love, the joy, the devotion, which flowed out from their lips and their lives—and their consciousness of spiritual power. . . .
>
> It is a movement, moreover, within the heart of the Church, not away from the Church.[24]

Even *Christianity Today*, evangelicalism's most influential periodical, by 1969, urged a tolerant attitude by churches toward Christians who speak in tongues.[25]

Besides liberal Protestants and Anglicans and conservative evan-

---

23. "Tongues: Updating Some Old Issues" (editorial), *Eternity* (March 1973), p. 8.

24. Philip E. Hughes, "From England, an Editorial," *Trinity* (Christmastide 1962–1963), pp. 20–22 (reprinted from *The Churchman* [September 1962]).

25. "The Gift of Tongues" (editorial), *Christianity Today* (April 11, 1969), pp. 27–28.

gelical leaders, numerous prominent Roman Catholic scholars and church officials began expressing their general approval of the pentecostal movement. Kilian McDonnell, president of the Institute for Ecumenical and Cultural Research, Collegeville, Minnesota, now himself a charismatic, was one of the first Catholics to conduct systematic research into the movement, and he wrote the most important early Catholic assessments of it in *Worship*,[26] *Journal of Ecumenical Studies*,[27] *Commonweal*,[28] *Dialog*,[29] and elsewhere. Bishop Emmett Carter of London, Ontario, Canada,[30] and Archbishop Philip Hannan of New Orleans,[31] (among other bishops) also praised charismatic renewal in the early 1970s. And Léon Joseph Cardinal Suenens, archbishop of Malines-Brussels, himself now a participant as well, spoke at the 1973 charismatic renewal conference at Notre Dame University, and gave his very enthusiastic endorsement to the movement, declaring, "In the name of the Church we thank you, for the future of the Church is coming out of this."[32]

But *some* prominent fundamentalist and evangelical thinkers remained quite negative about charismatic renewal and the pentecostal experience. Dispensational fundamentalists generally insist that the charismata disappeared at the close of the Apostolic era.[33]

---

26. Kilian McDonnell, "The Ecumenical Significance of the Pentecostal Movement," *Worship* (December 1966), pp. 608–629, and "New Dimensions in Research on Pentecostalism," *Worship* (April 1971), pp. 214–219.

27. Kilian McDonnell, "The Ideology of Pentecostal Conversion," *Journal of Ecumenical Studies* (Winter 1968), pp. 105–126.

28. Kilian McDonnell, "Holy Spirit and Pentecostalism," *Commonweal* (November 8, 1968), pp. 198–204.

29. McDonnell, "Catholic Pentecostalism: Problems in Evaluation," pp. 35–54.

30. G. Emmett Carter, "The Pentecostal Renewal in the Catholic Church," *Testimony* (First Quarter 1972), p. 1.

31. Philip M. Hannan, "We Thank God for the Charismatic Renewal!" *Testimony* (First Quarter 1972), pp. 2–3.

32. Quoted in Haughey, p. 551.

33. This is somewhat ironic, because most white classical pentecostals are, in fact, dispensational fundamentalists.

Typical of this position is J. Vernon McGee's argument. McGee, pastor emeritus of the independent Church of the Open Door, in Los Angeles, has been one of America's foremost dispensational fundamentalist spokesmen. He says,

> We have seen the importance of sign gifts [that is, "supernatural" *charismata*] at the beginning of the transitional period [between the dispensations of law and grace]. But these gifts disappeared. You may say to me, 'Are you sure they disappeared?' I want to say to you categorically and emphatically, that the sign gifts disappeared and the Scriptures said they would [citing 1 Corinthians 13].[34]

This position led to the charge commonly made by nonpentecostal dispensational fundamentalists and their kin since the advent of pentecostalism in 1901 that modern "charismatic manifestations" are, in fact, counterfeits—"Satanic," even.

As recently as 1978, John MacArthur, Jr., put forward ten problems—as he saw them—that made charismatic renewal incompatible with fundamentalism and much of conservative evangelicalism:

1. *The issue of revelation.* Charismatics claim that God is giving them the new revelation as they prophesy under the inspiration of the Spirit.
2. *The issue of interpretation.* Growing out of their approach to "new revelation," charismatics get strange meanings out of Scripture with an *ad lib* "this-is-what-it-means-to-me" approach.
3. *The issue of authority.* The charismatic emphasis on experience relegates Scripture to a secondary status of authority.
4. *The issue of Apostolic uniqueness.* Charismatics insist that the miraculous manifestations of the first century should be normative for today.
5. *The issue of historic transition.* Charismatic interpretation of Acts 2, 8, 10, and 19 uses specially selected historical events to build a theology of the Holy Spirit.

---

34. Quoted in Howard Ervin, *And Forbid Not to Speak with Tongues,* rev. ed. (Plainfield, N.J.: Logos International, 1971), p. 26.

6. *The issue of spiritual gifts.* Today's charismatics run a course perilously close to the church at Corinth, where spiritual gifts were counterfeited and practicers of pagan ecstasies ran amok.

7. *The issue of Spirit baptism.* Charismatics insist that every believer needs a second work of grace called "the baptism of the Holy Spirit."

8. *The issue of healing.* Charismatics confuse the biblical doctrine of healing by insisting that the gift of healing is still in use today.

9. *The issue of tongues.* Charismatics claim that the ecstatic prayer language practices in private is the same kind of tongues described in Scripture.

10. *The issue of spirituality.* True spirituality, say the charismatics, can be ours through the baptism of the Spirit; but Scripture teaches us to "walk in the Spirit," who already dwells in every Christian.[35]

Such a negative evaluation, however, has more to do with differences in biblical interpretation than it does with the fundamentalist versus charismatic view of scriptural authority per se. Christian churches still grounded in the principle of Scripture alone as the absolute rule of faith and conduct often declare that charismatic renewal is not in keeping with their tradition, but they cannot find a *convincing* scriptural argument for their opposition—only postbiblical interpretations now increasingly unacceptable among exegetical scholars.

Less severe, but still negative, in his criticism of the pentecostal experience was John R. W. Stott. In his widely circulated study, *The Baptism and Fullness of the Holy Spirit,* Stott did exegesis of relevant New Testament passages pertaining to Spirit baptism, and *separated* this experience of all Christians—identified with conversion—from the variety of spiritual gifts given by God to his people (including, in some instances, tongues). He concluded his 1964 essay by saying,

---

35. John MacArthur, Jr., *The Charismatics* (Grand Rapids, Mich.: Zondervan, 1978), pp. 199–200.

It is spiritual *graces* which should be common to all Christians, not spiritual *gifts* or spiritual *experiences*. The gifts of the Spirit are distributed among different Christians (1 Cor. 12); it is the fruit of the Spirit which should characterize all. . . . "I would appeal to you not to urge upon people a baptism with the Spirit as a second and subsequent experience entirely distinct from conversion, for this cannot be proved from Scripture.[36]

Nevertheless, as we have already seen, Stott took a much more accommodating stance on the matter by 1977.

Finally, Francis Schaeffer, another prominent evangelical writer (in *The New Super-Spirituality*), also puts forward a lingering negative assessment of neopentecostalism on the basis of what he feels is its weakened doctrinal commitment—its emphasis on "external signs" instead of theological "content"—and its "spiritual elitism." Schaeffer thinks that one reason why some theological liberals find charismatic renewal attractive is the fact that experience ("feeling") functions as the central "doctrine" of both pentecostalism (less so in classical pentecostalism than in neopentecostalism) and liberalism (with its roots in Schleiermacher, and later in existentialism). He declares,

One can . . . see a parallel between the new Pentecostals and the liberals. The liberal theologians don't believe in content or religious truth. They are really existentialists using theological, Christian terminology. Consequently, not believing in truth, they can enter into fellowship with any other experience-oriented group using religious language.[37]

---

36. Stott, p. 59.

37. Francis A. Schaeffer, *The New Super-Spirituality* (Downers Grove, Ill.: Inter-Varsity Press, 1972), p. 16. Two early attempts by evangelicals to "make peace" with pentecostals are Michael Griffiths, *Three Men Filled with the Spirit* (London: Overseas Missionary Fellowship, 1969); and Peter E. Gillquist, *Let's Quit Fighting About the Holy Spirit* (Grand Rapids, Mich.: Zondervan, 1974). See also the lighthearted, but serious, evangelical liberal critique, "Charismatics," *Wittenburg Door* (October–November 1980), pp. 1–32; and the radical evangelical assessment, "Charismatic Renewal," *PostAmerican* (now *Sojourners*) (February 1975), pp. 1–31.

REACTIONS FROM CLASSICAL PENTECOSTALISM

Since the initial emergence of charismatic renewal, classical pentecostals and neopentecostals have, in fact, enjoyed fellowship together and have had mutual "working relationships." Both participate in the Full Gospel Business Men's Fellowship International and in more localized ministries. Neopentecostals and classical pentecostals teach at Oral Roberts University, participate together in the Society for Pentecostal Studies, and both have been members of the official dialogues between pentecostals and the Vatican's Secretariat for Promoting Christian Unity. Furthermore, as already noted, with upward mobility classical pentecostalism has already lost many of its sectarian characteristics, and for that reason has moved closer to neopentecostalism. Protestant and Catholic neopentecostals often worship regularly in classical pentecostal churches (in addition to their own)—and, sometimes, vice versa. Many classical pentecostal congregations, moreover, without forsaking denominational identity, have gone so far as to remove the denominational title from their local church name, replacing it with a name that would appeal to a wider spectrum of people (e.g., Christian Center [after Melodyland], Christian Life Church, and The Church on the Way).[38] Such a change in name usually has been preceded by a distinct modification of worship style approximating that of charismatic renewal.

Already in 1961, Donald Gee, the British Assemblies of God leader, welcomed the fellowship of neopentecostals. Writing in *Pentecost,* he said,

> We are thrilled at what God is doing these days in bringing so many hundreds of our fellow-believers in the older denominations into Pentecostal blessing. This grace is being bestowed conspicuously, though by no means exclusively, among our friends of the Anglican Communion. They are speaking with new tongues as the Spirit gives them utterance, even as we. Let us unitedly worship God for this and other manifestations of His Spirit.[39]

---

38. See Jack W. Hayford, "The Church on the Way," *Logos Journal* (March–April 1972), pp. 20–22, 39.

39. Donald Gee, "To Our New Pentecostal Friends," *Pentecost* (December 1961–February 1962), back cover.

But American Assemblies of God leaders were not so quick to approve charismatic renewal. Both David du Plessis and Ralph Wilkerson lost their ministerial status in and were "disfellowshiped" by the denomination for their ecumenical activities. Yet, already by 1963, officials of the Assemblies of God and the Episcopal Church (which at that time, perhaps, embraced more neopentecostals than any other denomination) were already meeting together to "learn from each other about Christian faith and life." The church executives of both denominations indicated "a mutual recognition that we were servants of the same Father, the same Son and the same Holy Spirit. We are eagerly waiting to be led by the Spirit and believe that He will lead us as we continue our conversation together."[40] Then, in 1972, the executive presbytery of the Assemblies of God (U.S.A.) *endorsed* charismatic renewal (in principle, at least), wishing "to identify with what God is doing in the world today."[41] Finally, in 1980, du Plessis's ministerial credentials in the denomination were given back to him.

Nevertheless, until the mid-1970s, there remained much suspicion on the part of white classical pentecostals toward neopentecostalism. Ray Hughes, former general overseer of the Church of God (Cleveland, Tennessee) was one of charismatic renewal's severest critics from the classical pentecostal side (especially with respect to nonevangelicals and Roman Catholics who claimed the pentecostal experience). Hughes questioned basic neopentecostal theology and moral purity for (1) emphasizing an experience without major attention to belief and doctrine; (2) denying that speaking in tongues is a *normative* experience integrally linked to Spirit baptism; (3) affirming that glossolalia is enough to unite people of very different theologies (for example, evangelicals with Protestant and Anglican liberals, and Roman Catholics); (4) allowing such practices as social dancing, drinking, and smoking ("A body controlled by lust and sinful habits certainly could not be inhabited by

---

40. Quoted in "Episcopal and Pentecostal Leaders Confer," *Pentecost* (March–May 1963), p. 8.

41. See "American Assemblies of God Welcome Charismatic Movement," *Renewal* (December 1972–January 1973), p. 8.

the Holy Ghost"); and (5) regarding "separate" prayer meetings apart from formal services of worship as sufficient for corporate expression of spiritual gifts.[42]

Black pentecostals share another kind of critique of charismatic renewal. Scholars such as James Tinney, James Forbes, Ithiel Clemmons, and Gerald T. Sheppard have repeatedly been critical of the "whiteness" of the movement, its middle-class comfortableness, and its consequent apathy toward the concrete needs of the poor and the sin of racism. They argue that any brand of flamboyant Christian spirituality without a truly New Testament "logos" —one that demands a *sacrificial* response to the suffering of others —is itself only "marginally" Christian. In their opinion, William Seymour's original vision of the pentecostal experience as an eschatological event, signaling, among other things, the end of racism by a full implementation of the gospel message—empowered by the Spirit—has most often been missing in the development of neopentecostalism. Praying together, however often, these scholars insist, is not the same thing as really "fleshing out" the close kinship of humankind in a world still characterized by prejudice and injustice.

Although Ray Hughes did speak for the majority of the older generation of white classical pentecostal critics of charismatic renewal as late as 1974, that criticism (and that raised by leaders of the historic denominations and by nonpentecostal evangelicals) has waned dramatically since then. Opposition to neopentecostalism within white, middle-class church circles continues to turn into acceptance, if not outright approval.

---

42. Ray H. Hughes, "A Traditional Pentecostal Looks at the New Pentecostalism," *Christianity Today* (June 7, 1974), pp. 6–10. See also Bennie S. Triplett, *A Contemporary Study of the Holy Spirit* (Cleveland, Tenn.: Pathway Press, 1970), pp. 111–137.

Chapter Eight

The Reasons

for Success

I have already considered Gerlach and Hine's proposal of five factors crucial to the growth and spread of a modern religious movement:

1. Reticulate *organization* [that is, a weblike network]
2. Fervent and convincing *recruitment* along preexisting lines of significant social relationships
3. A *commitment* act or experience
4. A change-oriented and action-motivating ideology that offers (a) a simple master plan presented in symbolic and easily communicated terms, (b) a sense of sharing in the control and rewards of destiny, (c) a feeling of personal worth and power
5. The perception of real or imagined *opposition*.[1]

As these anthropologists have shown, the factors necessary for the rise and diffusion of a modern religious movement apply well to the pentecostal movement as a whole.[2] But a number of other reasons can be suggested for the emergence and success of neopentecostalism in particular.

1. Gerlach and Hine, "Five Factors Crucial to the Growth and Spread of a Modern Religious Movement," pp. 23–24.

2. See Gerlach and Hine, *People, Power, Change.*

THE ECUMENICAL MOVEMENT

"Unity in the Spirit" has become a central theological motif within the ecumenical movement. On the Protestant (and Anglican) side of that movement, a new emphasis upon the doctrine of the Holy Spirit was signaled by the appearance of Lesslie Newbigin's book *The Household of God* in 1954, in which, as we noted earlier, he maintained that Catholicism and Protestantism had been engaged in an "incomplete dialogue"—lacking the "Holy Spirit" aspect of theology, which is crucial to Christian unity. To remedy this incompleteness, Newbigin suggested conversations with a "third stream" of Christian tradition—the pentecostal—whose central theological element is

> the conviction that the Christian life is a matter of *the experienced power and presence of the Holy Spirit today* [emphasis mine]; that neither orthodoxy of doctrine nor impeccability of succession can take the place of this; that an excessive emphasis upon those immutable elements in the Gospel upon which orthodox Catholicism and Protestantism have concentrated attention, may, and in fact often does, result in a Church which is a mere shell, having the form of a Church but not the life; that if we would answer the question "Where is the Church?," we must ask, "Where is the Holy Spirit recognizably present with power?"[3]

The one-time WCC associate general secretary then went on to declare,

> Unless the living Spirit Himself takes the things of Christ and shows them to us, we cannot know them. Unless *He* unites us to the ascended Christ we cannot be united.[4]

In 1961, in New Delhi, the Third General Assembly of the

---

3. Newbigin, p. 95.

4. Ibid., p. 101. For comments by pentecostals on Newbigin's work, see Gee, *All with One Accord,* pp. 14–18; and Greg Forster, "The Third Arm 1," p. 6.

World Council of Churches reiterated this theological tenet that the Spirit functions as the key to Christian unity by saying,

> We believe that the unity which is God's will and his gift to his Church is being made visible as all in each place who are baptized into Jesus Christ and confess him as Lord and Savior are *brought by the Holy Spirit* [emphasis mine] into one fully committed fellowship.[5]

And Newbigin's plea for ecumenical-pentecostal contact was also realized largely, as noted, through the personal efforts of David du Plessis.

It is clear that the stress within the ecumenical movement on the doctrine of the Holy Spirit is one reason for the emergence and success of charismatic renewal—emphasizing the Spirit's presence and work—in denominations closely aligned with the ecumenical movement throughout the world. But it is the Roman Catholic Church, through Pope John XXIII and Vatican II, which has been primarily responsible for the development of a modern theology of the Holy Spirit pertaining to ecumenism. That theological emphasis (rooted in Pope John's "New Pentecost") is a prime factor to explain the growth and spread of the pentecostal movement within Catholicism.

VATICAN II

Stephen Neill declares, "Nothing in the records of the Vatican Council is more remarkable than the constant references, both in speeches and in documents, to the Holy Spirit."[6] Again, much of

---

5. Quoted in Harold E. Fey, ed., *A History of the Ecumenical Movement: 1948–1968* (Philadelphia: Westminster Press, 1970), p. 43.

6. Stephen Neill, *The Church and Christian Union* (London: Oxford University Press, 1968), p. 318. One can, perhaps, argue that Vatican II's stress on the Holy Spirit was the result of the failure of all other legitimations for doctrine, social policy, and so on. When legitimations (papal infallibility, for instance) fail or become suspect, then the Holy Spirit might be a very useful (extremely general and unspecific) legitimation for *any* cause or policy.

Vatican II's focus on the work of the Spirit can be traced to Pope John's prayer for a New Pentecost marked by unity in the Holy Spirit:

> May there be repeated thus in the Christian families the spectacle of the apostles gathered together in Jerusalem after the Ascension of Jesus to heaven, when the newborn Church was completely united in communion of thought and prayer. . . . And may the Divine Spirit deign to answer in a most comforting manner the prayer that rises daily to Him from every corner of the earth: "Renew your wonders in our time, as though for a new Pentecost."[7]

That the Spirit is, in fact, the center of Christian unity is affirmed in the Vatican Council's decree "On Ecumenism":

> It is the Holy Spirit, dwelling in those who believe, pervading and ruling over the entire Church, who brings about that marvelous communion of the faithful and joins them together so intimately in Christ that He is the *principle* of the Church's unity [emphasis mine].[8]

With respect to spiritual gifts in particular—so important in pentecostal theology—Vatican II accepted and encouraged the continued operation of *charismata* in the life of the church. The document entitled "The Church" declares,

> It is not only through the sacraments and Church ministries that the same Holy Spirit sanctifies and leads the people of God and enriches it with virtues. Allotting his gifts to everyone according as he will (1 Cor. 12:11), he distributes special graces among the faithful of every rank. By these gifts he makes them fit and ready to undertake the various tasks or offices advantageous for the renewal and up-building of the Church, according to the words of the Apostle: "The manifestation of the Spirit is given to everyone for profit" (1 Cor. 12:7). These charismatic gifts, whether they be the most outstanding or the more simple and widely diffused, are to be received with

---

7. Quoted in Kevin and Dorothy Ranaghan, *Catholic Pentecostals*, p. vi.

8. Quoted in Robert McAfee Brown, *The Ecumenical Revolution* (New York: Doubleday, 1967), p. 10.

thanksgiving and consolation, for they are exceedingly suitable and useful for the needs of the Church.[9]

If the ecumenical movement itself, together with its stress on the Holy Spirit as the principle of Christian unity, is one factor to explain the emergence and success of charismatic renewal, Pope John's New Pentecost, with its implications for Vatican II and the Roman Catholic Church thereafter, represents another factor—especially with respect to Catholic participation in the pentecostal movement since 1967 (two years after the close of the Vatican Council). For, by emphasizing the unifying work of the Spirit even more than ecumenical Protestantism had done, Vatican II officially sanctioned the operation of charismata in the contemporary Catholic Church.[10] Furthermore, the Vatican Council *encouraged* Roman Catholics to build positive relationships with their Protestant albeit—"separated"—brethren by visiting their services of worship and other meetings. These new relationships brought Catholics and Pentecostals together in a significant way and, obviously, first introduced Catholics to the pentecostal experience as a *legitimate* experience of Christian spirituality.[11]

WIDER ACCEPTANCE OF THEOLOGICAL DISSENT

The decade of the 1960s was marked by an increasing toleration of (even radical) theological dissent within the historic denominations. If the iconoclastic views of the late Episcopal Bishop James Pike of California and those of Bishop J. A. T. Robinson (formerly of Woolwich) could be tolerated (and sometimes applauded) within the Anglican Communion, it was far less difficult for this church

---

9. Quoted in James Byrne, *Threshold of God's Promise*, rev. ed. (Notre Dame, Ind.: Ave Maria Press, 1971), p. 72.

10. A case has been made for a woman, Elena Guerra, as the "real" forerunner of Catholic pentecostalism (rather than Pope John XXIII). See Val Gaudet, "Forerunner of the Charismatic Renewal!" *Testimony* (Third Quarter 1974), pp. 5–9.

11. For a report on an early Vatican II pentecostal-Catholic encounter, see Daniel J. O'Hanlon, "The Pentecostals and Pope John's 'New Pentecost,'" *View*, no. 2 (1964), pp. 44–47.

to accommodate such pentecostal priests as Dennis Bennett, Michael Harper, and Graham Pulkingham. The same was generally true of other historic denominations as well. Furthermore, wider acceptance of theological dissent within the institutional church (epitomized, perhaps, by the "death of God" movement in the late 1960s) actually helped bring about the growth and spread of charismatic renewal in those denominations. Thus, in 1968, Oral Roberts was welcomed into the ministry of the United Methodist Church. Roberts felt that if the United Methodist Church could embrace theological radicals, it could also accept pentecostals (even one as "notorious" as himself). And he was right.

GENERAL SPREAD OF SECULARIZATION

During the course of the second half of the twentieth century, the secularization of Western culture has become a fact of life. Among other scholars, Bryan Wilson suggests, simply, that religion has lost its influence on society, as evidenced by the atrophy of religious *practice* (as in Scandinavia); by the transformation of religious *institutions* into organizations that incorporate all the rational bureaucratic authority suppositions of other, nonreligious organizations of the wider (advanced, technological) society (as in the United States); and, most of all, by a fundamental change in religious thinking. He puts it this way:

> Men act less and less in response to religious motivation: they assess the world in empirical and rational terms, and find themselves involved in rational organizations and rationally determined roles which allow small scope for such predilections as they might privately entertain. Even if, as some sociologists have argued, nonlogical behaviour continues in unabated measure in human society, then at least the terms of non-rationality have changed. It is no longer the dogmas of the Christian Church which dictate behaviour, but quite other irrational and arbitrary assumptions about life, society and the laws which govern the physical universe.[12]

12. Bryan Wilson, *Religion in Secular Society* (Baltimore: Penguin Books, 1966), p. 10.

With the advance of secularization in the modern era, churchgoing itself, except in the United States, has been declining in proportion to population growth. People no longer feel *compelled* to attend church on Sunday merely for reasons of "social respectability." Furthermore, the "mainline" denominations—whose clergy and structures have been most thoroughly secularized—have been the ones particularly and most visibly affected by declining membership and attendance. Sociologist Peter L. Berger says,

> *If* there is going to be a renascence of religion, its bearers will *not* be the people who have been falling all over each other to be "relevant to modern man." To the extent that modernity and secularization have been closely linked phenomena in Western history, any movement of countersecularization would imply a repudiation of "modern man" as hitherto conceived.[13]

Among other things, secularization of the wider affluent and technological society has brought with it boredom, loss of meaning, and a painful sense of aimlessness in life; while increased permissiveness (also associated with secularization) has produced a new desire for discipline. In his classic study of American denominations, *Why Conservative Churches Are Growing,* Dean M. Kelley maintains that "conservative" (less secularized) churches are growing because they provide the meaning and insist on the discipline ("strictness") that an increasing number of people desire in order to regain direction for their lives.

It is apparent, moreover, that with the ever more pervasive rationalization and routinization of life inherent in modernity, the nonrational, the ecstatic, have again become appealing. In secular society, it is quite understandable that an *experiential* religious tradition that also provides meaning and discipline—such as pentecostalism—has become widely attractive. Both classical pentecostalism and charismatic renewal owe their growth and

---

13. Peter L. Berger, "A Call for Authority in the Christian Community," *Christian Century* (October 17, 1971), p. 1262.

spread, in large part, to the new enthusiasm for religious experience in Western culture today.[14]

YOUNG PEOPLE

In discussing secularization, Wilson points out that, in the West. the sense of mystery, the religious meaning of objects, has waned steadily with modernization. A demystified world means that everyday thinking has become more instrumental and matter-of-fact, that emotional involvement with nature, the community, and other humans more generally has been reduced, and that the external world has been drained of meaning.[15] Among young people, the "countercultural" movement of the 1960s was an attempt to challenge these trends—to recover the sense of mystery in the cosmos, to reject the matter-of-fact character of everyday life, to build community, and to relate emotionally with nature again. Thus the "back to the land" and ecology movements came into being, as did handicrafts and communes, new ("alternative") lifestyles, *and* enthusiastic religion (Eastern and Western), with a transcendent emphasis. Pentecostalism, with its inherent spontaneity—particularly as expressed in the Jesus People movement—was sufficiently compatible with countercultural lifestyles to gain acceptance among the young (the institutional church was not). It provided "instant community" and contributed to the restoration of meaning to life and the mystery behind it (including the possibilities of predictive prophecy, divine healing, and speaking "a heavenly language"). For the young, with whom even the eighteenth- and nineteenth-century revivalists had their greatest successes,[16] pentecostalism has been an attempt to escape the routinization of modern life in secular society, and it has been a major vehicle through which an answer to the current search for authenticity or reality in living (something more often *felt* than

---

14. For an attempt to deal with "secularism" in the context of charismatic renewal, see Edward O'Connor, *Pentecost in the Modern World* (Notre Dame, Ind.: Ave Maria Press, 1972), pp. 14–17.

15. Wilson, *Religion in Secular Society*, p. 78.

16. Ibid., p. 33.

learned) is carried—symbolized by the "One Way" slogan of the Jesus People movement (John 14:6).[17] Hence its emergence and success among young people should come as no surprise. Pat Boone, himself a former teenage idol, had this to say on the matter in 1970:

> These young people are searching for reality. The church, as they see it today, doesn't have it. They see its failures, double standards, lack of concern, and are turned off. Even much of what we call "evangelical Christianity" has way too little to offer them. Because doctrine, no matter how pure or correct it may be, is *not enough*.[18]

IN THE MIDDLE CLASS

Reasons for the growth and spread of charismatic renewal in the white middle class as a whole have already been put forth. Not unlike those reasons pertinent to the young in particular, they include the appeal to the alleviation of "affluent boredom." Pentecostalism represents something meaningful to do and experience *now*. In the pentecostal experience, the life to come can already be "tasted" in the here and now. Also, neopentecostalism has been one manifestation of the increased middle-class acceptance of emotional expression as part of everyday life. Males are now "allowed" to cry in public; speaking in tongues can be "therapeutic"; and nonverbal forms of communication (such as distinctive prayer postures, embracing, and the laying on of hands) are acceptable, even encouraged. At the same time, however, most of the nontransferable cultural traditions of classical pentecostalism have been rejected. Charismatic renewal became attractive to the white middle class because of its "legitimate," rational, educated clergy and lay leadership, and because of its generally nonrevivalistic evangelism. Kathryn Kuhlman and David du Plessis were officially

---

17. See, for instance, the testimonies of young people who were early participants in Catholic pentecostalism in Kevin and Dorothy Ranaghan, *Catholic Pentecostals*, pp. 58–106.

18. Boone, p. 184.

received by the Pope. Oral Roberts, the university president, was *welcomed* into the ministry of the United Methodist Church, while neopentecostal leaders such as Edward O'Connor, Donald Gelpi, and Josephine Ford continue to function as respected members of the theological academy. Social or psychic deprivation within charismatic renewal, as we have seen, has not been easily documented.[19]

STATISTICS

Any discussion of reasons for the diffusion and success of neopentecostalism remains incomplete without at least some attempt to deal with actual constituency statistics. Reliable statistics for classical pentecostalism are hard enough to find, but for charismatic renewal the problem is even more severe. First, unlike for a church or denomination, there has been no formal membership for the movement as a whole. Informal prayer groups come, go, and coalesce. Without one overarching organizational structure, numbers and turnover in the movement have been *very* hard to estimate. (Neopentecostal literature is purchased both by participants and nonparticipants; thus, publication and distribution figures are not definitive.) Second, enthusiastic religious groups, as a whole, are prone to exaggerate statistics, and charismatic renewal has been no exception here. Third, continuing growth and declines ensure that the various "estimates" from whatever source are quickly dated. Citing a 1967 source, Hollenweger suggested in 1972 that over 1,000 Presbyterian ministers, 700 Episcopal priests

---

19. From the sociological perspective, pentecostalism was a legitimated way to dismantle inhibition and to enjoy emotional release, which for a long time was limited in modern society. In some ways, it may be anticultural (or even countercultural), but it may also function as a safety valve, and may thus in the long run prevent emotions from running into socially nihilistic channels. It might be interesting to speculate why, in the 1900–1960 period, the lower socioeconomic levels of society needed this kind of release; and why, in the 1960s and 1970s, the middle class needed it. The need *could*, perhaps, be linked to the declining relative position of the middle class in a period of economic redistribution and the reduction of status differences (that is, a limited experience of "relative deprivation").

(10 percent of the total), and 10,000 Roman Catholics in the United States had received the pentecostal experience.[20] In 1971, *Melodyland Messenger* estimated that 300 Lutheran pastors, 500 Presbyterian ministers and 800 Baptist ministers in America were charismatic renewal participants;[21] while David du Plessis speculated in 1974 that 10 percent of all ministers of denominations affiliated with the National Council of Churches (about 10,000) had been baptized in the Holy Spirit.[22] Among all of the historic denominations in Great Britain, 300 clergy had experienced Spirit baptism by 1979 already, according to Michael Harper.[23] Of all the denominations, moreover, the Roman Catholic Church has displayed the most dramatic statistics: Edward O'Connor numbered 10,000 American Catholic pentecostals in 1971;[24] Edward Fiske of the *New York Times* estimated 15,000 to 50,000 in 1970;[25] and John Haughey of the Jesuit magazine *America* brought the total number of Catholic pentecostals in America to over 300,000 by 1973.[26]

More recent statistics are especially interesting. The 1979 Gallup survey, which did not distinguish between classical pentecostals and new charismatics, found that 19 percent of the total U.S. adult population identified themselves as pentecostal/charismatic (18 percent of all Roman Catholics, 22 percent of all Protestants, 20 percent of the Baptists and Lutherans, 18 percent of the Methodists, and 16 percent of the Presbyterians).[27] Then, according to the *World Christian Encyclopedia*, published in 1982, there are an estimated 51 million classical pentecostals and 11 million new

20. Hollenweger, *The Pentecostals*, p. 15.

21. *Melodyland Messenger* (February 1971), p. 4.

22. " 'Mainline' Charismatics," *Christian Century* (October 30, 1974), pp. 1006–1007.

23. Michael Harper, "Baptism in the Spirit," *Transmit* (September 1970), p. 2

24. O'Connor, *The Pentecostal Movement in the Catholic Church*, pp. 16–18.

25. Fiske, p. 37.

26. Haughey, p. 551.

27. Kantzer, p. 13.

charismatics within the total world population of Christians—numbering more than 1.4 billion. If this is correct, at least 5 percent of all Christians worldwide are pentecostal today.

Sources of financial support for program and paid personnel within charismatic renewal include, of course, the regular salaries given to neopentecostal clergy by their churches, as well as money collected and distributed by charismatic renewal organizations. But far more important, as Gerlach and Hine have stated, "Pentecostals give personally to fellow Pentecostals believing the recipient has been called by God to do a specific work. The giver believes in the work as much as the recipient—but thinks the recipient can do it better."[28]

Finally, we ought to say something about constituency "transience" within neopentecostalism. Again, any statistics at all are very hard to locate. Although it is apparent that once-avid participants do leave this movement—just like any other movement or church—there seems to be a tendency to do so "quietly." Dissident members of sectarian religious groups often quit ("defect"), then immediately begin vocally to "denounce" the group, its teachings, and leadership (become "apostate"). But charismatic renewal generally has not fostered this kind of transience. A good deal of theological and moral diversity is tolerated—if not in one group, then surely in another. Thus, those who do cease to identify with the movement as a whole probably do so, more often than not, for sheer loss of interest.

RELIGIOUS EXPERIENCE AND "INSTANTISM" IN MODERN CULTURE

We have already touched on the attraction of young people and the middle class more generally to charismatic renewal, because it offers something to do and experience *now*. The new enthusiasm for religious experience is one of the more surprising developments

---

28. Gerlach and Hine, *People, Power, Change*, p. 52.

of the past two decades in the larger society. Often, moreover, this enthusiasm has occurred in people who have *abandoned* churches and formal religion. Some are consciously seeking a personal encounter with God, but for others the search for experience is less consciously religious—involving the use of drugs, humanistic "therapies," even occult practices. In addition, very little *patience* is apparent in this quest; results are expected immediately. The enthusiasm for experience and impatience for that experience ("instantism") are integrally related in modern culture.

In classical pentecostalism, religious experience has indeed been a central feature and attraction. But the pentecostal experience here tended to be *cumulative* rather than *intrinsic* ("instantaneous"). In many pentecostal denominations, religious experience is still conceived to involve, at its core, *three* stages of development, not necessarily in short succession. Conversion ("a personal experience with Jesus") is the first. Second, there is sanctification as a distinct and identifiable experience (a *gradual* process in some pentecostal denominations, however). Third, Spirit baptism, with the initial evidence of speaking in tongues, is sought—followed, in due course, by one or more of the spiritual gifts. The whole experiential process may take many hours of personal and corporate prayer, with "pleading" and "tarrying at the altar" over a period of months or even years. Then, given the strong Arminian character of classical pentecostalism, even a Spirit-filled believer may "fall from grace" ("backslide") and have to "do the first works over" again—begin the experiential process anew. Furthermore, it is always quicker and far easier to backslide than to be converted, sanctified, and baptized in the Spirit.

In charismatic renewal, however, personal religious experience has been largely intrinsic (for example, the "NOW" experience of Oral Roberts). Conversion—personal commitment to Jesus as an act of will—is insisted on, but immediately thereafter Spirit baptism becomes a real possibility. Sometimes, moreover, conversion and baptism in the Holy Spirit occur virtually at the same time, so that the experiences of Spirit baptism and conversion can hardly be distinguished from each other.

In classical pentecostalism, traditionally much time was spent by a candidate for Spirit baptism *waiting* for the initial evidence of tongues. It was something that "just happened"—suddenly, sometimes after years of "seeking." But in charismatic renewal, and among its upwardly mobile classical pentecostal emulators, one could expect a much quicker response. Fluency in glossolalia, neopentecostals admit, comes only with much practice (it is, obviously, a form of "learned behavior"), but the first "sounds" can be articulated almost at once. Thus, Dennis and Rita Bennett say,

> When you receive Jesus as Savior, you believed in your heart and confessed Him with your lips [that is, conversion]. Now confess with your lips, but in the new language that the Lord is ready to give you. Open your mouth and show that you believe the Lord has baptized you in the Spirit by *beginning to speak*. Don't speak English, or any other language you know.[29]

It has not been uncommon in charismatic renewal for an outright nonbeliever to be converted to Christ and baptized in the Spirit (with the "beginning of speaking in tongues")[30] in the course of *one* experience of the laying on of hands. Hence neopentecostalism, more than traditional pentecostalism, has accommodated to the current enthusiasm for a "full" religious experience *now*.

INCREASED LEISURE TIME

It is clear that the greatly increased affluence and abundant spare time characteristic of large segments of modern society—including those in the historic churches, and even many of the pentecostal denominations today—contributed to the emergence and success of charismatic renewal. Multimillionaires and other well-to-do people in the movement, many of whom are connected

---

29. Dennis and Rita Bennett, pp. 69–72.

30. Ibid., p. 72.

with the Full Gospel Business Men's Fellowship International, constitute one important factor in its growth and spread. Included among the early ones were Demos Shakarian, one-time millionaire dairyman, and founder-president of the FGBMFI; Pat Boone, the entertainer and businessman; George Otis, an electronics manufacturer[31] and early patron of the Blessed Trinity Society.[32] Otis describes his life just before his involvement in charismatic renewal:

> That Saturday morning in Bel Air [California], with more than half of my life gone, something like a video replay surged before me. An audit of my life flashed by; listed among the Young Millionaires . . . a member of Young Presidents' Organization (acquiring the presidency of a million-dollar plus organization before the age of 40) . . . head of a well-known electronics firm with a Cadillac in the garage and an airplane at Santa Monica. I was a jet-setter for sure—and this world called me "a big success."[33]

Then he goes on to describe the degree to which his business duties (such as travel) enabled him, after his conversion, to witness to his faith and pentecostal experience throughout the world:

> Desire to proclaim Christ's magnificence has propelled me since that [FGBMFI] chapter meeting some half-million miles. I've traveled from the Arctic Circle to Tasmania and from Tahiti to India, to share with all who will listen—from the children of the night to polished mansion halls; in Rotary clubs, hotels and auditoriums; on aircraft carriers and in dung huts, television stations, government offices, Pentagon corridors, movie studios, monasteries, universities and churches.[34]

---

31. See George Otis, "High Adventure," *Full Gospel Business Men's Voice* (March 1972).

32. *Trinity* (Transfiguration 1963), p. 50.

33. Otis, "High Adventure," *Full Gospel Business Men's Voice* (March 1972), p.6.

34. Ibid., p. 29.

The affluence of many new charismatics (together with the sacrificial giving of ordinary laypeople as well) allowed prominent clergy in the movement like David du Plessis, Dennis Bennett, Michael Harper, Ralph Wilkerson, and a host of others to become world travelers in evangelism. The fact that corporate executives can leave their work for weeks at a time whenever they wish resulted in the feasibility of FGBMFI international airlifts in the late 1960s already.[35] It made possible the numerous international neopentecostal conventions, held since the 1970s, and a world tour, even sponsored by Melodyland Christian Center in 1972–1973[36]—all attended by wealthy supporting laypeople, prominent clergy and other leaders, and middle-class participants "on vacation." Active participation in charismatic renewal has most often required the contribution of time and money to *two* religious affiliations—to the movement *and* to one's own church (a departure from the long-standing Christian idea that there can be just *one* central religious loyalty). This kind of costly personal involvement, obviously, could not be so widespread without the increased availability of leisure time and the higher income levels characteristic of large segments of contemporary Western society. And it is manifestly apparent that charismatic renewal participants found the movement to offer an especially viable use for their money and spare time.

ANTIINSTITUTIONALISM

It has become almost a truism to speak of the pervasiveness of antiinstitutional sentiment in contemporary Western culture. There seems to be little interest in building new bureaucratic structures or superstructures to replace old ones. In the religious sector,

35. See, for instance, FGBMFI, *Airlift to London;* and Raymond W. Becker, "A Report of the 1972 Scandinavian-European Airlift," *Full Gospel Business Men's Voice* (October 1972), pp. 5–14, 19–22, 30–33, 35–38, 42–45.

36. See *Melodyland World Tour* (Anaheim, Calif.: Melodyland Christian Center, 1972).

this feeling is perhaps best illustrated by the virtual collapse of major efforts at organic church union that emerged in the 1960s and the weakening of the World Council of Churches and its regional counterparts, especially the National Council of Churches (U.S.A.). The prevalence of such antiinstitutional sentiment made charismatic renewal attractive as a movement of *spiritual* unity in diversity that sought to revitalize *existing* church structures rather than to tear them down to build new ones. In this connection, it is also important to underscore the contemporary viability of the persistence of a *movement* lacking coherent internal structure, hierarchy, or real membership—given the existence in modern society of a "looser" affiliation, carried by the mass media (such as books, magazines, newspapers, radio, television, cassette tapes, and large gatherings), without the need to bring people together for formal, as distinct from expressive (fellowship and evangelistic), purposes.

REDISCOVERY OF THE SUPERNATURAL

Like the contemporary quest for religious *experience,* the reality of increased affluence and leisure time, and the attempt to destructure society, the rediscovery of the "supernatural" by the middle class in contemporary Western society also contributed to the emergence and success of charismatic renewal. It is easy to understand why, in an age of the resurgence of predictive prophecy, "fore-telling" rather than "forth-telling" (Jeane Dixon and Edgar Cayce), psychic research (the late Bishop James Pike), astrology, interest in the occult, and investigations of "after-death experiences" (Elisabeth Kübler-Ross), pentecostal phenomena such as divine healing, glossolalia, prophecy, and exorcism[37] should also be attractive to those who, in past times, would have dismissed such concerns and activities as appropriate only for the uninstructed.

---

37. On exorcism in charismatic renewal, see Michael Harper, *Spiritual Warfare* (Plainfield, N.J.: Logos International, 1970), a cautious treatment of the issue.

CHARISMATIC RENEWAL AND OTHER CONTEMPORARY MOVEMENTS

Black Power

The emergence of charismatic renewal bears resemblance to the rise of other unstructured religious, quasi-religious, and secular movements in the 1960s and 1970s. We have already mentioned Gerlach and Hine's *People, Power, Change: Movements of Social Transformation*. This study is primarily a comparison of classical and neopentecostalism with "black power" as movements of social transformation. The authors, interestingly enough, discovered striking similarities between both movements in their decentralized structure, face-to-face recruitment, personal commitment, kind of ideology, and feeling of real or perceived opposition. Furthermore, Gerlach and Hine insist that pentecostalism may even be considered *conceptually* "revolutionary" (like black power), and black power transcendentally "religious" (like pentecostalism). Their reasoning is as follows:

> Our survey of pentecostalism in the United States shows that participants tend to be politically conservative. Furthermore, the pentecostal ethic militates against social change through social action. Although they envision radical political, economic, and social change here on earth, they expect this to be instituted through supernatural means. The social change associated with pentecostalism, especially in non-Western societies moving toward industrialization, is largely an inadvertent consequence of personal change, but is nevertheless real. It should be noted that many of the newer converts who have remained in their nonpentecostal churches, especially clergy and very active lay members, combine the radical personal change involved in the pentecostal experience with a radical approach to social action on nonreligious issues. Pentecostalism, we suggest, is conceptually revolutionary. It encourages an experience through which an individual believes himself to be radically changed; many converts behave accordingly in social situations.
>
> Black Power, on the other hand, is clearly a movement which seeks to accomplish social change with entirely human means. But it is religious in the sense that it requires the commitment of the indi-

vidual to something greater than self . . . transcending even the body of believers.[38]

If pentecostalism as a whole can be likened to black power in terms of transformative potential, neopentecostalism, specifically, can also be placed side by side in its development with other movements that emerged in the 1960s and 1970s.

The Human Potential Movement

Kilian McDonnell, in 1968, was probably the first scholar to suggest the similarity between charismatic renewal and what is now known as the human potential movement. There is in each of these movements (one religious, one secular), he points out, a "contemporary quest for transcendence and a new synthesis."[39] Very broadly, in the group dynamics of the human potential movement and in the prayer meetings of neopentecostalism are demonstrated similar experiments in "community building," interpersonal honesty, and nonverbal forms of communication (such as hand-holding and embracing), although the ideological bases for such actions are very different.[40]

By the late 1970s, human potential group dynamics and popular psychology in general had diffused throughout the movement in both its modernist and traditionalist segments. Already in 1976, Josephine Ford was making specific recommendations for the development of an egalitarian, Esalen-type structure and process for charismatic prayer groups. At the same time, however, she criticized the more "leader-directed" prayer groups and covenanted communities aligned with South Bend and Ann Arbor—groups based on strictly defined patterns of authority. But these, too, had developed with the use of human potential techniques.[41]

---

38. Gerlach and Hine, *People, Power, Change,* p. xix.

39. Kilian McDonnell, "Holy Spirit and Pentecostalism," *Commonweal* (November 8, 1968), p. 204.

40. For a somewhat contrary view on this comparison, however, see O'Connor, *Pentecost in the Modern World,* pp. 41–48.

41. See Ford, *Which Way for Catholic Pentecostals?,* pp. 102–134.

Psychologically informed mental and relational methods within charismatic renewal became even more popular with the healing ministry of Ruth Carter Stapleton, who, in 1978, founded her "Holovita" ("Whole Life") retreat center on a 30-acre ranch outside Dallas. Here she elaborated her spiritual therapy of renewal—with diet and exercise programs—into a total "design for healing" for people of *all* faiths (or none) who sought spiritual, emotional, and physical well-being.[42]

The Jesus People Movement

Another movement analogous in its development to charismatic renewal, and intertwined with it, was the Jesus People movement, which had been visible from about 1967 until 1972.[43] Both could be considered decentralized movements with many diverse segments. The Jesus People movement, composed primarily of countercultural young people, was generally open in its various groups to the pentecostal experience with its inherent spontaneity and its promised spiritual gifts. It was different from neopentecostalism, however, in that the Jesus People originally worshiped *outside* the already established churches, which they viewed as "hypocritical." But in its "maturity," the Jesus People movement began to take on more of the explicit characteristics of charismatic renewal and evangelicalism more generally. Ronald Enroth, an authority on the Jesus People movement, made the following observations in 1973:

> It appears that the "Jesus bandwagon" days of superficial fervor are giving way to more committed discipleship. One sign of this can be seen in the growing interest in serious Bible study. . . .
> Many of the Jesus people seem to have faded into the crowd—the Christian crowd. . . . [For] the young people are now attending established churches where their influence has been felt mainly in

---

42. See Kenneth L. Woodward, "Sister Ruth," *Newsweek* (July 17, 1978), pp. 58–62, 65, 66.

43. See Robert S. Ellwood, *One Way: The Jesus Movement and Its Meaning* (Englewood Cliffs, N.J.: Prentice-Hall, 1973).

terms of more informal worship and *a new emphasis on the Holy Spirit* [emphasis mine] . . . .

Another trend among young Christians who have been a part of the Jesus people movement is a return to the college campus and an increased concern to become more involved in the larger society.[44]

At the same time, the countercultural communes, collectives, and communities of the early days of the Jesus People movement (such as the Berkeley Christian Coalition and the Sojourners Fellowship in Washington, D.C.) which are still in existence became more formally structured—very similar in character to the Catholic pentecostal covenanted communities.[45]

44. Enroth, pp. 14–15, 17.

45. See James T. Richardson and M. T. V. Reddy, "Form and Fluidity in Two Contemporary Glossolalic Movements," in Bryan R. Wilson, ed., *Annual Review of the Social Sciences of Religion,* vol. 4 (Paris: Mouton, 1981), pp. 183–200.

Conclusion

The Achievement of
Charismatic Renewal

During the late 1960s and 1970s, there emerged on the American scene a large number of "new religious movements" or "cults," as their critics termed them. Most churches, denominations, and religious movements that are now "established" and well within the cultural mainstream *began* as cults—small minority groups of highly committed individuals following a strong, visionary, or "charismatic" leader with a new spiritual truth that has a potential impact on society at large. In seeking to renew the influence of religious truth on the social order, cults challenge both the comfortableness and the discontents of a static and spiritless status quo; and they are opposed—sometimes violently—by those whose established, but often sterile and loveless, ways they challenge. This opposition, however, strengthens such new religious movements, because it gives them a distinctive identity and a powerful motivation to do what they feel they must do.

Christianity itself began as a cult within Judaism; Lutheranism, as a cult within Catholicism; and Methodism, as a cult within Anglicanism—to name just a few. Jesus of Nazareth sought to "fulfill" Judaism, but he was rejected by the Jews, and his disciples were forced to start a new and separate tradition. Luther wanted to reform Catholicism from within, but he was excommunicated, and Protestantism was born as the consequence. And Wesley's "methodical" discipline of "entire sanctification," conceived within his "Holy Club" in Oxford, was meant to revitalize the Church of England. But Methodism—as a distinct and separate denomination—had to be organized even before his death, because the new Wesleyan method of moral purity was an affront to the staid and lax Anglican establishment.

And so it was with classical pentecostalism, too. Parham and Seymour were both visionary leaders with a conceptually revolutionary truth to renew and unify the whole of Christendom. But the new understanding of Spirit baptism, especially as it emerged from Azusa Street, was unacceptable to the middle class of the time. It was too "black." Speaking in tongues, spiritual healing, "possession" by spirits, and prophetic utterances were common occurrences in the shamanistic traditions of Africa, Latin America, and elsewhere long before the birth of the pentecostal movement. Although "Christianized" and "Americanized" in early pentecostalism, they continued to be practiced in the context of a well-developed oral liturgy, the core of which was derived from African rhythms, movement, and vocalization. (Even white classical pentecostalism retained these Africanisms until the 1970s, when upward mobility made them appear "too crude.") With the rejection of the pentecostal experience by the religious mainstream, pentecostalism had to go its own sectarian way—despite the movement's early visions of unity.

But charismatic renewal—the *new* pentecostalism—emerged and developed sixty years later in a different manner. This movement propagated the very same pentecostal experience. Yet, because of its solid middle-class and white origins, neopentecostalism was able—despite early opposition—to accommodate Spirit baptism to the religious mainstream in ways that working-class, black, and Latin pentecostals could not and would not do. In less than two decades, the movement made the *charismata* acceptable in mainline Christianity—to the point where a distinctively new charismatic denomination was simply unnecessary. And this *was* a great ecumenical achievement.

Charismatic renewal did accomplish a lot in the course of its development as a movement. First of all, by the early 1970s, it achieved positive recognition by mental health professionals who, in the past, had viewed the pentecostal experience as evidence of a subnormal psychological state. John Kildahl's assessment of the characteristic lifestyles of neopentecostal glossolalists is a good illustration of how well the new charismatics had made their case:

> One of the characteristics invariably noted by new tongue-speakers was a greater sense of power. This took the form of a stronger sense of identity and self-confidence in interpersonal relations. New tongue-speakers reported a greater sense of purpose and meaning in their lives and a deepening of its spiritual quality. Whereas religious matters often had been important to them before, after speaking in tongues they became increasingly involved with their religious convictions. They felt bolder in their business dealings, in their marriage relationships, and in teaching Sunday School. . . .
>
> The practitioners of glossolalia whom we surveyed were joyful and warm in one another's company. Their sense of community crossed ethnic, socioeconomic, and educational lines. Their common overhwelming experience surmounted their barriers.
>
> We noted a tremendous openness, concern, and care for one another . . . and the highest ethical mandates were part of their camaraderie. . . . They reported being less annoyed by frustrations, showing patience in their families and a deeper love for mankind in general.[1]

Published evaluations of this sort helped the movement considerably. And—by implication—they also aided classical pentecostalism achieve the legitimacy denied it by the mental health community for seven decades.

Secondly, with its emphasis on the recovery of the New Testament charismata, neopentecostalism also accomplished a surprising restoration of mysticism within middle-class, Western Christianity as a whole. Both Protestant evangelicalism, centered on a reverence for "propositional revelation" and Baconian inductive logic in its doctrine of biblical "inerrancy," and Protestant and Catholic liberalism, with *its* rationality and "demythologized" the-

---

1. Kildahl, pp. 83, 84.

ology, had lost the same sense of mystery in the cosmos. But Spirit baptism—in the context of charismatic renewal—made it possible, once again, for even "sophisticated" theologians to have a mystical experience of God. And that *was* a surprise.

Finally, and this is most important, neopentecostalism achieved what classical pentecostalism had set out to do in the beginning but could not accomplish. It earned respectability within the historic denominations and a place for the pentecostal experience in the religious mainstream. Practitioners of the charismata gained an intractable foothold in those churches and helped Protestantism into a new age of pluralism by their charismatic spirituality, which rivaled, and sometimes relativized, doctrinal diversities systemic to Christianity since the time of the Reformation. In its own strange way, neopentecostalism actually helped Protestantism become more "catholic" by opening it up to the mysteries of the Spirit at a time—in the 1960s and 1970s—when doctrinal certitude was being so hotly debated by theological elites.

These are the things that charismatic renewal achieved in the course of two decades of development—the *good* news about what it has left us. But the very successes of the movement in earning respectability meant that it no longer stood against anything as a corrective. (Even New York City's prestigious and *very* liberal Union Theological Seminary appointed two pentecostals to its faculty during the 1970s.) Thus, with ever-increasing accommodation to parallel religious and cultural forces, it lost its distinctiveness—its identity—-as a new religious movement. Very simply, its "newness" was gone.

By 1977, at the latest, neopentecostalism had reached "maturity," and its visibility peaked. Baptism in the Holy Spirit was now sufficiently diffused within the Protestant and Catholic mainstream so as to make charismatic renewal—as a movement with a goal—increasingly unnecessary. In the years following, the mass rallies centered on charismatic concerns decreased in size and broadened in their topical emphases. Neopentecostal publishers and journals either disbanded or extended their offerings to include a wider diversity of issues and perspectives treated. In Catholicism, "charismatic" renewal became integrated with other forms of spiritual renewal, including Eastern and Western meditative disciplines. And the concept of divine healing was expanded to encompass psychological as well as spiritual aids toward recovery. Protestant new charismatics, increasingly bewildered by the pluralistic neopentecostal environment, moved toward further accommodation with the evangelicals, and their leaders began espousing conservative evangelical theological concerns vocally. These issues included, on the one hand, a doctrinal stress on biblical inerrancy that gave charismatics a way to distinguish themselves from their "less orthodox" fellows who also claimed Spirit baptism, and, on the other hand, "church growth" as the principal measure of success for Christianity.[2]

Christians who identified themselves as charismatic included not only theological liberals of all stripes, but also, for instance, members of the distinctively gay Metropolitan Community Churches, founded by Troy Perry, a one-time classical pentecostal minister. MCC was established in 1968, and gradually came to regard itself as an extension of the larger charismatic renewal. And there were neopentecostal "cults" as well—among them, The Way International, and the highly controversial Children of God.[3] New charismatic theologians enhanced the pluralism even further by integrating Spirit baptism with everything from a liberal "process theology" (in the case of Donald Gelpi) to a radical Marxist-oriented "liberation theology."

To make matters even more confusing, Gallup reported in 1979 that, of all Americans surveyed who identified themselves as pen-

---

2. See, for instance, Jeffrey Fewkes, "Biggest Church in the World," *Renewal* (October–November 1981), pp. 16, 17, 19, 20; and "Going for Perpetual Growth," *Renewal* (December 1981–January 1982), pp. 36–38. See also Jamie Buckingham, "The World's Largest Pastorate," *Charisma* (June 1982), pp. 20–27. In the summer of 1982, in place of its earlier charismatic clinics, Melodyland Christian Center held a conference on church growth, featuring Paul Yonggi Cho, pastor of Full Gospel Central Church in Seoul, Korea. Cho's 200,000-member congregation (affiliated with the Assemblies of God) is the subject of the aforementioned articles.

3. See Richardson and Reidy.

tecostal or charismatic, only one-sixth had *ever* spoken in tongues —one-seventh of charismatic Lutherans, one-tenth of charismatic Catholics and Methodists, one-sixteenth of charismatic Baptists, and only a negligible portion of charismatic Presbyterians.[4] With so few neopentecostals who actually spoke in tongues, it became harder yet to distinguish "charismatics" from nonpentecostal "evangelicals," on the one hand, and "liberals," on the other.

In the course of its brief development and maturation as a movement, charismatic renewal did make a lasting contribution to ecumenical Christianity in the modern era. It brought together the most unlikely fellow-believers at all levels of church life, and it fostered a kind of "grass-roots" ecumenism that even the institutional ecumenical movement—from the World Council of Churches to Vatican II—could not match. But, like other experience-centered renewal movements before it, neopentecostalism did not live up to the potential envisioned by its early leaders. The problem was as old as that isolated by St. Paul in his letters to the church at Corinth. Here the apostle tried to combat the temptation on the part of the Corinthian believers to let ecstasy play a preemptory, amoral role in their lives, with only secondary attention either to the confession of Jesus as Lord or to matters of moral rectitude within the community of faith. Although the Corinthians were "not lacking in any spiritual gift," they were still full of dissension and rivaled the pagans in immorality (1 Cor. 5:1). Paul recognized that mere "spirituality"—even when rich with miracles and other proofs of power—is not to be equated with an authentically Christian faith and morality. The new charismatics, like the Corinthian church, too often glorified the gifts of the Spirit—and the experience of initiation behind them—more than the Giver. They stressed the extraordinary charismata but too often ignored the "fruits" of the Spirit that, ultimately, validate or invalidate the dogmas taught by *whomever* from *whatever* tradition. "By their fruits you shall know them."

What this all means, then, is simply that

---

4. Kantzer, pp. 13, 14.

the charismatic renewal of the 1960s and 1970s was both a unifying movement of deep spirituality and an ephemeral movement of 'divisive enthusiasm' (to use Gelpi's cogent term) in the white First World. Long before its mass rallies had time to gather in the United States and other Western nations, classical pentecostalism had taken root and grown exponentially in Latin America, Africa, and elsewhere in the Third World. Ironically, the greatest spiritual gift of neopentecostalism was the one least appreciated and least exercised, namely, the ecumenism of the Spirit that might have provided an experiential "bridge" back to pentecostalism's roots in the black church and its rivals in Hispanic pentecostalism. If that bridge had been bravely and humbly crossed, charismatic renewal could have wedded the moral, economic, and political fruits of the Holy Spirit more securely to the flamboyant public exercise of the charismata.[5]

As it happened, however, the neopentecostal movement plumbed the depths of ecstatic religion only to find diminishing returns even from the mysterious abyss of the meaning of the Spirit. Not unlike other movements of the Spirit before it, charismatic renewal had "run out of steam" by the late 1970s—but not out of abiding significance.

---

5. Sheppard, "Commentary." The place of charismatic renewal in modern American religion as a whole is taken up in Quebedeaux, *By What Authority*.

Annotated Bibliography

Acts. Los Angeles, 1967–1970. Bimonthly. *An independent neopentecostal news-magazine.*

Acts 29. Bath, Ohio, 1973–. Monthly. *Published by Episcopal Renewal Ministries.*

Aglow. Lynwood, Washington, 1969–. Bimonthly. *Published by the Women's Aglow Fellowship.*

Agora. West Covina, California, 1977–1981. Quarterly. *Published by dissident pentecostal intellectuals. Some of its surprising and controversial critiques can be found nowhere else.*

Agrimson, J. Elmo, ed. *Gifts of the Spirit and the Body of Christ: Perspectives on the Charismatic Movement.* Minneapolis, Minn.: Augsburg, 1974.

Anderson, Robert Mapes. *Vision of the Disinherited: The Making of American Pentecostalism.* New York: Oxford University Press, 1979. *Examines the rise of pentecostalism from its origins to the early Depression years. Anderson views pentecostalism as a movement of radical social discontent whose revolutionary thrust was expended in veiled, ineffectual, and misplaced attacks on organized religion and society. His evaluation of psychological and sociological factors leads Anderson to conclude that pentecostalism replaced feelings of social powerlessness in its adherents—who came from the most oppressed segments of American society—with feelings of inward religious power through baptism in the Holy Spirit. Frustration was changed into the confidence of being God's elect. See the lengthy reviews by Grant Wacker and Timothy L. Smith in* Religious Studies Review *(January 1982), pp. 15, 16, 18–20, 22–28.*

Armstrong, Ben. *The Electric Church.* Nashville, Tenn.: Nelson, 1979. *A very sympathetic history of the "electronic church" and an assessment of the accomplishments of its leading evangelists and teachers, including Oral Roberts, Pat Robertson, and Jim Bakker.*

Barfoot, Charles, H., and Gerald T. Sheppard. "Prophetic vs. Priestly Religion: The Changing Role of Women Clergy in Classical Pentecostal Churches." *Review of Religious Research* (September 1980), pp. 2–17.

Barnhouse, Donald Grey. "Finding Fellowship with Pentecostals." *Eternity* (April 1958), pp. 8–10. *An early editorial by a prominent evangelical Presbyterian leader calling for better pentecostal-evangelical relations.*

Barrett, David B., ed. *World Christian Encyclopedia: A Comparative Survey of Churches and Religions in the Modern World,* A.D. 1900–2000. New York: Oxford University Press, 1982. *An invaluable reference work that includes up-to-date information on classical pentecostalism and charismatic renewal. See the major review by Richard N. Ostling in* Time *(May 3, 1982), pp. 66, 67.*

Bartelman, Frank. *Another Wave Rolls In!* (formerly *What Really Happened at Azusa Street?*), ed. John Walker and John G. Myers. Monroeville, Pa: Whitaker Books, 1980. *A firsthand account of the Azusa Street revival by one of its white participants.*

Basham, Don. *A Handbook of Holy Spirit Baptism.* Monroeville, Pa.: Whitaker Books, 1969.

Bennett, Dennis. *Nine O'Clock in the Morning.* Plainfield, N.J.: Logos International, 1970. *A classic spiritual autobiography of the neopentecostal pioneer.*

Bennett, Dennis and Rita. *The Holy Spirit and You.* Plainfield, N.J.: Logos International, 1971. *Teachings on the Spirit-filled life widely accepted within charismatic renewal.*

Bess, Donovan. " 'Speaking in Tongues': The High Church Heresy." *Nation* (September 28, 1963), pp. 173–177. *A belittling account of neopentecostalism, centered on the Anglo-Catholic segment of the movement.*

Bittlinger, Arnold. *Gifts and Graces.* Grand Rapids, Mich.: Eerdmans, 1967. *A Reformed, churchly, and nonexclusivist interpretation of the charismata.*

———. *Gifts and Ministries.* Grand Rapids, Mich.: Eerdmans, 1973.

———, ed. *The Church Is Charismatic.* Geneva: World Council of Churches, 1981. *An assessment of the ecumenical impact of pentecostalism on the church as a whole.*

Bloch-Hoell, Nils. *The Pentecostal Movement.* Oslo: Universitetsforlaget, 1964. *A classic study of classical pentecostalism.*

"Blue Tongues." *Time* (March 29, 1963), p. 52. *An account of the "outbreak of tongues" within the evangelical Inter-Varsity Christian Fellowship at Yale.*

Boone, Pat. *A New Song.* Carol Stream, Ill.: Creation House, 1970. *A classic spiritual autobiography by the neopentecostal entertainer.*

Bourgeois, Patrick L. *Can Catholics Be Charismatic?* Hicksville, N.Y.: Exposition Press, 1976.

Breckenridge, James F. *The Theological Self-Understanding of the Catholic Charismatic Movement.* Washington, D.C.: University Press of America, 1980.

Bredesen, Harald. *Yes, Lord.* Plainfield, N.J.: Logos International, 1972. *A classic spiritual autobiography of the early neopentecostal leader.*

Bruner, Frederick Dale. *A Theology of the Holy Spirit: The Pentecostal Experience and the New Testament Witness.* Grand Rapids, Mich.: Eerdmans, 1970. *A sophisticated critical study of exegetical and theological problems related to the pentecostal experience.*

Buckingham, Jamie. *Daughter of Destiny.* Plainfield, N.J.: Logos International, 1976. *A sympathetic and very informative biography of Kathryn Kuhlman.*

Byrne, James E. *Living in the Spirit: A Handbook on Catholic Charismatic Christianity.* New York: Paulist Press, 1975.

Carothers, Merlin R. *Prison to Praise.* Plainfield, N.J.: Logos International, 1970.

_____. *Power in Praise*. Plainfield, N.J.: Logos International, 1972. *The function of the praise of God in charismatic renewal.*

Catholic Charismatic. New York, 1976–1980. Bimonthly. *Published by Paulist Press. A more modernist alternative to the largely traditionalist magazine,* New Covenant.

Charisma. Winter Park, Florida, 1975–. Monthly. *The major American magazine oriented to Protestant charismatic renewal since the collapse of* Logos Journal.

Charisma Digest (previously, *View*, a quarterly). Los Angeles, 1966–1969. Semi-annual. *A journalistic attempt by the Full Gospel Business Men's Fellowship International to gain an academic readership.*

"Charismatic and Socio-Political Movements." *Social Compass* 25 (1978), 1–163 (whole issue).

The Charismatic Movement in the Church of England. London: CIO Publishing, 1981. *An official report.*

"Charismatic Renewal." *PostAmerican* (now *Sojourners*), (February 1975), pp. 1–31 (whole issue). *Written from the perspective of "radical evangelicals," and containing an interview with Ralph Martin.*

"Charismatics." *Wittenburg Door* (October–November 1980), pp. 1–32 (whole issue). *A humorous "evangelical liberal" approach. Contains an interview with J. Rodman Williams.*

Christenson, Larry. *Speaking in Tongues: A Gift for the Body of Christ*. London: Fountain Trust, 1963.

_____. *Speaking in Tongues and Its Significance for the Church*. Minneapolis, Minn.: Bethany Fellowship, 1968.

_____. *A Charismatic Approach to Social Action*. Minneapolis, Minn.: Bethany Fellowship, 1974. *A conservative approach.*

Christian Life. Wheaton, Illinois, 1948–. Monthly. *A breezy Christian alternative to* Life, *focusing on religious celebrities. Contains sympathetic articles on various leaders of charismatic renewal, although the magazine itself is not "charismatic" per se.*

Christie-Murray, D. *Voices from the Gods: Speaking with Tongues*. London: Routledge & Kegan Paul, 1978. *A scholarly study.*

Clark, Stephen B. *Building Christian Communities*. Notre Dame, Ind.: Ave Maria Press, 1972. *A handbook on the covenanted community by a prominent Catholic charismatic intellectual.*

_____. *Man and Woman in Christ*. Ann Arbor, Mich.: Servant Publications, 1980. *A scholarly traditionalist study of the roles of Christian men and women in church and society.*

Crim, Keith, ed. *Abingdon Dictionary of Living Religions*. Nashville: Abingdon, 1981.

Culpepper, Robert H. *Evaluating the Charismatic Movement*. Valley Forge, Pa.: Judson Press, 1977. *A scholarly survey, emphasizing theology.*

Cutten, George B. *Speaking with Tongues: Historically and Psychologically Con-*

sidered. New Haven, Conn.: Yale University Press, 1927. *An early work ascribing glossolalia (as a psychological condition) to hysteria (extreme susceptibility to suggestion, with exaggerated sensations), ecstasy, or even catalepsy (suspended animation with rigidity of the body).*

Damboriena, Prudencio. *Tongues as of Fire: Pentecostalism in Contemporary Christianity.* Washington, D.C.: Corpus Books, 1969. *An interesting interpretation of the movement, written with scholarly sophistication.*

Dann, Norman K. "Spatial Diffusion of a Religious Movement." *Journal for the Scientific Study of Religion* (December 1976), pp. 351–360. *An assessment of the spread of the holiness movement.*

Davis, Rex. *Locusts and Wild Honey: The Charismatic Renewal and the Ecumenical Movement.* Geneva: World Council of Churches, 1978. *A favorable evaluation by a World Council of Churches staff member.*

Davison, Leslie. *Pathway to Power: The Charismatic Movement in Historical Perspective.* London: Fountain Trust, 1971.

Dayton, Donald. W. "The Evolution of Pentecostalism." *Covenant Quarterly* (August 1974), pp. 28–40. *A somewhat controversial study.*

Devine, Finbarr. *Charismatic Renewal for Catholics.* Los Angeles: S.C.R.C. Publications, 1976.

Doolittle, Robert. "Denominational Renewal." *Unitarian Universalist World* (May 1, 1975), p. 3. *Charismatic renewal in the Unitarian Universalist Association.*

Dunn, James D. G. *Baptism in the Holy Spirit.* Naperville, Ill.: Allenson, 1970. *One of the standard exegetical and theological studies.*

_____. "Spirit Baptism and Pentecostalism." *Scottish Journal of Theology* (November 1970), pp. 397–407.

_____. *Jesus and the Spirit.* Philadelphia: Westminster Press, 1975. *Very important.*

Du Plessis, David. "A Statement by Pentecostal Leaders." In Norman Goodall, ed., *Missions Under the Cross.* London: Edinburgh House, 1953, pp. 249–250. *Early declaration by various pentecostal leaders affirming ecumenism.*

_____ (with Bob Slosser). *A Man Called Mr. Pentecost.* Plainfield, New Jersey: Logos International, 1977. *A spiritual autobiography.*

_____. *The Spirit Bade Me Go.* Rev. ed. Plainfield, N.J.: Logos International, 1970. *A spiritual autobiography containing material not found in* A Man Called Mr. Pentecost.

Durasoff, Steve. *Bright Wind of the Spirit: Pentecostalism Today.* Englewood Cliffs, N.J.: Prentice-Hall, 1972. *A survey commissioned by Oral Roberts.*

Ellwood, Robert S. *One Way: The Jesus Movement and Its Meaning.* Englewood Cliffs, N.J.: Prentice-Hall, 1973. *A fine scholarly assessment.*

Enroth, Ronald M. "Where Have All the Jesus People Gone?" *Eternity* (October 1973), pp. 14, 15, 17, 28, 30. *The "routinization" of the Jesus People movement.*

Ensley, Eddie. *Signs of Wonder: Speaking in Tongues in the Catholic Church.* New York: Paulist Press, 1977.

Ervin, Howard M. *These Are Not Drunken, As Ye Suppose.* Plainfield, N.J.: Logos International, 1968. *A scholarly exegetical and theological defense of Spirit baptism from the perspective of early charismatic renewal.*

Fahey, Sheila M. *Charismatic Social Action.* New York: Paulist Press, 1977. *A left-of-center Catholic approach that provides an interesting contrast to Larry Christenson's* A Charismatic Approach to Social Action.

Farrell, Frank. "Outburst of Tongues: The New Penetration." *Christianity Today* (September 13, 1963), pp. 3–7.

Fichter, Joseph H. "Liberal and Conservative Catholic Pentecostals." *Social Compass* 21 (1974), 303–310.

_____. *The Catholic Cult of the Paraclete.* New York: Sheed & Ward, 1975. *An engaging social-scientific evaluation of Catholic pentecostalism by the eminent Jesuit sociologist.*

Fiske, Edward B. "Pentecostals Gain Among Catholics." *New York Times* (November 3, 1970), pp. 37, 56.

Flora, Cornelia Butler. *Pentecostalism in Colombia: Baptism by Fire and Spirit.* Rutherford, N.J.: Farleigh Dickinson University Press, 1976. *Extensive survey research interpreted in a very interesting manner.*

Flynn, Thomas. *The Charismatic Renewal and the Irish Experience.* London: Hodder & Stoughton, 1974.

Ford, J. Massyngberde. *The Pentecostal Experience.* New York: Paulist Press, 1970.

_____. *Baptism in the Spirit.* Techny, Ill.: Divine Word Publications, 1971.

_____. "Biblical Material Relevant to the Ordination of Women." *Journal of Ecumenical Studies.* (Fall 1973), pp. 669–699.

_____. *Which Way for Catholic Pentecostals?* New York: Harper & Row, 1976. *The traditionalist-modernist debate within Catholic pentecostalism came to a head with this articulate modernist perspective.*

Forster, Greg S. "The Third Arm 1." *TSF Bulletin* (London), (Summer 1972), pp. 5–9. *A very helpful interpretation of pentecostalism and the pentecostal experience by an Evangelical Anglican neopentecostal.*

_____. "The Third Arm 2." *TSF Bulletin* (London), (Autumn 1972), pp. 16–21.

Frost, Robert C. *Aglow with the Spirit.* Rev. ed. Plainfield, N.J.: Logos International, 1971.

Full Gospel Business Men's Fellowship International. *The Acts of the Holy Spirit Among Catholics Today.* Los Angeles: FGBMFI, 1974. *Testimonies.*

_____. *Catholics and the Baptism in the Holy Spirit.* Los Angeles: FGBMFI, n.d. *Early testimonies.*

Full Gospel Business Men's Voice. Costa Mesa, California, 1953–. Monthly. *Mainly testimonies of Spirit-filled classical pentecostals and neopentecostals.*

Gee, Donald. *All with One Accord.* Springfield, Mo.: Gospel Publishing, 1961.

An early ecumenical approach to Spirit baptism by the eminent classical pentecostal in the British Assemblies of God.

————. *Wind and Flame* (formerly *The Pentecostal Movement*). Nottingham, England: Assemblies of God Publishing, 1967. *A popular survey of the pentecostal movement by an insider whose long-term participation as a leader makes this a valuable historical source.*

Gelpi, Donald L. *Pentecostalism: A Theological Viewpoint*. New York: Paulist Press, 1971. *The first attempt to systematize a Catholic theology of the pentecostal experience.*

————. *Charism and Sacrament*. New York: Paulist Press, 1976. *A highly sophisticated liberal Catholic approach to the charismata and sacraments within the church.*

————. *Experiencing God: A Theology of Human Experience*. New York: Paulist Press, 1978. *The Jesuit author's own modernistic tendencies become even more apparent here as he integrates his own charismatic theology with the concerns and methods of "process theology" in this innovative study.*

Gerlach, Luther P., and Virginia H. Hine. "Five Factors Crucial to the Growth and Spread of a Modern Religious Movement." *Journal for the Scientific Study of Religion* (Spring 1968) pp. 23–40.

————. *People, Power, Change: Movements of Social Transformation*. Indianapolis, Ind.: Bobbs-Merrill, 1970. *An anthropological comparison of the dynamics of two movements, pentecostalism and black power. Both, the authors assert, are conceptually revolutionary.*

Goodman, Felicitas D. *Speaking in Tongues: A Cross-Cultural Study*. Chicago: University of Chicago Press, 1972. *A comparative anthropological study of glossolalia. The author believes that the common features of glossolalic behavior within different cultural contexts can be attributed to an altered state of consciousness.*

Hadden, Jeffrey K., and Charles E. Swann. *Prime Time Preachers: The Rising Power of Televangelism*. New York: Addison-Wesley, 1981. *A very interesting and informative sociological interpreation of the electronic church phenomenon and its leading personalities, including Oral Roberts, Pat Robertson, and Jim Bakker.*

Hamilton, Michael P., ed. *The Charismatic Movement*. Grand Rapids, Mich.: Eerdmans, 1974. *A fine collection of scholarly essays on charismatic renewal written from a variety of perspectives. Includes a recording of speaking in tongues.*

Harper, Michael. *As at the Beginning*. Plainfield, N.J.: Logos International, 1965. *An early popular history of charismatic renewal in the context of the history of pentecostalism more generally. Published in the United States by Logos in 1971 from the original Fountain Trust edition.*

————. *None Can Guess*. Plainfield, N.J.: Logos International, 1971. *A classic spiritual autobiography, and one of the best in this genre.*

————. *Spiritual Warfare*. Plainfield, N.J.: Logos International, 1970. *On exorcism.*

————. *A New Way of Living*. Plainfield, N.J.: Logos International, 1973. *On the charismatic renewal community spawned by Graham Pulkingham and the Episcopal Church of the Redeemer, Houston, Texas.*

Harrell, David Edwin, Jr. *All Things Are Possible: The Healing and Charismatic Revivals in Modern America.* Bloomington: Indiana University Press, 1975. *A high-grade historical assessment of the independent healing evangelists and their ministries during the pentecostal revival of 1947–1958. The author argues that these flamboyant men had a major impact on the charismatic renewal of the 1960s and 1970s. See the review by Harvey Cox in the* New York Times Book Review*(February 22, 1976), pp. 6, 22.*

Haughey, John C., ed. *Theological Reflections on the Charismatic Renewal.* Ann Arbor, Mich.: Servant Publications, 1978.

Healey, John B. *Charismatic Renewal: Reflections of a Pastor.* New York: Paulist Press, 1976.

Hine, Virginia H. "Pentecostal Glossolalia: Towards a Functional Interpretation." *Journal for the Scientific Study of Religion* (Fall 1969), pp. 211–226.

Hitt, Russell T. "The New Pentecostalism." Reprinted from an article in *Eternity* the same year in *Trinity* (Trinitytide 1963), pp. 24–27. *An early evangelical critique of charismatic renewal that provoked a major response from the Blessed Trinity Society in the same issue of its magazine.*

Hollenweger, Walter J. "Handbuch der Pfingstbewegung." 10 vols. Unpublished doctoral thesis, Faculty of Theology, University of Zurich, 1965–1967. *An essential reference work for the development of pentecostalism as a global religious movement. Available on microfilm from ATLAS, Board of Microtexts, Yale Divinity School Library, New Haven, Connecticut.*

_____. *New Wine in Old Wineskins.* Gloucester, England: Fellowship Press, 1973.

_____. *The Pentecostals.* Minneapolis, Minn.: Augsburg Publishing, 1972. *An abridged and updated version of the author's "Handbuch der Pfingstbewegung." All of Hollenweger's works are very important.*

_____. "Charismatic and Pentecostal Movements: A Challenge to the Churches." In Dow Kirkpatrick, ed., *The Holy Spirit.* Nashville, Tenn.: Tidings, 1974, pp. 209–233.

_____. *Pentecost Between Black and White: Five Case Studies on Pentecost and Politics.* Belfast: Christian Journals, 1974.

Hughes, Ray H. "A Traditional Pentecostal Looks at the New Pentecostalism." *Christianity Today* (June 2, 1974), pp. 6–10. *A critical response by an executive of the Church of God (Cleveland, Tennessee). His denomination, however, has accommodated considerably to charismatic renewal since the mid-1970s.*

Hummel, Charles G. *Fire in the Fireplace: Contemporary Charismatic Renewal.* Downers Grove, Ill.: InterVarsity Press, 1978. An *evangelical theological evaluation of the movement that is essentially positive.*

Hutch, Richard A. "The Personal Ritual of Glossolalia." *Journal of the Scientific Study of Religion* (September 1980), pp. 255–266.

Hutcheson, Richard G., Jr. *Mainline Churches and the Evangelicals: A Challenging Crisis?* Atlanta, Ga.: John Knox Press, 1981. *A well-researched study of the presence and contribution of evangelicals and new charismatics in the mainline denominations.*

Jensen, Jerry, ed. *Baptists* (1963), *Episcopalians* (1964), *Lutherans* (1966), *Methodists* (1963), and *Presbyterians and the Baptism of the Holy Spirit.* Los Angeles: Full Gospel Business Men's Fellowship International, 1963. *Early testimonies.*

Jones, James W. *Filled with New Wine: The Charismatic Renewal of the Church.* New York: Harper & Row, 1974. *An Anglo-Catholic theological assessment of the movement.*

Jorstad, Erling, ed. *The Holy Spirit in Today's Church: A Handbook of the New Pentecostalism.* New York: Abingdon, 1973.

Kantzer, Kenneth S. "The Charismatics Among Us." *Christianity Today* (February 22, 1980), pp. 13–17. *Commentary on the 1979 Gallup survey.*

Kelsey, Morton T. *Tongue Speaking.* New York: Doubleday, 1964. *A well-conceived, psychologically informed study of glossolalia by an early participant in charismatic renewal.*

Kerkhofs, J., ed. *Catholic Pentecostals Now.* Canfield, Ohio: Alba Books, 1977.

Kerr, John Stevens. *The Fire Flames Anew: A Look at the New Pentecostalism.* Philadelphia: Fortress Press, 1974.

Kildahl, John P. *The Psychology of Speaking in Tongues.* New York: Harper & Row, 1972. *Results of a ten-year study of neopentecostal speakers in tongues. One of the most positive of recent evaluations.*

Koenig, John T. *Charismata.* Philadelphia: Westminster Press, 1978. *A fine biblical study of the issue.*

Kroll-Smith, J. Stephen. "The Testimony as Performance: The Relationship of an Expressive Event to the Belief System of a Holiness Sect." *Journal for the Scientific Study of Religion* (March 1980), pp, 16–25. *The function of liturgy in the Church of God in Christ.*

Kuhlman, Kathryn. *I Believe in Miracles.* Englewood Cliffs, N.J.: Prentice-Hall, 1962. *Testimonies of dramatic healings.*

———. *God Can Do It Again.* Englewood Cliffs, N.J.: Prentice-Hall, 1969. *Testimonies of dramatic healings.*

———. *Nothing Is Impossible with God.* Englewood Cliffs, N.J.: Prentice-Hall, 1974. *Testimonies of dramatic healings.*

Lalive d'Epinay, Christian. *Haven of the Masses: A Study of the Pentecostal Movement in Chile.* London: Lutterworth Press, 1969. *A groundbreaking sociological study.*

Laurentin, René. *Catholic Pentecostalism.* New York: Doubleday, 1977. *A scholarly evaluation of Catholic pentecostalism, particularly in its European context.*

The Logos. Fort Wayne, Indiana, 1968–. Bimonthly. *Published by the Logos Ministry for Orthodox Renewal.*

Logos Journal. Plainfield, New Jersey, 1971–1981. Bimonthly. *Until the late 1970s, the leading Protestant neopentecostal magazine in the United States. Toward the end, its contents were almost indistinguishable from that found in leading nonpentecostal conservative evanglical magazines of the time.*

Lombard, Émile. *De la Glossolalie chez les Premiers Chrétiens et des Phénomènes Similaires: Étude d'Exégèse et de Psychologie.* Lausanne: Imprimeries Réunies, 1910. *Classic study viewing glossolalia as a kind of "automatic speech."*

Looney, John Thomas. "Nondenominational Charismatic Churches: Vision of a New Testament Community." Unpublished master of divinity thesis, Union Theological Seminary, New York, 1981. *An interesting study of sectarian tendencies within charismatic renewal, and a critical evaluation of the controversy surrounding Christian Growth Ministries by an objective one-time participant.*

Lovekin, Adams, and H. Newton Malony. "Religious Glossolalia: A Longitudinal Study of Personality Changes." *Journal for the Scientific Study of Religion* (December 1977), pp. 383–393.

MacArthur, John F., Jr. *The Charismatics: A Doctrinal Perspective.* Grand Rapids, Mich.: Zondervan, 1978. *A highly critical conservative evangelical evaluation of charismatic renewal. Negative, to say the least, but also representative of the long tradition of antipentecostal feeling among American fundamentalists.*

McDonnell, Kilian. "The Ecumenical Significance of the Pentecostal Movement." *Worship* (December 1966), pp. 609–629.

_____. "Holy Spirit and Pentecostalism." *Commonweal* (November 8, 1968), pp. 198–204.

_____. "The Ideology of Pentecostal Conversion." *Journal of Ecumenical Studies* (Winter 1968), pp. 105–126.

_____. "Catholic Pentecostalism: Problems in Evaluation." *Dialog* (Winter 1970), pp. 35–54. *A foundational evaluation.*

_____. "New Dimensions in Research on Pentecostalism." *Worship* (April 1971), pp. 214–219.

_____. "The Catholic Charismatic Renewal: Reassessment and Critique." *Religion in Life* (Summer 1975), pp. 138–154.

_____, ed. *The Holy Spirit and Power.* New York: Doubleday, 1975.

_____. *Charismatic Renewal and the Churches.* New York: Seabury Press, 1976. *One of the author's most important works.*

_____. *The Charismatic Renewal and Ecumenism.* New York: Paulist Press, 1978.

_____, ed. *Presence, Power, Praise,.* 3 vols. Collegeville, Minn.: Liturgical Press, 1980. *Contains almost all the important ecclesiastical documents pertaining to charismatic renewal from the beginning of the movement, with introductions. See the lengthy review by Vinson Synan in* Theology Today *(July 1982), pp. 187–193.*

_____, and Arnold Bittlinger. *The Baptism in the Holy Spirit as an Ecumenical Problem.* South Bend, Ind.: Charismatic Renewal Services, 1972. *Catholic and Protestant perspectives in contrast.*

McGaw, Douglas B. "Commitment and Religious Community: A Comparison of a Charismatic and a Mainline Congregation." *Journal for the Scientific Study of Religion* (June 1979), pp. 146–163.

McGuire, Meredith B. *Pentecostal Catholics.* Philadelphia: Temple University Press, 1982. *An altogether excellent sociological study of Catholic pentecostalism. Includes an interesting discussion of the movement's place among modern "sects" and "cults."*

MacNutt, Francis. *Healing* Notre Dame, Ind.: Ave Maria Press, 1974.

———. *The Power to Heal.* Notre Dame, Ind.: Ave Maria Press, 1977.

Marshall, Catherine. *Something More.* New York: McGraw-Hill, 1974.

Marshall, Michael. *Glory Under Your Feet: The Challenge of Catholic Renewal Today.* London: Darton, Longman and Todd, 1979.

Martin, Ralph. *Hungry for God.* New York: Doubleday, 1974.

———, ed. *New Wine, New Skins.* New York: Paulist Press, 1976. *Testimonies.*

———, ed. *The Spirit and the Church.* New York: Paulist Press, 1976. *Testimonies.*

Maust, John. "Charismatic Leaders Seeking Faith for Their Own Healing." *Christianity Today* (April 4, 1980), pp. 44–46. *On the shepherding controversy.*

Mead, Frank S. *Handbook of Denominations in the United States.* 7th ed. New York: Abingdon, 1980. *A handy reference volume that includes the history and essential beliefs of most pentecostal denominations.*

Mills, Watson, ed. *Speaking in Tongues: Let's Talk About It.* Waco, Texas: Word, 1973.

"Miracle Woman." *Time* (September 14, 1970), pp. 62, 64. *On Kathryn Kuhlman.*

Montague, George T. *The Spirit and His Gifts.* New York: Paulist Press, 1974. *A brief but well-conceived scholarly assessment.*

Morris, James. *The Preachers.* New York: St. Martin's Press, 1973. *Journalistic but valuable biographies of celebrity evangelists in the United States, including Oral Roberts and Kathryn Kuhlman.*

Mosimann, Eddison. *Das Zungenreden geschichtlich und psychologisch untersucht.* Tübingen: Mohr, 1911. *A classic study likening glossolalia to an hypnotic state.*

Mühlen, Heribert. *A Charismatic Theology.* New York: Paulist Press, 1979. *The author is a Roman Catholic theologian.*

National Courier. Plainfield, New Jersey, 1975–1977. Weekly. *A newspaper focusing on the charismatic renewal.*

Nauer, Barbara. *Rise Up and Remember.* New York: Doubleday, 1977. *A classic spiritual autobiography by a Catholic charismatic.*

Newbigin, Lesslie. *The Household of God.* New York: Friendship Press, 1954.

One of the first favorable assessments of pentecostalism from the ecumenical movement is contained in this book.

New Covenant. Ann Arbor, Michigan, 1971–. Monthly. *The first and most important Catholic pentecostal magazine.*

New Wine. Mobile, Alabama, 1968–. Monthly. *Published by Christian Growth Ministries.*

Nichol, John T. *Pentecostalism.* New York: Harper & Row, 1966. *A groundbreaking scholarly history of the movement.*

Nickel, Thomas R. *The Shakarian Story.* 2nd ed. Los Angeles: Full Gospel Business Men's Fellowship International, 1964. *An early biography of Demos Shakarian in booklet form.*

NSC Newsletter. Ann Arbor, Michigan, 1975–. *Published eight times a year by Charismatic Renewal Services.*

O'Connor, Edward D. *The Pentecostal Movement in the Catholic Church.* Notre Dame, Ind.: Ave Maria Press, 1971. *An excellent early discussion of the character of Catholic pentecostalism and how it differed both from classical pentecostalism and Protestant segments of charismatic renewal.*

_____. *Pentecost in the Modern World.* Notre Dame, Ind.: Ave Maria Press, 1972.

_____, ed. *Perspectives on Charismatic Renewal.* South Bend, Ind.: University of Notre Dame Press, 1975.

Opsahl, Paul D., ed. *The Holy Spirit in the Life of the Church.* Minneapolis, Minn.: Augsburg Publishing, 1978. *Theological studies from the Lutheran perspective.*

Ortiz, Juan Carlos, and Jamie Buckngham. *Call to Discipleship.* Plainfield, N.J.: Logos International, 1975. *A highly influential text within Catholic covenanted communities and the shepherding movement.*

Pentecost. London, 1947–1966. Quarterly. *A valuable historical source for the development of modern pentecostalism. Edited by Donald Gee for the Pentecostal World Conferences.*

Phillips, McCandlish. "And There Appeared to Them Tongues of Fire." *Saturday Evening Post* (May 16, 1964), pp. 31–40. *An important early report on charismatic renewal, sympathetic in its evaluation.*

Piepkorn, Arthur C. *Profiles in Belief, III: Holiness and Pentecostal Bodies.* San Francisco: Harper & Row, 1979. *A standard reference work on the holiness and pentecostal denominations in the United States. Introduction by Vinson Synan.*

Plowman, Edward E. "Mission to Orthodoxy: The 'Full' Gospel." *Christianity Today* (April 26, 1974), pp. 44, 45. *A report on charismatic renewal within Eastern Orthodoxy.*

_____. "The Deepening Rift in the Charismatic Movement." *Christianity Today* (October 10, 1975), pp. 52–54. *A report on the early stages of the shepherding controversy.*

Pneuma. Springfield, Missouri, 1979–. Semiannual. *Scholarly journal of the Society for Pentecostal Studies.*

Pope, Liston. *Millhands and Preachers: A Study of Gastonia.* New Haven, Conn.: Yale University Press, 1942. *A classic sociological study of the role of the churches, including the Church of God (Cleveland, Tennessee), in the strike of textile workers in Gastonia, North Carolina, during the 1930s.*

Pridie, J. R. *The Spiritual Gifts.* London: Robert Scott, 1921. *An early Anglican exegetical and theological treatise sympathetic to the basic pentecostal stance on the charismata.*

Pulkingham, W. Graham. *Gathered for Power: Charisma, Communalism, Christian Witness.* New York: Morehouse-Barlow, 1972. *The story of the intentional charismatic community developed by the Episcopal Church of the Redeemer, Houston, Texas.*

Quebedeaux, Richard. *The Young Evangelicals.* New York: Harper & Row, 1974. *The first study of its kind to show the accommodation of evangelical Christianity to modernity and the function of charismatic renewal within that process.*

————. *By What Authority: The Rise of Personality Cults in American Christianity.* San Francisco: Harper & Row, 1982. *An historical survey and contemporary evaluation of "celebrity leaders" in American Christianity, focusing on the television evangelists of the electronic church, including Oral Roberts, Pat Robertson, and Jim Bakker. The issue of religious authority more generally is also taken up in some depth.*

Ranaghan, Kevin and Dorothy. *Catholic Pentecostals.* New York: Paulist Press, 1969. *The first book on the Catholic charismatic renewal by two of its leaders. Still useful.*

————, eds. *As the Spirit Leads Us.* New York: Paulist Press, 1971. *Scholarly essays on Catholic pentecostalism.*

Randall, John. *In God's Providence: The Birth of a Catholic Charismatic Parish.* Plainfield, N.J.: Logos International, 1973.

"Rector and a Rumpus." *Newsweek* (July 4, 1960), p. 77. *Coverage of the outbreak of tongues in Dennis Bennett's parish.*

Renewal. Crowborough, East Sussex, England, 1966–. Bimonthly. *England's first and foremost charismatic renewal magazine. Edited by Michael Harper.*

Renewal News. Oklahoma City, Oklahoma, 1966–. Bimonthly. *Published by the Presbyterian Charismatic Communion.*

Richardson, James T., and M. T. V. Reddy. "Form and Fluidity in Two Contemporary Glossolalia Movements." In Bryan Wilson, ed., *Annual Review of the Social Sciences of Religion.* Paris; Mouton, 1981, pp. 183–220. *A comparison of charismatic renewal and the Children of God.*

Roberts, Oral. *The Call: An Autobiography.* Old Tappan, N.J.: Spire Books, 1971.

Robertson, Pat, and Jamie Buckingham. *Shout It from the Housetops: The Story of the Christian Broadcasting Network.* Plainfield, N.J.: Logos International, 1972.

Runyon, Theodore, ed. *What the Spirit Is Saying to the Churches*. New York: Hawthorn Books, 1975.

Samarin, William J. *Tongues of Men and Angels: The Religious Language of Pentecostalism*. New York: Macmillan, 1972. *Arguing that glossolalia in neopentecostalism, as a linguistic symbol of the sacred, signals transition, this was a groundbreaking work on speaking in tongues, and it is still one of the best studies available.*

Schwartz, Gary. *Sect Ideologies and Social Status*. Chicago: University of Chicago Press, 1970. *A sociological study of pentecostal belief systems as a response to social circumstances.*

Shakarian, Demos and Sherrill. *The Happiest People on Earth*. Lincoln, Va.: Chosen Books, 1975. *A spiritual autobiography.*

Sherrill, John L. *They Speak with Other Tongues*. New York: Pyramid Books, 1964. *Still a journalistic classic in its reporting of early neopentecostalism.*

"Speaking in Tongues." *Time* (August 15, 1960), pp. 53, 55. *A report on the controversy surrounding Dennis Bennett.*

Spirit. Washington, D.C., 1977–. Irregular. *A journal of issues related to black pentecostalism. Like Agora, another forum for dissident pentecostal intellectuals, mainly black. Some assessments here can be found nowhere else.*

Spittler, Russell, ed. *Perspectives on the New Pentecostalism*. Grand Rapids, Mich.: Baker Book House, 1976. *Fine scholarly essays.*

Spraggett, Allen. *Kathryn Kuhlman: The Woman Who Believes in Miracles*. New York: New American Library, 1971. *A very interesting parapsychological interpretation of the evangelist and her "gift" of healing.*

Stagg, Frank E., Glenn Hinson, and Wayne E. Oates. *Glossolalia*. New York: Abingdon, 1967.

Stanley, Gordon, W. K. Bartlett, and Teri Moyle. "Some Characteristics of Charismatic Experience: Glossolalia in Australia," *Journal for the Scientific Study of Religion* (September 1978), pp. 269–277.

Stott, John R. W. *The Baptism and Fullness of the Holy Spirit*. Downers Grove, Ill.: InterVarsity Press, 1964. *A generally negative assessment of the pentecostal view of Spirit baptism about which the prominent evangelical author later revised his thinking.*

Suenens, Léon Joseph Cardinal. *A New Pentecost?* New York: Seabury Press, 1974. *The great ecumenical leader links the pentecostal experience and charismatic renewal with ecumenism here.*

————, and Dom Helder Camera. *Charismatic Renewal and Social Action*. Ann Arbor, Mich.: Servant Publications, 1979. *A sometimes surprising dialogue on the topic.*

Sullivan, Emmanuel. *Baptized into Hope*. London: SPCK, 1980. *A study of contemporary Christian renewal movements, including charismatic renewal and the Catholic-evangelical convergence more generally—by a Franciscan.*

"Symposium: The Evangelical Movement." *Penthouse* (April 1978), pp. 70–72,

74, 82, 90. *An engaging discussion about the evangelical "resurgence." Moderated by Harvey Cox, with Bob Guccione, Charles Adams, Donald Dayton, Richard Quebedeaux, Robert Hoyt, Barbara Hargrove, Richard Lovelace, and Josephine Ford (who represented the charismatic renewal position).*

Synan, Vinson. *The Holiness-Pentecostal Movement in the United States.* Grand Rapids, Mich.: Eerdmans, 1972. *A groundbreaking historical study.*

————, ed. *Aspects of Pentecostal-Charismatic Origins.* Plainfield, N.J.: Logos International, 1975. *Fine scholarly essays.*

Taylor, James A. "A Search for Giants." *A.D.* (September 1974), pp. 20–23. *David du Plessis received his rightful recognition by the mainline religious media in this article.*

Testimony. Hanford, California, 1962. Quarterly. *Includes important testimonies by early neopentecostal leaders.*

Theological Renewal. Nottingham, England, 1977–. Bimonthly. *A more scholarly counterpart to* Renewal *for ordained ministers and theologians.*

Tinney, James S. "Black Origins of the Pentecostal Movement," *Christianity Today* (October 8, 1971), pp. 4–6. *See also the author's more developed views in* "The Blackness of Pentecostalism," Spirit, *no. 3 (1980), 28, 29, 31, 32. Both articles are controversial and very significant.*

Trinity. Van Nuys, California, 1961–1966. Quarterly. *The first neopentecostal magazine. Published by the Blessed Trinity Society and edited by Jean Stone.*

Triplett, Bennie S. *A Contemporary Study of the Holy Spirit.* Cleveland, Tenn.: Pathway Press, 1970. *A white pentecostal evaluation of Spirit baptism and its consequences, published for the Church of God (Cleveland, Tennessee).*

Tugwell, Simon *Did You Receive the Spirit?* New York: Paulist Press, 1972. *By one of the most sophisticated Catholic charismatic theologians.*

————, ed. *New Heaven? New Earth?: An Encounter with Pentecostalism.* London: Darton, Longman and Todd, 1976.

United Church of Christ. *The Life of the Spirit in the Life of the Church.* New York: Office for Church Life and Leadership, 1975. *A very positive evaluation for America's most liberal Christian denomination. Inadvertently left out of Kilian McDonnell's collection of neopentecostal ecclesiastical documents,* Presence, Power, Praise, *but available from Church Leadership Resources, United Church of Christ, 1400 North 7th Street, St. Louis, Mo. 63106*

Van Dusen, Henry P. "Force's Lessons for Others," *Life* (June 9, 1958), pp. 122, 124. *An early assessment of pentecostal, holiness, and other "sectarian" groups as a "third force" within Christianity. Groundbreaking recognition of this Christian stream by the late president of Union Theological Seminary in New York City.*

Vivier, Lincoln M. Van E. "Glossolalia." Unpublished M.D. thesis, University of the Witwatersrand, Johannesburg, South Africa, 1960. *A groundbreaking study that concludes that speaking in tongues is due to the "impact of a religious dynamism in all its power," and not to a "basic inherent weakness in the individual." Available on microfilm in a number of research libraries.*

Voigt, Robert J. *Go to the Mountain: An Insight into Charismatic Renewal.* St. Meinrad, Ind.: Abbey Press, 1975.

Von Trapp, Maria. *Maria.* Carol Stream, Ill.: Creation House, 1972. *A classic spiritual autobiography of this Catholic charismatic celebrity.*

Wagner, C. Peter. *Look Out! The Pentecostals Are Coming.* Carol Stream, Ill.: Creation House, 1973. *A popular and interesting evaluation of pentecostalism in Latin America by one of the foremost experts on "church growth."*

Warner, Wayne, ed. *Touched by Fire: Eyewitness Accounts of the Early Twentieth Century Pentecostal Revival.* Plainfield, N.J.: Logos International, 1978.

Wead, R. Douglas. *Catholic Charismatics: Are They for Real?* (formerly *Father McCarthy Smokes a Pipe and Speaks in Tongues*). Carol Stream, Ill.: Creation House, 1973. *A fascinating account of the "culture shock" experienced by classical pentecostals in having fellowship with Catholic charismatics whose lifestyles included habits and practices still considered "taboo" by traditional pentecostals.*

Wild, Robert. *Enthusiasm in the Spirit.* Notre Dame, Ind.: Ave Maria Press, 1975.

Wilkerson, David. *The Cross and the Switchblade.* Old Tappen, N.J.: Spire Books, 1964. *The story of Wilkerson's work among the delinquent subculture in New York City that led to the founding of Teen Challenge International.*

Willans, Jean Stone. *The Acts of the Green Apples.* Altadena, Calif.: Society of Stephen, 1973. *A spiritual autobiography of Jean Stone (now Willans) after her remarriage and move to Hong Kong to start a charismatic healing ministry.*

Williams, Cyril G. *Tongues of the Spirit.* Cardiff: University of Wales Press, 1981. *A rare consideration of psychological, social, and theological issues pertaining to glossolalia in relation to each other. See the review by Bryan Wilson in the* Times Literary Supplement *(July 3, 1981), p. 765.*

Williams, J. Rodman. *The Era of the Spirit.* Plainfield, N.J.: Logos International, 1971. *One of the first sophisticated attempts to fit the pentecostal experience into mainline (in this case, Reformed) Protestant theology.*

————. *The Gift of the Holy Spirit Today.* Plainfield, N.J.: Logos International, 1980. *A mature theology of charismatic renewal from the ecumenical Protestant perspective.*

————. *The Pentecostal Reality.* Plainfield, N.J.: Logos International, 1972.

Wilson, Bryan. *Sects and Society.* London: Heinemann, 1961.

————, ed. *Patterns of Sectarianism.* London: Heinemann, 1967.

Wilson, Dwight. *Armageddon Now! The Premillenarian Response to Russia and Israel Since 1917.* Grand Rapids, Mich.: Baker Book House, 1977. *The author focuses on white classical pentecostal attitudes.*

Wood, William W. *Culture and Personality Aspects of the Pentecostal Holiness Religion.* Paris: Mouton, 1965. *A psychological study of two small-town congregations of the Pentecostal Holiness Church.*

Woodward, Kenneth L. "Sister Ruth." *Newsweek* (July 17, 1978), pp. 58–62, 65, 66. *Cover story on Ruth Carter Stapleton.*

Worsfold, J. E., ed. *A History of Charismatic Movements in New Zealand.* London: Puritan Press, 1974.

Index

Acts, *155, 205;* and baptism in the
Holy Spirit, *12, 13, 27, 132, 151,
158;* and community living, *169;*
and social change, *167;* and spiri-
tual gifts, *16, 27, 184*
Administrators, *15*
Africa: classical pentecostals in, *48,
51, 239;* and neopentecostalism,
72, 77, 118, 192, 197; prepen-
tecostal religious traditions in, *21,
234*
Africanism, *29, 40, 170–171, 184,
234*
Aglow, 82
Agora, 114
Albert, Carl, *103*
Allen, A. A., *171*
All Saints Church, *47, 52–53, 56*
All Souls Church, *115–117*
American Lutheran Church (ALC),
65, 194, 196
Anabaptists, *19, 137*
Anderson, Robert Mapes, *27, 241*
Anglican churches. *See* Church of
England; Episcopal churches
Anglican Renewal Ministries, *82*
Ann Arbor covenanted community,
77–78, 136–138, 141, 150
Ann Lee, Mother, *19–20*
Antiinstitutionalism, *226–227*
Antisacramentalism, *26, 33*
Apostles, *15*

Apostolic Church, *45, 48*
Apostolic Faith, 30
Apostolic Faith Gospel Mission,
Azusa Street, *30–31*
Apostolic Faith Mission, South
Africa, *110–111*
Apostolic uniqueness issue, *205*
Argentina, *49*
Arminianism, *32, 223*
Arminius, Jacob, *32n5*
Asceticism, *40. See also* Moral
negativism
Asia, *48, 50, 51, 52*
Assemblies of God, *209;* and church
government, *3, 34;* du Plessis and,
84, 111, 112–113, 114, 209; and
education, *187–188;* in Great Brit-
ain, *46;* and laymen, *119;* and Na-
tional Association of Evangelicals,
37, 50; of Nigeria, *48;* and Pen-
tecostal Assemblies of Canada, *49;*
and social change, *51, 166;* and
theology, *37, 43, 45*
Atonement, *37*
Augustine, *19*
Australia, *49–50, 72, 77, 118, 192,
197*
Austria, *48*
Authority: human, *90–92, 135–142,
252;* spiritual, *32, 43, 131–134,
153, 181, 205*
Autonomy, of local church, *3, 88*

Azusa Street Mission, 29–31, 88, 179, 185, 234; Shakarians and, 119; and women, 33

Backsliders, 32, 223
Baker, Joan, 61–62
Baker, John, 61–62
Bakker, Jim, 83–84, 126, 154
Bakker, Tammy, 126
Baptism, water, 13, 44, 159–161, 180, 197
Baptism and Fullness of the Holy Spirit, 206
Baptism in the Holy Spirit, 3, 5, 12–14, 15, 177, 179, 206, 223; and conversion, 9, 13, 36, 43, 143–144, 155, 159, 206–207, 223; and culture, 192, 234; evangelism and, 9, 38; and human authority, 135; and mystery, 236; as preaching qualification, 56, 99; and sanctification, 29, 41, 43, 46, 223; and social change, 166–170; speaking in tongues evidencing, 20, 27, 29, 44, 155–148, 209, 223; and water baptism, 13, 159–161, 197
Baptists: and classical pentecostalism, 5, 26, 34, 38, 42–43, 45; and neopentecostalism, 5, 143, 196, 197, 198, 221, 238
Baptists for Life and Growth, 82
Baptist World Alliance, 197
Barnhouse, Donald Grey, 202
Barratt, Thomas, 46–47, 52–53
Basham, Don, 145; and Christian Growth Ministries, 139, 140; and prayer groups, 147; and Spirit baptism, 155–156, 158, 161
Baxter, Ern, 139, 140
Bel Air Presbyterian, 65
Belgium, 197
Bennett, Dennis, 65, 91, 93, 216, 226; and Christian Growth Ministries, 140; in Great Britain, 70; in New Zealand, 71; and St. Luke's, 63–64, 70; and St. Mark's, 10–11, 61–63, 186, 194; and spiritual gifts, 156, 158, 224; and Stone, 64, 122
Bennett, Rita, 156, 158, 224
Berg, Daniel, 49
Berger, Peter L., 217
Berkeley Christian Coalition, 231
Bethany Fellowship, 97
Bible, 26; authority of, 32, 43, 131–134, 153, 181, 205; inerrancy of, 37, 131, 180, 181, 235, 237; interpretation of, 37, 176, 180, 205, 206
Bible institutes, 187
Bittlinger, Arnold, 72, 84, 154, 158
Black classical pentecostalism, 28–31, 185, 186, 234, 253; and church government, 3; and fundamentalism, 4; and neopentecostalism, 5, 171, 173, 183–185, 210, 234; and social change, 166; worship by, 17, 29, 181–183, 234
Black power, 228–229
Blessed Trinity Society, 64–65, 91, 122–124, 247; collapse of, 66, 123–124; du Plessis and, 64, 93; socioeconomic levels in, 11, 225
Block-Hoell, Nils, 23, 26
Bloy, Francis, 63, 194
Boardman, William, 35–36
Boddy, Alexander, 42, 47, 52–53, 54, 55–56
Boddy, Mrs. Alexander, 53
Books, neopentecostal (general), 96, 117
Bookstall, 96
Bookstores, 96
Boone, Pat, 92, 164–165, 219, 225
Boston, 77
Braxton, Lee, 120
Brazil, 48, 49, 50, 51, 52
Bredesen, Harald, 65, 66, 71, 91, 164
Bruner, Dale, 159

Burnett, Bill, 72
Burton, William, 48
Bushnell, Horace, 35

Calling, 33, 99
Call to Discipleship, 141
Calvinism, 32n5
Cambridge Daily News, 70
Cambridge Inter-Collegiate Christian Union (CICCU), 114
Camisards, 19
Camp meetings, 24, 36, 38, 41
Canada, 49, 77, 196–197
Card playing taboo, 189
Carnell, Edward J., 153
Carter, Emmett, 204
Carter, Jimmy, 80
Catalepsy, 244
Catholic Apostolic Church, 20
Catholic Charismatic, 138
Catholics. *See* Roman Catholics
Cayce, Edgar, 227
CBN University, 126
Challenging Counterfeit, 96
Charisma, 82
Charismata. *See* Spiritual gifts
Charismatic leaders, 88–92, 93, 98
Charismatic Movement in the Church of England, 84
Charismatic renewal, as term, 145
Charismatic Renewal Services, 78, 83
Charismatic revival, 145
Children of God, 237
Chile, 48–49, 50, 51, 52
China, 48
Cho, Paul Yonggi, 237n2
Christenson, Larry, 65–66, 91, 93–94, 245; and baptism with the Holy Spirit, 158; and Germany, 68, 69; and Great Britain, 68, 69, 116–117; and prayer groups, 148; and speaking in tongues, 157, 158; and worship patterns, 172
Christian Advance, 65, 71, 123, 124

Christian and Missionary Alliance, 36
Christian Broadcasting Network (CBN), 125
Christian Center, 208
Christian Digest, 130
Christian Growth Ministries, 82, 139–142
Christian Interdenominational Fellowship, 72
Christianity, beginnings of, 233
Christianity Today, 203
Christian Life, 82
Christian Life Church, 208
Chrysostom, 19
Church government, 3, 26, 34, 43, 198
Church growth, as success measure, 237
Church Is Charismatic, 84
Churchman, 68, 203
Church of Christ, 82, 164, 196, 254
Church of England, 54–55, 67–68, 84, 196, 197, 208; Bennett and, 93; and dissent, 215–216; and Methodism, 233–234
Church of God (Anderson, Indiana), 36
Church of God (Cleveland, Tennessee), 50; and education, 187–188; and footwashing, 44; and holiness people, 36, 43, 45; and neopentecostals, 209, 247; and women, 34; worship patterns in, 182–183
Church of God Evangel, 41
Church of God in Christ, 3, 34, 45, 188
Church of the Nazarene, 36, 196
Church of the Way, 208
Circuit riders, 24
City of Faith, 109
Clark, Dick, 165
Clark, Steve, 77, 78, 138, 151–152
Class. *See* Socioeconomic levels

Classical pentecostalism, *3–5, 12–17, 23–57, 175–192, 195, 239, 241;* deliverance ministry in, *17, 141;* democratized ministry of, *25, 33–34, 127;* du Plessis and, *84, 110, 112–114;* and evangelism, *23–24, 32, 38–39, 40, 41, 142, 176;* and experience, *32, 39, 209, 217–218, 223;* in Germany, *43, 46, 47, 72;* Harper and, *118;* and Irvingites, *20;* and mental health community, *235;* neopentecostal accommodation of, *84;* neopentecostalism viewed by, *183–184, 208–210;* and ordination, *33–34, 99, 127–128, 131;* and respectability, *185, 236;* Roberts, *106–107, 108;* and Roman Catholic charismatics, *50, 84, 163, 208, 255;* and social change, *33, 51, 166, 176, 210, 228–229;* and speaking in tongues, *3, 14, 16, 27, 29, 37, 41, 44, 53, 156, 177, 209, 223, 224;* statistics on, *221;* as term, *198;* in United States, *23–46, 50, 51, 55, 221;* worship patterns in, *29, 31–32, 46, 170–171, 181–184, 195, 234.* *See also* Black classical pentecostalism; Cultural baggage; White classical pentecostalism
Clemmons, Ithiel, *188, 210*
Cleveland, *77*
Coe, Jack, *171*
Coffee, taboo on, *44*
College of Bethel, *27–28*
Colleges, *187. See also* Universities
Commitment act, *211. See also* Conversion
Commonweal, 204
Communion, *33, 44, 46, 161, 180*
Communities, *168–169, 231. See also* Covenanted communities
Conference on Charismatic Renewal in the Christian Churches, *79–80*
Conferences. *See* Conventions

Confidence, 53
Conformity, *32*
Congregationalism, *26, 34, 198*
Conventions *83;* ecumenical, *111–112;* international pentecostal, *50, 78–80, 93, 111, 121, 186, 226;* *Keswick interdenominational, 35–36, 46, 52;* Presbyterian, *199–200;* Sunderland, *53–54*
Conversion, *13, 36, 176, 223;* and baptism in the Holy Spirit, *9, 13, 36, 43, 143–144, 155, 159, 206–207, 223;* and sanctification, *42–43, 223*
Conversionist sect model, *176*
Copeland, Kenneth, *142*
Core groups, *136–137*
Corinthians: and baptism in the Holy Spirit, *12;* and order, *17, 172–173;* and social change, *167;* and spiritual gifts, *3, 15, 134, 157, 158–159, 173, 203, 205, 207, 214, 238*
Cornelius, *13*
Council of the Presbyterian World Alliance, *199–200*
Countercultural movement, *218*
Covenanted communities, *77–78, 136–138, 141, 150, 167–168*
Cross and the Switchblade, 73–74
Crouch, Jan, *126*
Crouch, Paul, *126*
Cruz, Nicky, *96*
Cults, *233, 237, 250*
Cultural baggage (classical pentecostal), *4, 29–44 passim, 162–165, 176, 192, 199, 219, 255;* of moral negativism, *32–33, 36–37, 40, 43–44, 189–190, 209–210;* in worship services, *17, 29, 40, 170–171, 184, 234*
Czechoslovakia, *197*

Damboriena, Prudencio, *35, 51*
Dancing, social, taboo on, *33, 189, 190, 209*

Darby, J. N., *33n6*
Darnall, Jean, *130*
Dartmouth College, *67*
Darwin, Charles, *35*
Davis, Kingsley, *1*
"Death of God" movement, *216*
Decentralized structure, *87–88, 94, 178*
Deliverance ministry, *17, 141*
Democratic attitudes, *25, 33–34, 127*
Demon possession, *17, 141*
Denominations, *177–178;* classical pentecostal, *3, 23, 34, 42, 44–46, 176–177, 185;* holiness, *36;* neo-pentecostal, *177–179*
Deprivation, *143, 183, 191, 220*
Dialog, 204
Directory of Catholic Charismatic Prayer Groups, 80
Discrimination, *39*
Dispensationalism, *33, 37, 180, 181, 204–205*
Distinguishing between spirits, *15*
Diversity, *6–9, 44, 151–153, 209, 215–216*
Divorce, *44*
Dixon, Jeane, *227*
Drinking, taboos against, *32, 37, 44, 189, 190, 209*
Dunamis Fellowship, *82*
Dunn, James, *108, 159*
du Plessis, David, *59, 60, 91, 93, 100, 100–114, 219–220, 226, 254;* Assemblies of God and, *84, 111, 112–113, 114, 209;* and Australia, *72;* and Blessed Trinity Society, *64, 93;* and Catholic pentecostal conferences, *78;* and Christian Growth Ministries, *140;* and ecumenical movement, *8, 60, 67, 84, 111–113, 199–200, 213;* and FGBMFI, *120;* and fundamentalists, *195–196;* and Great Britain, *69, 116;* and South Africa,

72; statistics by, *221;* and unity, *8, 152–153;* and worship patterns, *170–171*
Duquesne University, *73–75, 149*
Durasoff, Steve, *121*
Dutch Reformed Church, *110–111*

Eastern Orthodox Christians, *7, 94*
Ecumenical movement, *7–8, 185–187, 199–201, 212–215, 234, 238–239;* and communion, *161;* du Plessis and, *8, 60, 67, 84, 111–113, 199–200, 213. See also* World Council of Churches
Editors, *94–97*
Education: classical pentecostals and, *25, 33, 50–51, 187–188, 208;* neopentecostals and, *82, 98–99, 188–189, 208. See also* Universities
Elect, self-conception as, *175*
Electronic church, *83–84, 108–109, 124–126, 164*
Elim Pentecostal Alliance, *44, 45–46*
Emotion, *1, 218;* classical pentecostalism and, *4, 145, 183, 220n19;* holiness movement and, *36;* neopentecostalism and, *145–146, 183, 189, 219, 220n19*
Empiricism, *24, 26*
Enroth, Ronald, *230–231*
Ephesians, *15, 158*
Episcopal churches, *82, 196, 197, 209, 215–216;* Bennett and, *10–11, 61–64, 70, 93, 186, 194, 216;* and intentional communities, *168–169;* statistics on, *220–221;* Stone and, *64, 122*
Episcopal Church of the Redeemer, *168–169*
Episcopal Renewal Ministries, *82*
Ervin, Howard, *65, 71, 91, 154, 181*
Eternity, 202–203
Ethics, *35–37. See also* Sanctification
Ethiopia, *197*

Europe, *19–20, 43–57 passim, 166–167, 197. See also* Germany; Great Britain

Evangelical Brethren, *197*

Evangelicalism, *153–154, 202–203;* Harper and, *114–115;* and mysticism, *235–236;* neopentecostal accommodation with, *9–10, 83–84, 237–238;* opposition from, *194, 195, 204, 205–207, 249;* and spiritual authority, *131–132*

Evangelicals in the Church of England, *83*

Evangelism, *23–24, 211;* classical pentecostalism and, *23–24, 32, 38–39, 40, 41, 142, 176;* by conversionist sect, *176;* holiness people and, *36;* neopentecostalism and, *9–10, 104, 121, 142–147, 178, 181*

Evans, Leonard, *151*

Evolutionism, *35*

Ewald, Todd, *66*

Exclusiveness, *175*

Existentialism, *207*

Exorcism, *17, 141, 195*

Experience, *2, 39, 151, 155, 178, 211, 217–218, 219;* vs. biblical/doctrinal sources, *32, 146, 209, 212;* and instantism, *222–224;* and leadership, *126, 178;* liberals and, *207;* Schleiermacher and, *35*

Faith, *15, 127–173*

Faith confessionalists, *142*

Falwell, Jerry, *84*

Far East, *48, 50, 51, 52*

Farrow, Lucy, *29*

Feeling, *151, 207. See also* Experience

Fellowship, *147, 151*

Fellowship of Charismatic Christians in the United Church of Christ, *82*

FGBMFI. *See* Full Gospel Business Men's Fellowship International

Filadelfia Church, *47*

Finances, *89, 99, 103, 191, 222, 226*

Finland, *47*

Fiske, Edward, *221*

Foot washing, *44, 180*

Forbes, James, *79, 210*

Ford, Josephine Massyngberde, *76, 136, 137–138, 142, 220;* and dispensationalism, *181;* and human potential movement, *229;* and sexism, *131*

Formalism, *35*

Fountain Trust, *69, 91, 117–118, 148*

France, *19, 48, 50*

Francescon, Louis, *49*

Francis Xavier, *19*

Free Churches, *54, 196*

Frost, Robert, *66, 162*

Full Gospel Business Men's Fellowship International (FGBMFI), *59–60, 82, 91, 99, 208, 225–226;* and Great Britain, *71;* Malachuk and, *96;* Roberts and, *60, 71, 106, 119;* Shakarian and, *60, 71, 93, 95, 119–122, 225;* in South Bend, *76;* and Stone, *122–123;* and young people, *129–130*

Full Gospel Business Men's Voice, *60, 82, 95, 120, 121*

Full Gospel Central Church, *237n2*

Fundamentalism, *10, 145, 146, 181;* classical pentecostalism and, *4, 34, 37, 146, 180, 189;* and human authority, *137;* opposition from, *194, 195–196, 204–206, 249;* and individualism, *24;* and social change, *33, 166;* and spiritual authority, *131–132*

Gallup Poll, *80, 84, 125, 221, 237–238*

Gambling taboo, *189, 190*

Gasson, Rafael, *96*

Gay churches, *237*

Gee, Donald, *54, 55–56, 113, 182,* *208*

Gelpi, Donald, *138, 152, 181, 220,* *237, 239*

Gerlach, Luther, *191;* and Black Power, *228–229;* and financial support, *222;* and opposition, *39,* *211;* and pentecostal movement structure, *87, 89, 211;* and recruitment, *142–143, 211*

Germany, *192, 197;* Anabaptists in, *19;* Christenson and, *68, 69;* classical pentecostalism in, *43, 46, 47,* *72;* Irvingites in, *20*

Ghana, *197*

Gift, 72

Gift of tongues, *3, 14, 18, 156. See* *also* Speaking in tongues

Gifts. *See* Spiritual gifts

Glossolalia. *See* Speaking in tongues

Graham, Billy, *106*

Great Britain, *43–57 passim, 67–71,* *77, 81–82, 192, 197;* Harper and, *68–69, 91, 93, 95, 114–118; opposition in, 56, 196;* prepentecostal glossolalia in, *19–20;* statistics in, *51, 221;* Welsh Revival in, *26,* *46, 52*

Great Saint Mary's, *70*

Greeley, Andrew, *2*

Gregersen, Dagmar, *47*

Group for Evangelism and Renewal, *82*

Groups, *36–37, 147. See also* Communities; Prayer groups

Guerra, Elena, *215n10*

Guilt, for sin, *176*

Hagen, Kenneth, Sr., *142*

Hannan, Philip, *204*

Harper, Jeanne, *115, 116*

Harper, Michael, *6–7, 68–69, 83, 91* *–100 passim, 114–118, 216, 226;* and Australia, *72, 118;* on Boddy, *54;* and Catholic renewal, *80,* *118;* and dispensationalism, *181;* on du Plessis, *110;* and emotion, *145–146, 189;* and New Zealand, *71, 118;* and prayer groups, *148–* *149;* and social change, *167;* and South Africa, *72, 118;* statistics by, *221;* and *Trinity, 116, 123;* and unity, *8, 128, 132, 151;* and worship patterns, *172–173*

Haughey, John, *221*

Healing, *15, 16, 25–26, 37, 158,* *197, 237, 247;* Anglican tradition of, *195;* Kuhlman and, *100–104,* *130, 171;* MacNutt and, *171–172;* opposition to, *40, 194, 206;* Parham and, *27, 28;* Roberts and, *104, 105;* Stapleton and, *130,* *171, 230*

Helpers, *15*

Hezmalhalch, Thomas, *48*

Hine, Virginia, *191;* and Black power, *228–229;* and financial support, *222;* and opposition, *39,* *211;* and pentecostal movement structure, *87, 89, 211;* and recruitment, *142–143, 211*

Historic transition issue, *205*

Hitt, Russell, *202*

Holiness people, *24–47 passim, 115,* *143, 162–165, 189–190, 194*

Holland, *48, 197*

Hollenweger, Walter, *82–83, 154,* *155;* on Shakarian, *119;* and socioeconomic levels, *191;* and speaking in tongues, *157;* and Spirit baptism, *155, 159–160;* statistics by, *51, 220–221;* on Stone, *122;* and worship patterns, *183*

Hollywood First Presbyterian, *65*

"Holovita" retreat center, *230*

Holy roller, *17*

Holy Spirit, *132–134, 153, 155, 212* *–215. See also* Baptism in the Holy Spirit

Holy Spirit Teaching Mission, *139*

Hoover, Willis, 48
Horton, Wade, 183–184
Household of God, 200, 212
Howbury Hall, 53
Hughes, Phillip, 68, 203
Hughes, Ray, 209–210
Huguenots, 19
Human authority, 90–92, 135–142, 252
Human potential movement, 171, 229–230
Humbard, Rex, 126
Hutchinson, Sister, 29
Hysteria, 244

Immersion, baptism by, 44, 180
India, 48, 51
Individualism, 24
Indonesia, 50, 51, 52
Industrial society structure, 25
Instantism, 222–223
Intentional communities, 168–169
Interchurch Features, 114
Interdenominationalism, 26, 34, 35, 121, 161. *See also* Unity
International Church of the Four-square Gospel, 45, 164
International Convention of Faith Churches and Ministries, 142
International Missionary Council, 111–112
Inter-Varsity Christian Fellowship, 66, 129
Iowa, University of, 77
Irving, Edward, 20
Irvingites, 20
Italy, 50, 51

Jansenists, 19
Jeffrey, George, 45
"Jerks," 30
"Jesus only" groups, 43, 45, 179–180
Jesus People, 130, 136, 139, 164, 218, 219, 230–231

Joel, 16
John, 13, 15
John XXIII, 213–214, 215
John Paul II, 83, 137, 197
John the Baptist, 12
Journal of Ecumenical Studies, 204
Judaism, 233

Kant, Immanuel, 35
Keifer, Ralph, 74, 75
Kelley, Dean M., 217
Keswick conventions, 35–36, 46, 52
Kildahl, John, 90, 143, 144, 235
King, Martin Luther, Jr., 166
Kübler-Ross, Elisabeth, 227
Kuhlman, Kathryn, 92, 100–104, 130, 134, 219–220; and Christian Growth Ministries, 140; and education, 102, 188; and worship patterns, 184
Küng, Hans, 137

Laity, 33–34, 119–120, 127, 128–129, 175–176, 178
Lake, John, 48
Lambeth Conference, 197
Lamont, Robert, 103
Latin America: classical pentecostalism in, 48–52 *passim*, 199, 239; and neopentecostalism, 77, 197, 199; prepentecostal religious traditions of, 21, 234
Laying on of hands, 13–14
Leadership, 56, 81, 87–126, 128
Lecturers, 97–99
Leisure time, increased, 224–226
Liberalism, 10, 24; classical pentecostalism and, 4; conversionist sect and, 176; neopentecostalism and, 132, 154–155, 207, 235–236, 237, 238; opposition from, 194; and spiritual authority, 131
Liberation theology, 237
Life magazine, 201

Liturgical order, *31–32, 50, 172–173, 182–184*
Logic, *1, 235–236*
Logos, 71, 93, 95
Logos International, *92, 96–97*
Logos Journal, 97, 124, 249
Logos Ministry for Orthodox Renewal, *82*
Los Angeles, *77*
Los Angeles Episcopal diocese, *196*
Los Angeles Times, 29
Louis XIV, *19*
Luke, *12, 13, 41, 159–160*
Luther, Martin, *233*
Lutheran Church in America, *196*
Lutheran Renewal International, *82*
Lutherans: cult beginnings of, *233;* and neopentecostalism, *65, 82, 94, 194, 196, 197, 198, 221, 238*

MacArthur, John, Jr., *205–206*
Mackay, John, *111, 199–200, 201*
MacNutt, Francis, *171–172*
Magazines: classical pentecostal, *30, 53, 208;* national news, *63, 80, 100, 194, 201;* neopentecostal, *60–72 passim, 81, 82, 91–97 passim, 114–124 passim, 130, 138, 139–140, 151, 249 (see also* New Covenant); nonpentecostal Catholic, *204;* nonpentecostal evangelical, *68, 202–203*
Maguire, Frank, *61, 62, 68, 116*
Malachuk, Dan, *96–97, 103, 154*
Mark, *12*
Marshall, Catherine, *131, 133–134*
Martin, Dean, *164*
Martin, George, *128–129*
Martin, Ralph, *77, 78, 93, 95*
Marty, Martin E., *188*
Marxists, *166–167, 237*
Mason (C. H.) Theological Seminary, *188*
Mass conversions, *24*
Matthew, *12*

McDonnell, Kilian, *127, 198, 204, 254;* and cultural baggage, *17, 170;* and human potential movement, *229;* and social change, *166*
McGee, J. Vernon, *205*
McPherson, Aimee Semple, *45, 49–50, 134*
McPherson, Rolf, *45*
Meaning, *218, 219*
Media, *36, 40–41, 83;* electronic, *108–109, 124–126, 164;* print, *30–31, 36, 52, 78, 91, 92, 94–97, 117. See also* Magazines; Newspapers
Meeking, Basil, *188*
Melodyland Christian Center, *66, 91, 93, 124, 140;* and church growth, *237n2;* and ordination, *128, 131*
Melodyland Messenger, 221
Membership, *23–24, 87, 175, 178*
Mental health professionals, *235. See also* Psychology
Methodist Pentecostal Church, *48*
Methodists, *233–234;* and classical pentecostalism, *26, 27, 34, 38, 45, 48, 221;* and holiness movement, *35, 45;* and neopentecostalism, *82, 91, 106–108, 196, 197, 216, 220, 221, 238;* and social change, *167*
Metropolitan Community Churches (MCC), *237*
Mexico, *49, 51*
Michigan, University of, *77–78*
Michigan State University, *75, 76–77, 78*
Michigan State weekend, *76*
Middle class: and classical pentecostalism, *38, 44, 162–165, 170–171, 184, 187, 191, 219, 234;* neopentecostals and, *6, 162–165, 170–171, 179, 184, 188, 192, 210, 219–220, 234*
Military, prohibitions about, *44*
Miracles, *15, 16, 158*

Miraculous gifts, 16
Missions, to alcoholics and prisoners, 33
Missouri Synod Lutherans, 198
Mjorud, Herbert, 194
Modernist authority attitudes, 137
Montanists, 18–19
Montanus, 18
Montefiore, Hugh, 70
Morality, 178. See also Perfection, personal
Moral negativism, 32–33, 36–37, 40, 43–44, 189–190, 209–210
Mormon Church, 20
Morris, James, 101
Moule, Handley, 55–56
Movement, as term, 5–7, 227
Mumford, Bob, 139, 140
Mysticism, 2, 218, 227, 235–236

National Association of Evangelicals (NAE), 37, 50, 180, 185
National Council of Churches, 113, 221, 227
National Courier, 97
National Service Committee Newsletter, 83
National Service Committee of the Catholic Charismatic Renewal, 82
Nazarenes, 36, 196
Neill, Stephen, 213
Nelson, Nels, 49
Netherlands, 48, 197
Newbigin, Lesslie, 200–201, 212, 213
New Covenant, 78, 83, 93, 95, 137; and Ford, 138; New Wine and, 140; and Trinity, 124
New Pentecost, 213, 214, 215
Newspapers: pentecostal, 30–31, 38–39, 41, 83, 97; secular, 29, 30, 31, 53, 70, 78
New Super-Spirituality, 207
Newsweek, 63, 80, 194
New Wine, 139–140

New York, 77
New York Times, 221
New Zealand, 71, 77, 118, 192
Nichol, John, 36, 50, 176–177
Nigeria, 48, 51
Nondenominational charismatic churches, 136, 142, 181
Nonmiraculous gifts, 16
North America, 49, 77, 192, 196–197. See also United States
Norway, 20, 46–47, 52
Notre Dame University, 75–77, 78, 149, 167–168
"NOW" experience, 223
Nurture, Bushnell and, 35
Nystrom, Samuel, 49

O'Connor, Edward, 76, 94, 188, 220; and dispensationalism, 181; and laying on of hands, 14; and movement (term), 5–6; and prayer groups, 149; and social change, 167–168; and speaking in tongues, 158; and Spirit baptism, 160; statistics by, 221; and water baptism, 160
"One Way" slogan, 219
Openness, 9
Opposition, 211, 233; to classical pentecostalism, 39–44, 56; to neo-pentecostalism, 193–196, 204–207, 209–210
Optimism, 24–25, 33
"Oral Roberts and You," 108
Oral Roberts Evangelistic Association, 105–106, 107
Oral Roberts University (ORU), 82, 91–92, 100–109 passim, 188–189, 208
Order, liturgical, 31–32, 50, 172–173, 182–184
Ordination, 33–34, 99, 127–128, 131
Organizational leaders, 92–94, 97–99

Origen, *19*
Orlando, *77*
Ornamentation, taboos on, *40, 47*
Orphanages, *33*
Orthodoxy, historic, *9, 153, 154–155*
Ortiz, Juan Carlos, *141*
ORU. See Oral Roberts University
Otis, George, *164, 225*
Ozman, Agnes, *27*

Packer, James, *83*
Palmer, Everett, *194*
Pamphlets, neopentecostal, *96*
Parham, Charles Fox, *26–28, 29, 30, 42, 88, 234*
Paul, *13, 159–160, 238;* and order, *17, 172–173;* and spiritual gifts, *15, 157, 203, 238*
Paul, Jonathan, *47*
Paul VI, *79, 103–104, 197*
Pentecost, 208
Pentecostal Assemblies of Canada, *49*
Pentecostal Evangel, 41
Pentecostal Fellowship of North América (PFNA), *50, 185, 186*
Pentecostal Holiness Church, *36, 43, 44, 45;* and education, *187, 188;* Roberts and, *104, 105, 106*
Pentecostal World Conferences, *50, 93, 111, 186*
Pentecost Day, *13, 16, 20*
Pentecost for England, 52
Penthouse symposium, *138*
People, Power, Change, 87, 228–229
Perfection, personal, *33, 175. See also* Sanctification
Perry, Troy, *237*
Person, God as, *9*
Peter, *13, 16*
Philip, *13*
Pike, James, *70, 195, 215, 227*
Plog, Stanley, *179*
Poland, *48*

Polhill, Cecil, *53, 54, 56*
Pork, forbidden, *44*
Portland (Oregon), University of, *77*
Practice, *127–173*
Prayer groups, *6, 80, 147–150, 172, 184, 210*
Praying, with uplifted hands, *101, 171, 184*
Preachers, *56, 97–99. See also* Ordination
Preaching, revivalistic, *32*
Presbyterian Charismatic Communion, *82*
Presbyterian, *65, 82, 94, 196–197, 220–221;* Assemblies of God and, *45;* and du Plessis, *199–200;* and Irvingites, *20;* and speaking in tongues, *238*
Presence, Power, Praise, 198, 254
Press. *See* Media
Prethus, Lewi, *47*
Priesthood, of all believers, *175*
Prince, Derek, *139, 140*
Princeton Theological Seminary, *67, 199–200*
Process theology, *237, 246*
Prophecy, *15, 18, 158, 185, 227;* and human authority, *135;* and spiritual authority, *43, 133–134*
Prophets of the Cévennes mountains, *19*
Protestant ethic, *33*
Psychology, *143, 171–172, 183, 235, 243–244, 246, 250*
Psychology of Speaking in Tongues, 90
Publicity. *See* Media
Publishers, *78, 92, 94–97*
Pulkingham, Graham, *66, 168–169, 216*
Pylkkanen, William, *47*

Quakers, *20*

Ramabai, Pandita, 48
Ranaghan, Dorothy, 73, 75, 160, 163, 165; and dispensationalism, 181; and social change, 168
Ranaghan, Kevin, 73, 160, 163, 165; and cultural baggage, 162–163; and dispensationalism, 181; and social change, 168; and spiritual authority, 153
Ranters, 20
Rationalism, 35
Rauschenbusch, Walter, 24n1, 35
Recruitment. See Evangelism
Redemption, 176
Reformed churches, 82, 110–111, 197
Remarriage, 44
Renewal, 69, 82, 91, 93, 95, 114, 117, 118
Republicans, 11
Respectability, 98–99, 185, 188, 236; in Great Britain, 54–55, 118; Kuhlman and, 100; and worship patterns, 184
Resurrection, 37
Revelation, 43, 158, 205, 235. See also Bible
Revivalism, 3, 29–31, 34; conversionist sect and, 176; cultural baggage of, 32–33, 162–163, 190; for evangelism, 23–24, 32, 36, 38, 41, 104, 176; and holiness movement, 36; and liturgical order, 183; and spiritual gifts, 25–26, 29; and young people, 218
Rigins, S. J., 28
Roberts, Evan, 46
Roberts, Oral, 91–92, 104–109; and Boone, 164; and education, 82, 91 –92, 100–109 passim, 188–189, 208; and FGBMFI, 60, 71, 106, 119; and Kuhlman, 100; "NOW" experience of, 223; and television, 83–84, 108–109, 126, 164; and United Methodist Church, 91, 106 –108, 216, 220

Robertson, Pat, 83–84, 100, 124– 126, 140, 154, 164
Robinson, J. A. T., 215
Roman Catholics, 12, 50, 72–80, 83, 187, 196, 197, 204, 236–237, 250; and classical pentecostalism, 50, 84, 163, 208, 255; and education, 12, 73–78, 189; and FGBMFI, 76, 120; Harper and, 80, 118; and healing, 103–104, 171–172, 237; and human authority, 136–137; and laity, 128–129; leadership among, 94; Lutheranism and, 233; prayer groups among, 80, 149–150; and scriptural authority, 131, 153; and social change, 167–168; and socioeconomic levels, 191–192; and Spirit baptism, 158, 159, 160 –161; and spiritual gifts, 158, 197 –198, 214–215, 238; statistics on, 220–221; and unity, 7, 132, 151– 152, 212, 213–215; and water baptism, 159, 160–161
Romans, 158
Rootlessness, 25
Run Baby Run, 96
Russia, 20

St. Louis, 77
St. Luke's Episcopal Church, 63–64, 70
St. Mark's Episcopal Church, 10–11, 61–63, 122, 186, 194
Salter, James, 48
Samarin, William, 157
Samaritan converts, 13
Sanctification: classical pentecostalism and, 35, 37, 42–43, 45, 179– 180, 223; and holiness movement, 24–25, 35, 37, 41, 42–43, 46, 115; Methodism and, 26, 35, 233 –234. See also Baptism in the Holy Spirit
Sanford, Agnes, 130

Scandinavia, *20, 46–47, 51, 52, 192*
Schaeffer, Francis, *207*
Schleiermacher, F. D. E., *35, 207*
Schuller, Robert H., *84*
Schweizer, Eduard, *159*
Science, *24, 176*
Scofield Reference Bible, 33, 180
Scottish Journal of Theology, 108
Scripture. *See* Bible
Seattle, *63–64, 70, 77*
Second coming, *36, 37, 38, 181. See also* Dispensationalism
Secretariat for Promoting Christian Unity, *118, 208*
Sectarianism: and classical pentecostalism, *4, 40, 50, 52, 54–56, 175–177, 179, 208;* and neopentecostalism, *5, 51, 137, 250*
Secularization, *1–2, 216–218*
Segments, in pentecostal movement, *89*
Segregation, racial, *31, 34. See also* Black classical pentecostalism; White classical pentecostalism
Self-criticism, *51*
Seminaries, *67, 188, 199–200, 236*
Separation from the world, *32, 35, 165, 176. See also* Moral negativism
Servant Publications, *78, 97*
"700 Club," *124–126, 164*
Sexism, *131*
Seymour, William Joseph, *28–30, 31, 33, 42, 88, 210, 234*
Shakarian, Demos, *91, 100, 119–122, 188;* and Christian Growth Ministries, *140;* and FGBMFI, *60, 71, 93, 95, 119–122, 225*
Shakers, *19*
Shamanistic traditions, *234,*
Shepherding, *138–142, 198*
Sheppard, Gerald T., *210*
Sherrill, John, *74*
Simpson, Charles, *139, 140, 141*
Slain in the Spirit, *101, 184*

Smidt, Gerhard, *47*
Smith, Joseph, *20*
Smith, Robert Pearsall, *35–36*
Smith, Timothy L., *188*
Smoking, taboo against, *32, 44, 189, 190, 209*
Social change, *33, 51, 166–170, 176, 210, 228–229*
Social Gospel, *24, 35*
Society for Pentecostal Studies, *82, 188, 208*
Socioeconomic levels: in classical pentecostalism, *3–4, 25, 34, 38, 176–177, 179, 190–191, 220n19;* in neopentecostalism, *11–12, 180–181, 191–192, 220n19. See also* Middle class
Soda pop taboo, *44*
Sojourners Fellowship, *231*
SOMA (Sharing of Ministries Abroad), *82*
Songs, Gospel, *32*
South Africa, *48, 51, 72, 118, 192, 197*
South Bend covenanted community, *136–138, 141, 167–168*
Southern Baptists, *198*
South Pacific, *197*
Speaking in tongues, *15, 155–158, 197, 253, 254;* classical pentecostals and, *3, 14, 16, 27, 29, 37, 41, 44, 53, 156, 177, 209, 223, 224;* in holiness movement, *36;* neopentecostals and, *63, 66, 90–91, 116, 144, 148, 156–158, 172, 173, 184, 195, 209, 224;* opposition to, *194–195, 206;* prepentecostal, *18, 19–21, 234;* and psychology, *143, 243–244, 246, 250;* and revivalism, *25–26;* as Spirit baptism evidenced, *20, 27, 29, 44, 155–158, 209, 223;* statistics on, *238;* and worship patterns, *148, 172, 173, 184, 195*
Speaking in Tongues, 69, 117

Spirit baptism. *See* Baptism in the Holy Spirit
Spiritual authority, 32, 43, 131–134, 153, 181, 205
Spiritual gifts, 3, 5, 12–17, 37, 41, 158–159, 177, 202–203, 234, 238 –239; and democratized ministry, 127; opposition about, 43, 204– 205, 206–207; as preaching quali- fication, 99; prepentecostal, 18– 21; Roman Catholic and, 158, 197–198, 214–215, 238; and wor- ship patterns, 172–173, 184–185. *See also* Healing; Prophecy; Speak- ing in tongues
Spiritual inflation, 17–18n36
Spittler, Russell, 188
Spontaneity, 7, 29, 32, 176, 178, 183
Sprinkling, baptism by, 180
Stanford University, 67
Stapleton, Ruth Carter, 79–80, 130, 171, 230
Statistics, 51–52, 220–222. *See also* Gallup Poll
Stendahl, Krister, 202
Stephanou, Eusebius, 93, 94, 95
Stone, Donald, 122
Stone, Jean, 64, 65, 66, 100, 122– 124, 130–131; and Great Britain, 68, 69; and socioeconomic level, 191; and spiritual gifts, 184–185; and *Trinity*, 64, 91, 95, 123–124
Stott, John R. W., 83, 115, 117, 206 –207
Subjectivism, 24, 32, 187
Suenens, Léon Joseph Cardinal, 79, 94, 204
"Sunday Night Live with Oral Roberts," 108–109
Sunderland, 47, 52–54
Supernatural, 2, 218, 227, 235–236
Sweden, 20, 47
Synan, Vinson, 188

Teachers, 15
Teen Challenge International, 51, 73, 255
Television, 83–84, 108–109, 124– 126, 164
Tent meetings, 38, 104, 105
Tertullian, 19
Thelle, Agnus, 47
Theological Renewal, 82
Theology, 8–9, 35–37, 153–155, 179–181, 215–216
Thessalonians, 37
They Speak with Other Tongues, 74
Third Force/stream, 52, 60, 200, 201, 212, 254
Third World, 52, 166–167, 192, 239. *See also* Africa; Latin Amer- ica
This Is That, 134
Time magazine, 63, 100, 194
Tinney, James, 210
Tobacco, taboo against, 32, 37, 44, 189, 209
Tolerance, 23, 215–216
Torrey, Reuben Archer, 4, 46
Traditionalist authority attitudes, 137
Transdenominationalism, 4, 7–8
Transience, 40, 222
Trapp, Maria von, 92
Treeing the devil, 30
Trinitarians, 179–180
Trinity, 64, 67–68, 91, 95, 116, 123 –124

Unions, prohibitions about, 44
Union Theological Seminary, 236
Unitarians, 179–180
United Church of Canada, 197
United Church of Christ, 82, 196, 254
United Methodist Church, 91, 106– 108, 196, 216, 220
United Pentecostal Church, 45

United Reformed Church, *82, 197*
United States: classical pentecostalism in, *23–46, 50, 51, 55, 221;* neopentecostalism in, *59–67, 73–81, 82, 196, 220–221;* prepentecostal glossolalia in, *20*
Unity, *6, 7, 8, 9, 128, 132, 151–153, 212, 213–215, 234;* and antiinstitutionalism, *227;* Christian Growth Ministries and, *141;* FGBMFI and, *121. See also* Ecumenical movement
Universities, *66–67, 73–78, 129–130, 167–168. See also* Oral Roberts University
"Unsecular man," *2*

Valdez, A. C., *50*
Van Dusen, Henry P., *201*
Van Nuys, California, *64. See also* Blessed Trinity Society; St. Mark's Episcopal Church
Vatican II, *197–198, 213–215, 238*
Vatican's Secretariat for Promoting Christian Unity, *118, 208*
View, 130, 151
Vincent Ferrer, *19*
Vingren, Gunnar, *49*
Virgin birth of Christ, *37*
Visser 't Hooft, Willem, *112*
Voice of Healing, 41
Voluntary association, *23, 24, 175*

Wardleys, *19*
Warren, J. A., *29*
Water baptism, *13, 44, 159–161, 180, 197*
Way International, *237*
Weber, Max, *88, 177*
Weblike network, *89–90, 211*
Welsh Revival, *26, 46, 52*
Wesley, John, *33, 35, 233–234*
Westminster Confession of Faith, *37*

Which Way for Catholic Pentecostals? 137–138
White classical pentecostalism, *31, 34, 185–186, 209, 210;* and Africanisms, *234;* and church government, *3;* and fundamentalism, *4, 37, 180, 204n33;* and social change, *166*
White neopentecostalism, *171, 179, 180–181, 210, 219, 234*
Why Conservative Churches Are Growing, 217
Wigglesworth, Smith, *49–50, 53, 54*
Wilkerson, David, *51, 73–74, 164*
Wilkerson, Ralph, *91, 93, 140, 154;* Assemblies of God and, *209;* Blessed Trinity Society and, *64–65, 66;* and demon possession, *141;* and FGBMFI, *71, 226*
Willans, Richard, *124*
Williams, J. Rodman, *94, 133, 146–147, 161, 181*
Wilson, Bryan, *175–176, 177–178, 216, 218*
Wine, in communion, *44, 180*
Women, *33–34, 130–131*
Women's Aglow Fellowship, *82*
Word of God community, *77–78, 136–138, 141, 150*
Word of knowledge, *15, 134, 158*
Word of wisdom, *15, 158*
Working class, *34, 38, 179*
World Action Singers, *108*
World Christian Encyclopedia, 221
World Council of Churches (WCC), *7, 50, 84, 186, 187, 197, 238;* and antiinstitutionalism, *227;* Bittlinger and, *84, 154;* du Plessis and, *111–112, 113;* and Holy Spirit, *212–213*
Worldliness, *1–2, 4, 35, 36–37. See also* Cultural baggage
Worship, 204

Worship patterns, *31–32, 46, 170–173, 181–185, 195*
WYAH, *125*

Yale University, *66–67, 129*

Young people, *129–130, 218–219*

Zaire, *51*
Zimmerman, Thomas, *188*
Zion College, *53–54*